THE LION'S ROAR OF THE ULTIMATE NON-DUAL BUDDHA NATURE

A Text by Ju Mipham Namgyal
and Explanation by Tony Duff

TONY DUFF
PADMA KARPO TRANSLATION COMMITTEE

First edition, April, 2015
ISBN paper book: 978-9937-572-79-8
ISBN e-book: 978-9937-572-80-4

Janson typeface with diacritical marks and
Tibetan Classic Chogyal typeface
designed and created by Tony Duff

Produced, Printed, and Published by
Padma Karpo Translation Committee
P.O. Box 4957
Kathmandu
NEPAL

Committee members for this book: translation and composition, Tony Duff; assistant translation, Tamaś Agócs; editorial, Jason Watkin of Purica and Lama Richard Roth; cover design, George Romvari of Purica.

Web-site and e-mail contact through:
http://www.pktc.org/pktc
or search Padma Karpo Translation Committee on the web.

CONTENTS

Introduction v

The Lion's Roar That is a Great Thousand Doses of the Sugata Essence by Ju Mipham Namgyal 1

Posing the Question 5

Giving the Answer 5

The presentations of other traditions 6

The first reason 6

The second reason 6

Stating our own tradition 10

The first reason 10

The ordinary way 10

The extraordinary way 11

The second reason 17

The third reason 20

Dispensing with some mistaken positions 26

The element in being not empty being truly established 27

The element being a cut-off empty condition ... 28

Wisdom in being impermanent being compounded 30

A THOROUGH COMMENTARY TO THE LION'S ROAR THAT IS A GREAT THOUSAND DOSES OF THE SUGATA ESSENCE BY TONY DUFF 45

Introduction 47

The vocabulary of buddha nature—garbha, dhātu, gotra, potential, seed of a buddha, sugata essence and tathāgata essence; the importance of the teaching on sugata essence

The Text: Prefatory section 57

The title; the prostration; the expression of worship

The Text: Body of the text 62

Introduction, the need to establish sugata essence using scripture and reasoning; posing the question, giving the answer; the presentations of other traditions; presenting the positions of early Tibetans; refuting the positions of early Tibetans; the first reason; the second reason; stating our own tradition; the first reason; the ordinary way; the extraordinary way; the second reason; the third reason; dispensing with some mistaken positions; dispensing with the view that the element being not empty is truly established; dispensing with the view that the element is a cut-off empty condition; dispensing with wisdom in being impermanent taken to be compounded

The Text: Concluding section and colophons .. 156

TEXTS CITED 169

GLOSSARY OF TERMS 173

SUPPORTS FOR STUDY 193

TIBETAN TEXT 199

INDEX 229

INTRODUCTION

This book presents a text called the *Lion's Roar That is a Great Thousand Doses of the Sugata Essence*, written by the Tibetan master Ju Mipham Namgyal. Mipham, who lived in the nineteenth and twentieth centuries [1846–1912 C.E.], was a particularly learned scholar of the Nyingma tradition of Tibetan Buddhism. He was a prolific writer whose works have become amongst the most important for establishing and presenting the views of the Nyingma tradition. Having faith in an author because of seeing his good qualities usually leads to an enhanced ability to understand his work and that is true here, so it is recommended that you find and read a biography of Mipham in conjunction with reading this book.

The text here is one of a pair of "lion's roar" texts by Mipham, the other being the *Lion's Roar Proclaiming Other Emptiness*[1]. The Buddha used the term "lion's roar" and explained its meaning in several discourses, some of which are quoted towards the end of Mipham's text in this book. In essence, the Buddha used "lion's roar" to refer

---

[1] The two lion's roar books should be read in tandem. To make that possible Padma Karpo Translation Committee has also published an English translation of the *Lion's Roar Proclaiming Other Emptiness*. Publication data for that and all other publications cited in this book can be found in the Texts Cited section of this book.

to the ultimate teachings on reality that he presented in the sutra teachings.

The Buddha taught the sutra teachings in three successive waves called the three turnings of the wheel of dharma. In which of these three turnings did he teach the ultimate teachings on reality? Some Tibetan Buddhist masters, such as Tsongkhapa, have had the view that the teachings given on emptiness in the Prajñāpāramitā sutras of the middle or second turning of the three turnings of the wheel of dharma were the ultimate teachings on reality. However, Indian masters and most Tibetan masters have had the view that the teachings given on buddha nature in the final or third turning of the wheel of dharma were the ultimate teachings on reality. In fact, there should be no argument over this because the Buddha himself very clearly said in the discourses of the final turning that the final turning was where he gave the ultimate teachings of the sutras.

The disagreement just mentioned that happened in Tibet over where the ultimate teachings of reality were given in the sutra teachings is not a point of interest in this book. A complete treatment of the issue, culminating in the acceptance that they were given in the final turning of the wheel is contained in *Other Emptiness, Entering Wisdom Beyond Emptiness of Self*. That book and the other "lion's roar" text mentioned above provide sufficient, helpful background to this book that they should be considered to be required reading for it. In addition, Padma Karpo Translation Committee has published a wide range of books that cover the topic of the ultimate teaching on buddha nature and its sub-topic called "other emptiness" in depth. All of them will be helpful background material for this book, so all of them have been listed in the Supports for Study chapter at the end of this book.

The Buddha taught several types of teaching within the final turning, so the next question is, "Which teachings in particular of the final turning are the ultimate teachings on reality?" Again, the Buddha himself said very clearly that the teaching of buddha nature, most commonly referred to as the "tathāgata essence" or "sugata essence"[2], given in the final turning was the lion's roar, the ultimate teaching given in the sutras. The group of final turning sutras that convey that ultimate teaching is named "the definitive meaning essence sutras" because they teach the definitive meaning that is the very essence of all sutra teachings.

In Buddhism, teachings are defined as either provisional or definitive in meaning. Anything that is provisional in meaning is regarded as true because it was spoken by the Buddha but is not a final understanding; it was taught provisionally with the intent that it would lead on to the final understanding. The final understanding is found in teachings that are definitive in meaning. The term "definitive meaning" is used in two ways: in the first way it means a teaching that demonstrates the final understanding and in the second way it means the thing itself that is pointed to by the definitive meaning teachings. Thus we talk about the definitive meaning sugata essence as the teaching on sugata essence contained in the set of definitive meaning essence sutras and also as the actual sugata essence itself, what it really is. This dual usage of definitive meaning in relationship to the sugata essence is important to understand when reading this book.

Buddha nature was taught in the middle turning of the wheel, though not extensively. It was taught there as part of the primary teaching of that wheel that all dharmas, meaning all phenomena—and that includes the sugata essence—are empty of a self. It was taught there mainly under the name "tathāgata essence" meaning the essence or seed from which a tathāgata can come, the tathāgatas being the buddhas, the ones who have "gata" gone to "tathātā" things as they actually are.

---

[2] The Sanskrit names for tathāgata essence and sugata essence are tathāgatagarbha and sugatagarbha respectively.

Buddha nature was taught in the final turning of the wheel from various perspectives. For example, as in the first and middle turnings, it was taught as a seed or essence of mind that would turn into buddhahood under the influence of the right causes and conditions, that is, by practising the path to enlightenment. However, in the definitive meaning sutras it was taught not as something to be produced through causes and conditions but as actual buddhahood present in the mind that had simply to be uncovered. Moreover, whereas in the middle turning it was taught to be empty, it was additionally taught in the definitive meaning sutras to have a nature of luminosity—a metaphor for knowing—and that that luminosity spontaneously and from the very outset contains all of the good qualities of buddhahood.

This teaching of the sugata essence as actual buddhahood, as unified emptiness and luminosity with all the good qualities of buddhahood spontaneously existing in it, is the definitive meaning teaching of the sutras. It is the most profound teaching of all of the sutras which at root is no different from the teachings of the highest tantras, such as Mahāmudrā and Dzogchen. It concerns non-dualistic wisdom that is totally beyond all of the elaborations, the conceptual stuff, of dualistic mind. This is a very profound topic, so it is easy to misunderstand the teachings on it. Therefore, there is a strong need to clearly and correctly establish what the sugata essence actually is and what the Buddha's teachings on it actually meant. That is exactly what Mipham's text and this book attempt to do.

As mentioned above, Mipham wrote a pair of "lion's roar" texts. Each one explains sugata essence from a different angle. Briefly, the text here, *Lion's Roar That is a Great Thousand Doses of the Sugata Essence*, answers the crucial question, "How it can be known for certain that sentient beings have sugata essence in their mindstreams?" It is a crucial question because, if beings do not have a sugata essence, the whole Buddhist teaching becomes a nice but useless exercise in philosophy. Mipham's text answers the question using a verse from one of the most important texts on the definitive meaning sugata essence, a text of Maitreya's teaching called *The Great Vehicle Treatise on the Highest Continuum*. Having proved in that way that all beings do have sugata essence, the *Lion's Roar That is a Great Thousand Doses of the Sugata Essence* goes on to explain overall the definitive meaning teachings on sugata essence. In doing so, it quotes many sutras and authoritative treatises on them to show and verify what the Buddha intended. In the Tibetan tradition, a text that provides many different quotations from authoritative sources is called "a one thousand doses" text, meaning "a text with many doses of what authorities have to say". Mipham's text is "a great" one thousand doses text because it does not stop at taking quotations from one specific area of the Buddhist sutras, but takes them broadly from both middle and final turnings. In other words, his text condenses a large amount of teaching from various sources down into one, convenient text on definitive meaning sugata essence, which is why it was titled "a great one thousand doses of the sugata essence". In short, this lion's roar text proves that all beings have sugata essence then goes on to give a clear, overall presentation of the definitive meaning sugata essence teaching.

Now, a specific and important topic within the overall definitive meaning teachings on sugata essence is that sugata essence is empty. In the final turning, the Buddha explained that sugata essence is empty in the same way as all things are empty as taught in the middle turning. However, he went further and explained that it is also empty in the sense that its own entity is *empty* of everything that is *other* than it. This topic is therefore called "empty of other" or "other emptiness". A proper understanding of other emptiness leads to the view that the sugata essence is actual buddhahood sitting in the mind, waiting simply to be uncovered, which is a hallmark of the ultimate teachings on reality. The text *Lion's Roar Proclaiming Other Emptiness* focusses on this specific and important topic of the definitive meaning teachings on sugata essence.

How to use this Book

The text in this book, *Lion's Roar That is a Great Thousand Doses of the Sugata Essence* is terse, uses much technical vocabulary, and is about an extremely profound subject. In order to unravel it for the reader, I have written a long commentary that goes through the text in detail, making the text as accessible as possible. The commentary takes each line or section of Mipham's text and explains it thoroughly, sometimes explaining each word, sometimes explaining each phrase. You will get most out of the book by reading the commentary in conjunction with the Mipham's text.

It is important to remember that Mipham's text reveals the most profound of the Buddha's teachings. Because of that, even well-trained Tibetans have difficulty understanding this material. As Mipham himself says:

> This approach is so profound that it was said that even the mighty lords of the tenth level, like trying to see a form in the darkness of night, have difficulty in realizing it just as it is, let alone ordinary people.

Therefore, do not be discouraged if it is hard to understand, for it is hard to understand! Rather, read and re-read the book and think carefully about what is being said. Then some of the meaning will become clear.

It is also important to remember also that texts like this were intended as supports for oral teaching in which the meaning is transmitted directly from person to person. In other words, this book will open the door to understanding the definitive meaning sugata essence for those not well versed in it and will further the understanding of those who have some knowledge of it already. However, it would be wrong to expect that you can pick up a book like this and learn the subject simply by reading the book. At some point you will need verbal instruction, obtained in person, from someone who has received a proper transmission of these teachings in order to get more than a mere intellectual understanding of this extremely profound subject.

Next, it is necessary to understand that this most profound teaching of all of the sutras is the same teaching as that of the highest tantras such as Mahāmudrā and Dzogchen. One Dzogchen text, using exactly the same wording and with exactly the same meaning as found in the definitive meaning sugata essence teachings says:

> The self-arising wisdom, completely pure by nature sugata essence, spontaneous-existence buddha is the buddha at the beginning before all buddhas.

And another one says:

> The self-arising wisdom sugata essence is Samantabhadra.

This is a very important point for practitioners of those tantric systems. For example, these days many people try to practise Dzogchen in isolation, thinking that the so-called lower teachings are unnecessary. However, all Tibetan practitioners of Dzogchen that I have met at least know the definite meaning sugata essence teaching because it is the same teaching as presented in the Dzogchen tantras. A book like this, which presents the definitive meaning sugata essence teaching, should be regarded as very valuable by practitioners of those tantric systems.

Sanskrit and Diacriticals

Sanskrit terminology is properly transliterated into English with the use of diacritical marks. These marks often cause discomfort to less scholarly readers and can distance them from the work. However, the text here deals with technical issues, therefore diacritical marks have been used throughout. A few words such as samsara and nirvana and sutra that have become part of the English language have been left without diacritical marks for ease of reading.

The IATS system of transliteration of Sanskrit, the one generally in use in academic circles, is hard for non-scholars to read. Therefore, we have modified that system slightly to make the transliterated Sanskrit more readable for those who do not know the system. This same approach seems to be commonplace amongst translators of Tibetan Buddhism. In it:

ca is written as cha ;
cha is written as chha ;
ṅ is written as ng ;
ṛ is written similarly as ṛi ;
ś is written the way it sounds, as śh ;
ṣ is written similarly as ṣh .

Sources

Several editions of the Tibetan text were consulted during the translation, some of which had many mistakes. We found that a very recent edition of Mipham's works made by Tibetans in China was remarkably free of errors and used that for the final translation. We were guided in the work by a very detailed oral commentary that I received from the exceptionally learned and accomplished Nyingma teacher, Khenpo Palden Sherab, in 1986, when I was an active member of the Nālandā Translation Committee.

Further Study

Generally speaking, Padma Karpo Translation Committee has amassed a range of materials to help those who are studying this and related topics. Please see the supports for study chapter at the end of the book for the details.

Tony Duff,
Swayambhunath,
Nepal, April 2015

Ju Mipham Namgyal
Mural on the wall of Dzogchen Monastery, Tibet.
Photograph by the author, 2007

The Lion's Roar That is a Great Thousand Doses Of the Sugata Essence

by

Ju Mipham Namgyal

NAMO GURAVE

In the primordially stainless dharmatā of mind sits
The definitive meaning personified in the Warrior Mañjuśhrī
Whose sharp sword of ascertaining logic continuously
Severs the total stupidity that weaves the web of becoming.

Now I will give the actual explanation.

The essence of the speech of all the conquerors gone in the three times, the centre of their minds, the single central issue amongst all the teachings of the sutras and tantras, is only this all-pervasive sugata essence. This approach is so profound that it was said that even the mighty lords of the tenth level, like trying to see a form in the darkness of night, have difficulty in realizing it just as it is, let alone ordinary people.

Moreover, when the teacher, the sugata, spoke, he sometimes elucidated the entity of the sugata essence by teaching its emptiness and sometimes elucidated the nature of the sugata essence by teaching its primordial possession of the good qualities of enlightenment—the strengths and so on. The two must be unified without contradiction, but, due to not trusting in the extremely profound key point of the two truths inseparable, some stay in a view of permanence in which sugata essence is not empty of an entity and some, having grasped it as a mere, bare emptiness, stay on the side of understatement, having a nihilistic view in which it is not possible to define the sugata essence as primordially possessing—being inseparable from—the good qualities of kāyas and wisdoms. The noise of those people as they establish and refute in their desire to establish their own points of view is like a tumultuous ocean. However, those who have had the good fortune to receive the guru's foremost instructions on this matter have had the nectar of the most excellent quintessence seep into their hearts, causing them to trust in the fact of empty dhātu and luminous wisdom that are unified without contradiction. Having that trust, they stay in a place where any grasping at extremes in relation to appearance and emptiness has collapsed, then speak about this topic as follows.

Generally speaking, the word of the tathāgata was indeed spoken on the basis of valid cognition; it is correct authoritative statement, recorded in scripture, that is not deceptive. Nevertheless, its non-deceptiveness has to be ascertained. For that, generally speaking you use the three analysers to ensure that the scripture is completely pure and particularly you ensure that there is no reasoning that undermines the meaning of the words in the texts and that there are logical proofs that show it to be correct. Now it is not all right to leave aside reasoning that ensures the purity of scripture and simply trust what is said in a text for the reason that it is undeniable that, generally speaking, there are both true and counterfeit scriptures and the true scriptures moreover are divided into scriptures that are provisional and definitive in meaning.

In view of that, ordinary people cut exaggerations with hearing and contemplation and on top of that those who can use the three valid sources of knowledge to achieve certainty in regard to the topics they intend to enter produce within themselves an irreversible trust in those topics. A person who has not in that way achieved certainty for himself through his own valid cognition will not be able to establish certainty in others who are arguing against him. Such a person is comparable to someone who is obscured in regard to flesh-eaters yet claims "There is a flesh-eater in front of me"—his words will not be able to produce trust in either himself or others.

Therefore, experts take the approach of speaking in accord with correct logic. When a certain stance is established through reasoning, one's opponents are naturally quieted and one's own people become exuberant. When a certain stance is not provable by reasoning, even if many people embellish the argument however they do, the grounds for argument against it only increase, like springs popping up in the wetlands.

For those reasons, you enter into this, the tradition of the conquerors and their great sons together with their lineages, none of which are disturbed by sophists. If you then abandon attachment to all positions and with an honest mind evaluate this matter with pure reasoning that correctly establishes how the sugata essence was presented, you will see that the two assertions of permanence mentioned above—one having the sugata essence truly established and therefore not empty and the other having it as a cut-off empty condition that is without good qualities—are both undermined by reasoning and do not have valid proofs. Together with that, you will see that the thesis here—that beings do have an essence which has both an entity that is empty and a nature that primordially possesses the good qualities—is not undermined by reasoning and does have valid proofs."

Posing The Question

The question to be asked is "What is the proof of the existence of the element, sugata essence, in the mindstream of migrators?"

Giving The Answer

The *Great Vehicle Highest Continuum* gives this proof:

> Because the complete buddha's kāya radiates,
> Because suchness is without differentiation,
> And because the species exists, all bodied beings
> Perpetually have the essence of a buddha.

Its meaning will now be determined using reasoning. In regard to how its meaning is understood, there are two systems to be addressed: the presentations given by other traditions and the presentation of our own correct tradition.

1. The Presentations of Other Traditions

Early Tibetans explained that "the complete buddha's kāya radiates" means simply that the wisdom dharmakāya pervades all objects; that "suchness" is equivalent to a mere, bare emptiness; and that "the species exists" means simply that it is possible to become a buddha. They stated the meaning in only a few words that did not directly get at the key points that are the essence of the *Highest Continuum* text.

1.1. The First Reason

Merely that the dharmakāya pervades all objects does not prove the fully characterized species. That the knowledge of a buddha in appearing as part of others' mindstreams pervades objects means that it exists in all things, but its merely existing in them is not cause for them all to become buddha. Because of seeing that the dharmakāya of one's own mindstream has not become manifest at present, one has doubts about this.

1.2. The Second Reason

The meaning of the species is not found at all in mere assessed emptiness. In your way of thinking, you assert that the species is like a seed which shifts status to being a sprout, with the species having none at all of the good qualities of a buddha at present but, after it has been taken hold of by the condition of the path, having them from the very beginning. In your assertion, the aspect of emptiness of true existence as a non-affirming-negation is uncompounded, devoid of the ability to perform a function, making that part of your assertion totally unacceptable. And in your assertion, the compounded seed can, conventionally speaking, transform into a sprout, but the factor on top of that of being a seed lacking true existence means that it never could transform into a sprout.

Furthermore, the proof that it is possible to become a buddha by a key point of being empty of true existence also is just spouting unexamined ideas. If mind were truly established, it is true that there simply could be no becoming a buddha, but if it were without true establishment, there would be no ascertainment of becoming a buddha. All phenomena—earth, stones, and so on—are without true existence, but who is capable of proving that anything without true existence could become a buddha? Positing the species only as the ability to abandon obscurations by referencing lack of true existence also is useless—you yourselves assert that it makes no sense only to reference emptiness to abandon the obscurations to knowledge, that following it there must be adornment with an infinite accumulation of merit—but then you make the meaningless assertion of a sugata essence in relation to this sort of non-affirming negation! Doing so, your sugata essence becomes the ordinary species that the śhrāvakas and pratyekabuddhas have; it does not establish that beings could become buddhas because with merely this the agreed requirement that all-knowing wisdom will arise after the obscurations to knowledge have been abandoned cannot be proved and, as well as that, there is no factor of knowing in the non-affirming negation's entity so at the time of buddhahood too it will be impossible for it to know anything.

If you are enamoured of this approach of a species that transforms into being compounded, you could assert simply that the seeds of threefold knowledge, love, and capacity that have existed from beginningless time in the mindstreams of all sentient beings and exist as the love that carnivorous beasts, cannibal demons, and the like have for their offspring, and the way that they recognize help and harm, and so on, could, through being taken hold of by the path and thereby removing the obstructions to them and increasing them, become their full-blown form in a buddha who has them. It would be much better to do that than to assert the species in relation to non-affirming negation. In that case, the cause that creates them has to be the result and it follows that the cause which is a momentary, compounded thing must be the creator, but you put that aside and assert the cause as a non-thing which is uncompounded and not a creator, which is very weird!

One person who thinks that way, further thinks, "All that is without truth is not the species, but only what is mind in nature being without truth is accepted as the species", but his "mind being without truth making it possible" has no ability to create something. The moments of the dharmin mind can be said to produce the next moments of mind, because of which it seems that this uncompounded species is not required by you, so you should abandon it!

If there is a group who thinks, "We are not positing this on the basis of a separated two truths; we assert the species as the actuality that is the inseparability of the luminosity of the dharmin mind and the emptiness of the dharmatā" and if moreover they are asserting this in relation to an uncompounded item—the unchanging wisdom of the pair consciousness and wisdom—then yes, because it is established in that way by scripture and reasoning, that is very much how it is. However, if someone has his mind set on the dharmin to be unified with the empty condition as momentary consciousness then thinks, "This gradually shifts in status to being buddha", that is useless. It is useless because a claim like that has the consequence that the species would be both compounded and uncompounded and then, in view of that, the uncompounded factor having no capability to produce what is needed would mean that the species was only an imputed species and the compounded factor being the fully characterized species able to create a result would mean that the intent of the Great Vehicle sutras, all of which maintain that the naturally present species is the uncompounded dharmadhātu, has been totally lost.

Thus, while your mind cannot let go of a species posited in cause and effect terms in which there is a creating cause and created result, you verbally claim the dharmadhātu of complete purity as the naturally present species, but this goes nowhere other than displaying how the position you hold to with your mind and your words about it are contradictory. If the unchanging dharmadhātu is to be claimed as the buddha species, it follows that to start with what is being designated with the term "dharmadhātu" has to be identified as unassessed superfact, the great unity of the two truths, the fact of the non-dwelling Middle Way. If you do not identify it as such and make your assertions in regard to a mere assessed superfact, it is like seeing a group of monkeys in the forest and, due to your confusion, taking them to be gods of the Heaven of the Thirty-Three. Doing so, you take what is not dharmadhātu for dharmadhātu then assert that as the buddha species, and then, taking that species as your meditation's referenced object, you assert that as meditation on Prajñāpāramitā and assert that meditation to be the cause of the svabhāvikakāya, and so on. Nevertheless, all the classifications that you make in your system are established by what it says in the Prajñāpāramitā sutras and elsewhere to be a counterfeit path that only resembles the Great Vehicle.

The fact of the dhātu that is the unity of the two truths removed from all webs of elaboration, which is to be known by personal self-knowing, and which is called "the complete purity nature, dharma-dhātu" and "emptiness", is taught in all the Great Vehicle sutras and commentaries on their intent as that which is the fully-characterized species of buddha and what becomes the svabhāvikakāya having the two purities. Thus, it would not be all right to assert this naturally present species other than as uncompounded. And then, following on from its being uncompounded, your way of assertion in which it has by its very nature done the work of creating a result other than itself then done the work of stopping itself is not acceptable, and moreover, you have no choice but to assert the good qualities of the resulting dharmakāya as a disconnected result. That that is so was taught by the regent, the great being of the tenth level, in the *Highest Continuum* and moreover clearly taught by the glorious guardian noble one Nāgārjuna in his *In Praise of Dharmadhātu*. Therefore, our tradition follows those texts, asserting the uncompounded dharma-dhātu as the species. By doing so, that dhātu being the actuality of all phenomena, its entity is without birth and cessation and its personage is inseparable appearance-emptiness, so there is no falling into sides.

This is how it is. Compounds, which appear to arise and to cease, are not established as they appear and therefore no occurrence in the innate disposition of the dhātu of shrouding by them is ever known. Due to that, the dhātu is primordially pure of cause-and-result samsara and has no meeting and parting with the appearances of the nature, spontaneously-existing un-outflowed luminosity. It is by this key point that the actual mode of the sugata essence has to be identified.

2. Stating Our Own Tradition

2.1. The First Reason

The meaning of the first line of the verse "because the dharmakāya radiates" is as follows. A truly complete buddha's ultimate kāya, the dharmakāya whose qualities are equal to space, at some point becomes evident or radiates or becomes manifest from the mindstream of a person who prior to that had all the fetters of an ordinary person, which proves that "the sugata essence exists now in the mindstreams of sentient beings". There are two ways that this proof is accepted to work: an ordinary way and an extraordinary way.

2.1.1. The ordinary way

The ordinary way is as follows. If a sentient being who has manifested the wisdom dharmakāya exists, it is necessarily the case that a species that makes becoming a buddha possible exists in the mind, and, if such a species absolutely does not exist, then that would not be tenable. What *In Praise of Dharmadhātu* says fits with that:

> If the element exists, by doing the work
> You will see the pure form of the purest of gold.
> If the element does not exist, you might do the work,
> But it will end in only hardship being produced.

2.1.2. The extraordinary way

The extraordinary way is as follows. You might think, "The proof just shown, using the example that crops can grow in a field, establishes simply that this mind of ours is a cause that can become buddha. But how is a species that has the distinction of primordially having the good qualities of a buddha proved?" That too is proved by scripture and reasoning, which establish that the buddha bhagavats, the ones having the wisdom kāya whose personage has been utterly distinguished as uncompounded do not have a compounded, impermanent nature.

For scripture it is said in the *Nirvana Sutra* that:

> For a monk with perfect discipline it would be easier to become a Forder or even die than to say about the uncompounded Tathāgata that "The Tathāgata is compounded".

And:

> Son of the family, now look at the Tathāgata as a permanent kāya, an indestructible kāya, a vajra kāya, not a kāya of flesh, the dharmakāya.

And also:

> It would be easier to touch one's whole tongue to a blazing wood fire or even die than to say the words "The Tathāgata is impermanent". One should not listen to such words.

The factor merely of non-affirming negation does not make nirvana possible; the same scripture says:

> Whenever what is called "the emptiness of emptiness" is sought, nothing at all is found. Such "nothing at all" exists even for the naked ascetics, but emancipation is not like that.

And:

> What that emancipation is is the element that is not artificial; it is the tathāgata.

And the *Vajra Cutter* moreover says:

> Those who see me as form,
> Those who know me as sound,
> Have entered a path which is wrong.
> Those beings do not see me.
>
> The buddhas are viewed as dharmatā,
> The guides as the dharmakāya.
> The dharmatā is not to be known so
> It cannot be known by consciousness.

It is demonstrated by those and other sources, and the sutras of definitive meaning teach it more extensively than any others.

And then for reasoning, there is the following. If that ultimate result of being equal in taste due to being non-dual with the primal dharmadhātu, all-knowing wisdom, is impermanent due to being newly compounded by causes and conditions, then it has the faults of these and other consequences:

- it would not be self-arising wisdom;
- the pain of change would not have been abandoned;
- it would have a factor of ceasing and arising again and again;
- being destructible by its very nature, it would be deceptive;
- it would not be a lasting refuge because as soon as it arose, it would cease;
- it would dwell for a short while only, whenever the assembly of causes for it was complete;
- it would not have gone into equal taste with all phenomena;
- it would not have gone beyond all extremes;
- the arising, etcetera which are the nature of mental mind would not have ceased;

- it would not be under its own control but would be under the control of other, the formatives;
- and so on.

By claiming it to be so, a vast array of faults comes from viewing the vajra kāya as impermanent, so you should reject this bad path then view the non-dual wisdom kāya as having the excellences of being uncompounded and permanent.

If you think, "Uncompounded wisdom is impossible when evaluating with merely the reasoning that depends on the ordinary sight of this shore, because a common basis for consciousness and permanence is impossible", that is useless. Although it is necessarily the case that the short-lived consciousnesses that are conscious of objects are impermanent, wisdom in which awareness and knowable are one taste, wisdom having the vajra of space pervading space, is not comparable to them because all the phenomena of samsara and nirvana are all-at-once comprehended in the wisdom's state of the uncompounded's self-output, unchanging luminosity, so, primordially there being no production and cessation in its entity, it is established by the knowing awareness of ultimate analysis.

That being so, wisdom like that is the great uncompounded of not dwelling in any of the extremes compounded or uncompounded. It is definitely not like a bare non-thing. Both things and non-things are dharmins; the former are produced in dependence and the latter are imputed in dependence. Thus, analysis done on them from the perspective of the authentic shows that they are compounded, accumulated, fictional, and deceptive. The sugata essence, being the authentic, the great uncompounded dharmatā of all phenomena of things and non-things, is non-deceptive. What the *Root Prajñā* says fits with that:

> The pure nature is not artificial and
> Has no reliance on other.

And:

> Thing and non-thing are compounded.
> Nirvana is uncompounded.

That that ultimate dharmakāya wisdom has the nature of pervading all becoming and peace and of being equality, uncompounded, and unchanging superfact, is established by the scriptures of the definitive-meaning sutra section and by the reasoning of ultimate analysis. Such wisdom is seated right now without increment or decrement in sentient beings' mindstreams, as the wisdom dharmakāya nature in the mode of dharmatā that could one day become manifest. In terms of its appearance, that nature might have been freed from the adventitious stains or not and so be present as having been manifested or not. However, in terms of its actual situation, because it has a changeless, uncompounded nature it has not an speck of the differences earlier and later and bad and good. The *Highest Continuum* says:

> How it was before, so it is later.
> It is the unchanging dharmatā.

And:

> That which is mind's nature, luminosity,
> Is like space without change;
> The adventitious stains of passion, and so on, come from conceiving the not authentic
> Do not change it into affliction.

Those and other sources show that all the phenomena of samsara are changing and unstable and although it appears as though all of them are making shifts within the state of that dharmatā, you must know as was said again and again that the mind's purity, sugata essence, is like space, without shift and change. The dhātu of luminosity which as above is uncompounded does not have shrouding by confusion, so is by nature completely pure, and in the not confused innate disposition's self-output, the spontaneously existing strengths, and so on, that are the good qualities of the fruitional dharmas are present without separation, like the sun and its rays.

The *Highest Continuum* says the same thing too:

> The element is empty of that which has the characteristic
> Of being separable, the adventitious.
> It is not empty of that which has the characteristic
> Of being not separable, the unsurpassable dharmas.

All the faults of samsara come from the confused mind that grasps at the selves of I and dharmas. At the same time, that confused mind primordially does not shroud, does not merge with the primal innate disposition, luminosity, rather, it is adventitious to it, like clouds are to the sky, which is why those faults can be divided off and separated from the element, and that in turn is why the element's entity is empty of, unshrouded by, those faults. The element, having no connection to being spoiled by confusion, is luminous by its own nature and is not empty of but has the ultimate good qualities that are not separable from the self-arising wisdom that has engaged the just thatness of all phenomena, because it has the innate disposition of those good qualities being in and inseparable from its own entity, so it is like the sun and its rays.

If the naturally present species like that is established as the entity of the dharmakāya uncompounded by causes and conditions and primordially possessing the buddha qualities, then, because it makes becoming a buddha possible, the wisdom dharmakāya must be seated free from increment and decrement in the mindstreams of all sentient beings. If the path is cultivated, it will be established by the force of the thing that it is possible to become a buddha. And then, that dharmakāya at the time of buddhahood being uncompounded could not possibly have been newly compounded by causes and conditions, therefore it is established that "it is seated right now as the entity of a buddha".

Some people having pondered what was just said think, "If it is seated right now as the entity of buddhahood, why does that all-knowing wisdom not dispel the obscurations of those sentient beings?" And others, clinging to the understanding of the common vehicles, think

"Buddhahood is the result and sentient beings are the cause, so if the result exists in the cause, your argument is undermined by the reasoning that people who eat food are eating their excrement, and other such reasonings". These people have not had their minds trained in the meaning of the extremely profound, definitive-meaning sutras, but have been instructed using merely the understanding of the texts of the ordinary teachings, so they will have doubts but they cannot be blamed for that.

They might not be to blame for their doubts, nevertheless what they are thinking does not apply. The dharmatā luminosity wisdom exists in everybody without difference. However, when it comes out as this mind of ours of adventitious confusion that together with its object is named "samsara", it does not know just as it is the dharmatā that exists in us. It is like for example when one is sleeping that, solely due to mind consciousness, boundless appearances of body and objects and eye consciousness and the rest arise. At that time, although the mental consciousness grasps and observes perceiving subject and perceived object as separate items, it is unable to know its actual mode of being in which separate grasped at and grasper do not exist. It does not know its actual mode of being, yet has not changed to something other than its actual mode of being and this is similar to the fact that all phenomena reside in emptiness but their merely doing so does not mean that everyone necessarily knows it, which happens because there can be confusion in which the way things are and the way they appear are not synchronised.

Thus, mind is dharmin and the essence's wisdom is dharmatā, and we show that from the standpoint of buddhas and sentient beings being the way things are and the way they appear, respectively, because of which our way of showing it undermines your reasoning of result existing in the cause—it ends up being that our reasoning is of a different type than yours.

This first reason proves, using the reason of the dharmakāya at the time of fruition being clearly manifest, that the species at the time of the cause exists primordially endowed with the good qualities. In the way things are, there is no earlier and later cause and effect. However, in the way things appear it is necessary to posit cause and effect, because of which the cause is proved from the effect, which is called "the reasoning of reliance".

2.2. The Second Reason

The meaning of the second line of the verse "because suchness is without differentiation" is as follows.

All dharmas of samsara and nirvana are without differentiation, are one taste in the great actuality of emptiness that is primally luminous. Thus, buddhas and sentient beings also are without differentiation in superfact, which is the equality of becoming and peace. Therefore, that the seemingly apparent sentient beings who have been manifested by adventitious confusion also have not wavered in the slightest from actuality, the dharmatā of superfactual truth, is established by the reasoning of dharmatā, so it is ascertained that sentient beings have a buddha's essence. And in the sutras too, it is said that all dharmas primally are luminous, primally are nirvana, and primally are the nature of a manifest buddha.

You might think, "Well, as you said about others who came earlier, if the existence of the species is proved merely by there being no differentiation in suchness, there is the consequence that the species exists in earth, stones, and the like as well". In reply, if "the species" we are talking about must be posited as the faultless cause of buddhahood in which the two obscurations that arise due to the confused mind have been abandoned to exhaustion and the intelligent mind that is not confused about the nature of the knowable has been developed, then, given that for the sugata essence there is no practising of the path in relation to what is not mind—the material things of earth, stones, and so on—even though conventionally speaking there is no differentiation in suchness, it is not necessary to posit that the species exists in all of what is not mind. It is due to mind that earth, stones, and so on appear, it is not that mind arises due to external earth, stones, and so on, something which is illustrated by and to be understood through the example of the appearances of a dream and the awarenesses at that time. By understanding that this mind that makes the three realms has seated in it, like water has wetness, the dharmatā sugata essence having a nature of unoutflowed, superfactual virtue, the appearances of samsara and nirvana are simply the play of consciousness and wisdom respectively, so do not need to be different items. It has been most strongly proclaimed that in the fact of the authentic all appearances do not waver from the state of dharmatā primordial buddhahood so do not depart from the state of the tathāgata—the *Verse Summary Prajñāpāramitā* says:

> The purity of form is to be known as the purity of fruition.
> The purities of fruition and form will be the purity of all-knowing.
> The purities of all-knowing, fruition, and form
> Are analogous to the realm of space—not differentiable, not divisible.

According to that, that which is the purity of the perceiving subject having been liberated from the obscurations also is the purity or nature of the perceived object—visual form, and so forth—because aside from merely one's own manner of seeing being gradually freed from the obscurations of own-appearance, the factual entity resides primordially free from obscuration. Thus, if you exhaust the stains of the element's perceiving subject that knows and with that become buddha, it will be pure of perceived objects without exception, none remaining. It is like clearing away an eye disease causes the sight of floaters to be cleared automatically.

You might think, "Yes, but when one person becomes a buddha, it will be that all of impurity's appearances will cease". However, it is not so—each being has his own obscurations that produce his own appearances, so each has his own way of seeing in which actuality and appearance are contradictory.

You might think, "Yes, but at the level of a buddha where actuality and appearance always are synchronised, a buddha either has all this appearance of impurity or does not. If he has it, all dharmas would not be manifest, complete buddhahood, and if he does not have it, his knowing the paths that beings constantly travel and the rest would not be possible." All-knowing wisdom, within the state of being one-taste with all the dharmas of samsara and nirvana in their entirety, effortlessly and spontaneously knows all of them, and, while not departing from seeing everything in its own way as the great purity, it also sees the appearances of the six classes of migrators in the way that they appear to them. There is the key point that, as a result of the obscurations of the dualistic appearances of perceived object and perceiving subject having been exhausted in their entirety, this type of seeing comprehends all dharmins in an un-merged yet all-complete way within the space of dharmatā. Due to that key point, the equal taste wisdom free of all arising and cessation sees them all at once. Let alone the beings seeing this shore, even those dwelling on the levels have difficulty comprehending this!

That sort of thing has been spoken of in the bodhisatva sutras:

> All dharmas being the same in equality
> Is realized as such by self-arising.
> Therefore, the authentic manifest buddhas,
> The tathāgatas, have the same way of seeing.

And it has been said:

> By knowing the mind which is naturally luminous accordingly, it is because of that that by means of the prajñā that has one moment of mind there is what is called "unsurpassed, truly complete enlightenment, manifest complete buddhahood".

In accord with that, the master Chandrakīrti said:

> The sky is not differentiated in different vessels and
> Likewise compounded things are not differentiated in
> suchness because of which

Having made them known as one taste in the authentic,
You of excellent knowledge know knowables by the
instant.

The great wisdom that is non-dual with the dhātu pervades all dharmas and sees them without effort, pervading them in the manner of the moon and stars appearing in the ocean and seeing them within the state of complete pacification of thought. This great wisdom is the dharmatā of self-arising luminosity wisdom seated in the ground that, exhausted of its obscurations in their entirety, has become manifest as it actually is. It is known to be so precisely because it becomes manifest in that way, thus if you rely on a correct reasoning of dharmatā used in an ultimate analysis, you will acquire an irreversible trust in it. However, if you evaluate this with some other, less far-reaching kind of mind, you will see many rubbishy contradictions and concepts:

- you will prove that there is no wisdom at the level of the buddha or that, even if it does exist, it is equivalent to the ordinary dualistic mind that changes;
- you will assert that a buddha does not see the makeup of sentient beings or alternatively that a buddha has impurity's appearances;
- you will not be able to prove that the knowledges of nature and extent have entities of equal taste;
- and so on.

2.3. The Third Reason

The meaning of the third line of the verse "because the species exists" is that "the species that can become a buddha does exist in all sentient beings" because it is established that the adventitious stains can be abandoned and that the dharmakāya primordially having the good qualities exists in all beings without difference.

If there is a species that in that way can become a buddha existing in all sentient beings, it is ascertained that those bodied beings have the buddha essence because in their buddha phase their dharmakāya of a buddha also is established as an uncompounded entity so, from the point of view of the entity, there is no difference of earlier and later and those being bad and good.

By means of this third reason one knows that the result is created from a cause, which is the reasoning of the cause doing its work. In this case, it is not that the mere existence of a cause is taken to mean that there will be the production of a result. That is so because of the key points that the dharmatā suchness species is unchanging; that it at the time of the fruition has no good or bad in its entity; and that the adventitious stains can be separated from it no matter how long they persist, so it is impossible for the species to become spent, losing its ability to become buddha.

That causal species that exists is no different in entity from the dharmakāya at the time of its result; and if the dharmakāya of the time of result exists, then also at the time of a sentient being it must exist without increase and decrease; and although they are designated as earlier cause and later result, in fact they are one taste in the entity of the changeless dharmadhātu. Those three reasons prove that all sentient beings have the tathāgata essence, due to the correct reasoning of presence by the force of the thing.

By this reasoning that proves in that way that the tathāgata essence exists in all sentient beings, there is no difference between ultimate emancipation, the tathāgata, and the actuality of all dharmas in superfact. Moreover, if one knows that they arise due to the tathāgata essence itself, then a single ultimate vehicle is proved. Others who, speaking of "the sugata essence", have systems that get the meaning of the Great Vehicle back to front, saying that it does not exist in the makeup of sentient beings, does not exist at the time of buddhahood, does not possess the good qualities at the time of the cause but newly has them at the time of the result, and so on, speculate endlessly over the reasoning that establishes a single, ultimate vehicle. For that reason, those interested in the topics of the supreme vehicle must acquire a mind that has thoroughly mastered the subject matter being presented here.

What we have posited above, the existence of an element that at the time of sentient beings primordially has the good qualities, is a profound topic of the inconceivable, which is why the Buddha taught it as the ultimate of profound topics, instructing his retinues, "Trust in my words and you will not be deceived. This is difficult to understand on your own". Therefore, the sophists with their limited intellects argue back and forth about this ultimate of the profound topics, but all of their arguments—such as "the consequence is that there exists a mind that is a common basis for buddhas and sentient beings", and so on—are based in convention, so are just useless talk, which was said like this in the *Definitely Unravelling the Intent Sutra*:

> The character of the formative realms and superfact
> Is a character free of same or different.
> Those who comprehend them anyway as same or different
> Have engaged them not in accord with how they are.

According to that, both the dharmatā of mind—the essence element—and the dharmin mind must not in any way be proclaimed as same or different. They do not depart from the way things are, the fact of dharmatā, yet that does not contradict the possibility of the confused way they appear. It is more than that, for anything else would have faults such as there being no emancipation, confusion not being possible for anyone, and so on. Because the non-synchronisation of the way things are and appear does exist, it is proved that confused sentient beings exist and also that their abandoning confusion by engaging in the path then becoming buddhas also exists.

The reasoning of superfactual analysis establishes that all dharmas are empty. However, that does not negate the essence's good qualities because that person—the one whose works are the basis for the above explanations—maintained verbally[3] that the unsurpassable qualities exist but have an empty entity. Thus, the meaning taught by the middle turning, that all the dharmas of total affliction and complete purification are empty, is likewise established here because the sugata essence too has the nature of emptiness. Nevertheless, the buddha essence is taught here with the added feature of having no meeting and parting with what has the nature of emptiness, the appearances of kāyas and wisdoms, which is the intent of the definitive meaning sutras of the final turning. Due to that approach alone it is special compared to what is taught in the middle wheel, therefore the sutras and commentaries on their intent commend the meaning taught in the final turning as supreme. Note though that not all of the sutras included in the final turning speak that way—it is only the definitive meaning sutras that teach the buddha essence that do so. This can be clearly understood from other sutras that teach the species element, such as the one that shows it using the example of cleaning a jewel, and so on.

That being so, both the emptiness taught in the middle turning and the kāyas and wisdoms taught in the final turning must be known as unified appearance-emptiness. The issue of which of the sutras of the middle and final wheels is definitive in meaning should be understood only in the way that all-knowing Longchen Rabjam maintained, which is that both wheels can be definitive meaning, without need of eliminative differentiation. In his approach, not only is there none of the contradiction in which making one of the two definitive meaning entails making the other provisional meaning, but from grouping them together there is the sort of sugata essence that can be made out as the meaning of causal tantra, through which the key point of the foremost instructions of the Vajra Vehicle appears.

---

[3] This refers to Maitreya. The author assumes that the audience understands, through the wording used in the explanation for the third reason that has been given so far, that the explanation is based on the texts of Maitreya that were written down by Asaṅga after receiving Maitreya's verbal explanations in person.

Because of his approach, the need to understand those teachings of the Buddha as coming down to a single key point is upheld and, moreover, it can be understood that the pair Nāgārjuna and Asaṅga, and the others involved are of one mind in regard to this ultimate meaning, as is clearly seen from Nāgārjuna's *In Praise of Dharmadhātu*, *Enlightenment Mind Commentary*, and so on and Asaṅga's *Highest Continuum Commentary*, and so on.

Master Nāgārjuna also said that sort of thing:

> The sutras that show emptiness,
> As many as were taught by the conqueror,
> All turn away the afflictions
> But do not degrade the element.

In accordance with that, the result to be accomplished through analysis with superfactual analysis, the fact of the vajra-like inseparable ultimate truth, is the dhātu that is invincible in the face of the sophist's type of mind, so there is no basis for entering into arguments over superfact.

Now, I will explain how the element is seated in the mindstreams of those sentient beings. From the standpoint of actuality's own entity, all dharmas are contained within the space of that dharmatā and the dharmatā's own entity having no birth and cessation, all of them are residing in equality. Thus there is no good and bad of samsara and nirvana, and so on, and there are no factors of this shore and that shore, self and other, greater and smaller, and so on, and there are none of the distinctions of earlier and later times, and so on. It is the single unique sphere of dharmadhātu, without shift and change.

It is like that in actuality, but if we do this in terms of confusion's adventitious appearances, it is that appearances of the objects of body and mind of three-realmed samsara shine forth and then, although at this point the dharmatā's nature is not being seen, the dharmatā is not non-existent—it is there without the slightest wavering from its own nature. Thus, the dharmatā of mind like that having been enclosed by adventitious stains is not visible but it is present in the pith or centre as an essence, so is spoken of as a "gotra" meaning "species" or "garbha" meaning "essence". It has been taught that its being seated as such is to be understood through its illustration by the nine examples of a treasure under the earth, and so forth. Furthermore, the element is defined as having three phases in relation to the adventitious stains—impure, pure and impure, and utterly completely pure—though there is no such distinction in the element's own entity. It is as the *Highest Continuum* says:

> Because the wisdom of the buddha has entered the mass of sentient beings,
> That stainless nature is non-dual and
> That, the species of buddha, is accurately designated as the fruition,
> So it is said that all migrators have the essence of a buddha.

And:

> This is the nature dharmakāya,
> Suchness, and the species …

And:

> According to the sequence impure,
> Impure and pure, and utterly completely pure,
> The names "sentient being,
> Bodhisatva, and tathāgata" are given.

For someone who does not understand it that way, when he says, "sugata essence", his mind has an idea of it as something which, like Juniper sitting in a basin, is somewhere or other in the cage of the five aggregates, an imprecise idea that will be clearer or murkier depending on his level of confusion. That will be carried over into his efforts at refuting others' ideas and establishing his own, which can only end up with others crying aloud, "Oh no!" when they see how his idea is not consistent with the intended meaning of the Great

Vehicle. For that reason, it is pointless to broadcast this account of the buddha essence in the places of close-minded sophists who have not trained their minds in the Great Vehicle. This account of the profound is not to be taught to the immature and not to the Forders because they are not suitable vessels for hearing this profound dharma—which is why the Buddha started teaching them dharma with no self, impermanence, and so forth. And it is not to be taught to them because it must be proved by reasoning, but, because they will not be able to prove it with their seeing of this shore only, it can only turn into a topic of over- and under-statement for them.

A person's mind should be trained first in the tenets of the lower Buddhist schools. Following that, he needs to gain an outstanding level of certainty in the meaning of un-assessed great emptiness. When he has gained that, if he is gradually taught the story of the sugata essence, he will come to trust the primal situation.

Thus it is said that, "Though the path is completely pure, it cannot be established by reasoning; it has to be realized in direct experience". For that, you have to expose the stupidity of those who think, "If it does not become a path of the seeing of this shore, then it is not a valid path", then become expert in the key points of how to practise the path.

3. Dispensing with some Mistaken Positions

There are three parts to dispensing with some positions that come from wrong ideas about the nature of the element: dispensing with the view that the element in being not empty is truly established; dispensing with the view that the element is a cut-off empty condition; and dispensing with wisdom in being impermanent taken to be compounded.

3.1. Dispensing with the View that the Element in Being Not Empty is Truly Established

This matter has been discussed in the *Noble One, Descent Into Laṅgka* like this:

> The bodhisatva Mahāmati asked the Bhagavat, "Sir, how is the Buddha's teaching in the sutras that the tathāgata essence that dwells in an enclosure of stains is permanent, stable, and eternal different from the Forder works advocating a self? The Forder works moreover advocate a self by way of its being without good qualities, and so forth".
>
> In reply, the Bhagavat instructed, "Theirs is not the same. The buddhas have taught tathāgata essence with the meanings of the words three doors of complete emancipation, nirvana, and the unborn. Then, in order completely to get rid of immature beings being scared by no self, they teach the domain of the no-discursive-thinking place without appearance as a doorway to teaching the tathāgata essence—in regard to this Mahāmati, the bodhisatva mahāsattvas who arise in the future and the present should not strongly cling to a self."

And:

> Furthermore, the Buddha taught that there is no emancipation for those who have the perception of things; if something is not empty of self-entity, even though it might exist empty of other dharmas, that would not fulfill the function of emptiness. Of the seven ways of being empty, the worst is the emptiness of one and another one; in that case "what is to be abandoned" and the like is infinite. And moreover Mahāmati, the tathāgata is not permanent, not impermanent. Why is that? It is because both of them will be faulty.

And:

> You have been gripped by the māra of elaboration.
> You are to go beyond existence and non-existence.

And:

> If there existed a dharma that was superior to nirvana, that supreme dharma too will be like an illusion and a dream.

And so forth. In line with the meaning of such scripture, even with analysis by reasoning it is, due to the key point that the sugata essence has an empty entity, possible for it to be mind's dharmatā, pervade all objects, be permanent for all time, be inconceivable, and to shine forth without bias as every aspect of the good qualities. However, those words do not mean that not being empty of a self-entity it is truly established, for if it were truly established in that way then everything that it could be—the dharmatā of other dharmas, and so forth—would forever be impossible. As well as that, for a valid cognizer of superfactual analysis, the result to be accomplished that has been determined by such a valid cognizer could never be reached by anyone because in the aftermath of all dharmas having been analysed down to being without true existence, an establishment of even one true establishment does not remain, like darkness does not remain when there is light. A valid cognizer of conventional analysis also cannot establish a true establishment, because for it there might be true establishment but merely by that that dharma cannot ever be established as not empty. Given that that cannot be established through either of the two valid cognizers, going after any proof of it would be like chasing a sky flower, so attempting to prove it ends up in meaningless weariness.

3.2. Dispensing with the View that the Element is A Cut-off Empty Condition

Those who do not understand the type of reasoning used in connection with the dhātu of unified appearance-emptiness and take a different approach to it, taking the species, the dharmadhātu, and emptiness as mere assessed superfactual truth, a non-affirming negation, make proofs that contradict the texts that advocate the primordial possession of the good qualities. The *Samādhi of Wisdom Mudrā Sutra* says:

> Saying, "We are not bound in not desiring dharma
> And pursuing gain, we train for enlightenment",
> A future group of advocates who
> Like to talk will say that everything is empty.

And:

> "Emptiness unborn is not made by anyone.
> It is not seen, does not come, and does not shift—
> That reference we properly train in as emptiness".
> Those who speak thus are robbers of dharma.

And:

> If consumed with thinking about a non-existent dharma,
> Anyone who is immature will be fettered by that agitation.

And the *Verse Summary Prajñāpāramitā* says:

> Even if he realizes "these aggregates are empty", a bodhisatva
> Is coursing in concept labels, which is not faith in the unborn.

The *King of Samadhis* says:

> "Existence" and "nonexistence" both are extremes.
> This pure and impure also consists of extremes.
> Therefore, having utterly abandoned both the extremes,
> Experts will not engage in dwelling in the middle, either.

The *Sutra for the Benefit of Angulimālā* says:

> Oh my! There are two beings in this world who destroy the holy dharma. Both those who have the view of an extremely empty condition and those in the world who advocate a self destroy the holy dharma, ruining the holy dharma with their mouths.

And it has been said:

> If one clings to emptiness, the antidote that removes all views, as a thing or non-thing, that is a view that is incurable.

And it has been said again and again in the sutras and treatises on them:

> With empty and not empty you have not gone beyond all references; all of them must be abandoned.

In other words, even if those people have done an examination using reasoning, the aspect they have of a non-affirming negation that has merely severed true establishment involves a severance of that to be negated which has been merely imputed by a grasper that is associated with thought, due to which they have not arrived at actuality freed of exaggerations about it. Because this is easy to fathom, there is no need to say much about it here.

The mere factor of emptiness of truth that is a non-affirming negation is not the fully characterized dharmadhātu and actuality. However, it is all right for beginners to involve their minds with it merely as a doorway to the fully characterized one. A sutra says:

> Mañjuśhrī, compared to a bodhisatva who gave whatever is needed to the Three Jewels for one thousand god-years, another bodhisatva who for the smallest finger snap analysed with the thought, "All compounds in becoming are impermanent. All compounds are suffering. All compounds are empty. All compounds are without self", would create uncountably greater merit.

3.3. Dispensing with Wisdom in Being Impermanent Taken to be Compounded

You might wonder, "Ground sugata essence becomes manifest as it really is, all-knowing wisdom, like the sun becomes free of clouds.

Is that wisdom permanent or impermanent?" The sutras sometimes say that all-knowing wisdom is permanent and sometimes say that it is impermanent. Here is what they mean.

Conforming to the mind-set of others, disciples whose ground has not been entirely transformed, the scriptures say, "all-knowing wisdom is impermanent". In regard to that, the *Complete Commentary on Valid Cognition* says:

> A valid cognizer of permanence does not exist
> Because of a valid cognizer knowing substantial existence,
> And because knowables are impermanent
> Their one also is impermanent.

This is what is means. All-knowing is impermanent because it arises from the path's causes such as the arousing of enlightenment mind, meditation on emptiness, and so forth, so it is not tenable to say that it arises without cause. As well as that, all-knowing is impermanent because it is a direct perception valid cognizer of all dharmas. If valid cognition is a non-deceptive mind, then the valid cognizer that evaluates existing things must in accordance with that be a non-permanent one. Because its object, the knowable, is impermanent, the valid cognizer that evaluates it also is impermanent, arising as something having a succession of moments. On the other hand, if it were permanent, because it would be established by valid cognition as empty of the ability to perform a function, it would be ascertained to be empty of actions in their entirety of evaluating objects, and so on. Thus, it is totally untenable to say that all-knowing wisdom is permanent, and so is established to be impermanent. Similarly, all things are designated as impermanent and all non-things as permanent, but there is no basis for it to be permanent, so a dharma that is a fully characterized permanent will not be found at all.

That approach has to be taken for the Forders, who are outside the Buddhist tradition, and for those of the common vehicle who have not trained their minds in the approach in which there is a transformation within the entity of the inconceivable dharmatā. From the point of view of consciousness, the situation of the way things appear, there is no other way that all-knowing could shine forth.

Despite that, from the point of view of wisdom of entire transformation, all-knowing is established as permanent. In the end, that the knowables set out in the proof of impermanence have momentary arising and ceasing and the perceiving subject wisdom also arises having a succession of moments, and other such observations, only appear that way in the appearances of those who have not entirely transformed the ground. In the fact of how things are that has been established according to suchness, that is not the only way that it is established; in that fact, there is no dharma at all that arises for even a single moment, and if that is the case, then why state the obvious, which is that the succession that starts at the time of such an arising, and so forth, is not established? It is like for example a dream from its own view has various appearances with boundless time successions with an earlier beginning and a later end and has directions but they are not established as such.

Thus, when the fact of that dharmatā without birth and cessation has, in accordance with what it is, been entirely transformed into ultimate wisdom, it is the wisdom kāya of inseparable knower and knowable. And, when there has been no transformation of it, mind's innate disposition or the unified dharmatā that is by nature luminous is still changeless. Therefore, it has in it no distinction of earlier and later, so is called "the species which is present in the nature". What has change is the adventitious stains separable from it, which arise in a succession of momentary arisings and ceasings, and this non-equality of samsara and nirvana, good and bad, and so on, appears as undeniably not deceptive to those having the dualistic appearances of not having done the transformation. However, arising and ceasing dualistic dharmas are not established in the innate disposition, rather, dharmas abide in the great equality within which state all factors of changes of time and direction are all at once comprehended, and that does exist as the object of the personal self-knowing wisdom of the noble ones, and it is not spoiled by change of the three times, thus it is designated using the convention "the great permanence", because it is something that exists but without momentary arising and cessation.

It is like this. All the knowables of time and direction, such as the changeable things and the non-things like space, and so on, are included in that dharmatā in equal taste, but that dharmatā is not contained by any dharmins that have change, and so on. It is like the sky is a container of the clouds but the sky is not contained within the clouds.

That being so, the dharmatā great equality and the dhātu with its innate disposition of luminosity are present simultaneously in a single unique sphere of self-arising wisdom that naturally pervades all things. However, having adventitious stains, its own nature has not become manifest. Through the power of the abandonments and realizations belonging to the five paths that dispel the stains, it will be gained as the great wisdom in which knower and knowables are inseparable. When that happens, you will have gained the great all-knowing wisdom that while not thinking, effortlessly and spontaneously knows that all awarenesses, because they are unchanging self-arising wisdom, are of equal taste in the innate disposition of dharmatā.

Now that approach will not lead to self-arising wisdom being born from causes. In the authentic, the dharmakāya free from the adventitious stains has been reached as a disconnected result—it seems to be something newly arisen from causes, but ends up appearing that way only in the way things appear when there has been no transformation. On the other hand, in the fact of the authentic, the entity of the dharmakāya that is the dharmatā's nature has no birth and disintegration; according to the ultimate intent of the sutras of the profound, all dharmas primally are manifest buddhahood in equality, or from the beginning peaceful nirvana, or luminosity by nature, and so on. These ultimate intents are topics that even the bodhisatvas have difficulty contemplating, let alone ordinary people!

Nevertheless, if you trust in what is so, you will devote yourself to this approach because it is commended as being equivalent to obtaining the prophecy of having become irreversible from buddhahood.

If in accordance with that approach you view the tathāgata's wisdom kāya as permanent, merit will arise. It is said in the *Sutra Called "Samādhi due to Miracles that Fully Ascertain Utter Peace"*:

> Mañjuśhrī, compared to some sons or daughters of the family who gave whatever gifts were desired to the four retinues in each of the world realms of the ten directions for ten million god aeons, another son or daughter of the family who, having devotion to meaning that would accord with what is, says the words:
>
> > The tathāgata is permanent.
> > The tathāgata is eternal.
>
> will be creating a countless greater merit.

And the *Great Nirvana Sutra* says:

> Kāśhyapa, sons or daughters of the family should always with a one-pointed mind assiduously apply themselves to these two words: "The buddha is permanent and abiding".

And:

> If someone assiduously works at the perception of permanence in regard to the inconceivable, that is the place of going for refuge.

And as well as that it says in sutra:

> Viewing the kāya of the tathāgata as impermanent is not going for refuge at all and if the vajra kāya is viewed as impermanent, immeasurable disadvantages will arise.

Having understood what they are saying, it is then necessary that you bow to the meaning of the authentic.

❁ ❁ ❁

In that way, sugata essence's own entity, free of all elaborations of existence and non-existence, eternalism and nihilism, and so on, is the single unique sphere of the inseparable truths, equality. Within the state of that actuality, all dharmas of appearance and becoming have become one taste, just thatness. Seeing in accord with that is to see the fact of the authentic without removal and addition, so there is separation from grasping consciousnesses in their entirety, which is the excellent view that realizes superfact. It is as the *Showing the Dharmas Conducive to Enlightenment Sutra* says:

> Mañjuśhrī, the one who, in regard to all dharmas being non-dual in being without not being equal, sees them without duality has the correct view.[4]

And as the *Sutra Petitioned by Ākāśhakoṣha* says:

> There is things and non-things consciousness
> And what is residing in the authentic limit.
> Those expert in the view do not grasp
> Things and non-things.

And as the bodhisatva sutras say:

> In superfact, in face of the noble ones' prajñā and wisdom, any dharmas to be thoroughly known, or abandoned, or meditated on, or made manifest are not present at all.

Nevertheless, in the case of making good distinctions using the valid cognizer of conventional analysis:

- you know what is true as true such as knowing the path of the noble ones to be non-deceptive;

---

[4] This is not easy to read, but it is how the original reads. It is the style of expression of their time.

- you know what is not true as not true, such as knowing that advocating liberation by meditating on a self is a wrong view;
- you know what is impermanent as impermanent, such as knowing that all compounded things are momentary;
- you know what is permanent as permanent, such as knowing that sugata essence, self-arising wisdom, is always unchanging;
- you know what is non-existent as non-existent, such as knowing that the self and the appearances of grasped-at and grasper are not established by nature;
- you know what is existent as existent, such as knowing that the-way-things-appear of interdependent origination is infallible cause and effect and knowing that the dharmatā sugata essence with the good qualities spontaneously present naturally exists in all sentient beings;
- and so forth.

That is the style in which prajñā that is not twisted apprehends the mode conventionally of things, so through engaging what is to be known in that way you attain vast good qualities because it is a root of virtue that is without delusion.

Using that style of correctly understanding the matter at hand, the sutras teach many dharmas generally and specifically and especially, although there is no self of a person, they refer to sugata essence, which beyond both the elaborations of self and non-self, as the great self, and so on, teaching it as the supreme good qualities of transcendence which are spoken of as purity, bliss, permanence, and self. The sugata essence exists as the changeless good qualities of peaceful, cool, perfect, ultimate, great non-abiding nirvana and in order for one to know that it does exist, the *Nirvana Sutra* says:

> What is called "self" is any dharma that is permanent in the authentic. That which has become an owner that is unchanging and unshifting is called a "self".

Having heard the explanation of this profound sugata essence given above, even simply accepting and devoting yourself to it will produce immeasurable benefits. It is as the *Highest Continuum* says:

> The intelligent one accepting this object of the conquerors
> Will be a vessel for the buddha qualities.
> Through delighting in the inconceivable good qualities,
> He surpasses the merit of all sentient beings.
>
> Someone in pursuit of enlightenment decorates every day the dharma kings with gold and gems
> Numerous as the atoms in the buddha fields by offering such to them.
> In comparison, if someone else hears some words from this and having heard moreover has devotion to it,
> He will gain much greater merit than what came from the generosity.
>
> An intelligent one wanting unsurpassed enlightenment for many aeons even
> Works effortlessly to keep stainless discipline of body, speech, and mind.
> In comparison, if someone else hears some words from this and having heard them moreover has devotion to it,
> He will gain much greater merit than what came from the discipline.
>
> Someone whose absorption removing the fire of afflictions of the three becomings
> Has reached the abodes of the gods and Brahma cultivates the method of shiftless complete enlightenment.
> In comparison, if someone else hears some words from this and having heard moreover has devotion to it,
> He will attain much greater merit than what came from the absorption.

This is something whose profundity and depth are difficult to fathom, so if you know of it and have devotion to it, it will be very meaningful, though this teaching that is the lion's roar of the irreversible, the essence of the supreme vehicle that shows the story of sugata essence, is of the utmost profundity, so it is difficult for those of little previous training and inferior intellect to have devotion to it. The *Compendium of the Tathāgata Sutra* says:

> This wisdom of mine
> Is doubted by those of immature mind.
> They do not do the transformation,
> Like an arrow shot into the sky falls.

The *Sutra Gathering All the Threads* says:

> Fools like them are blessed by māra to go to the bad migrations, therefore, they are thought of as faulty. Those who propound the dharma bestowed by the Tathāgata also are thought of as faulty.

The *Sutra Petitioned by Brahmadatta* says:

> If you teach the dharma that was well spoken,
> Those of evil conduct will find it disagreeable.
> Having produced doubts about the dharma, those without faith
> Will become insane for many tens of millions of aeons.
> Their thoughts lacking in faith make them evil-doers.
> Moreover, they cannot protect their minds filled with hate.
> Having completely abandoned all that is of value,
> Those without faith cling to the dregs.
> Priding themselves and always haughty,
> Those without faith do not respect others.

And:

> They foment disagreement with non-dharmic words.
> Those who stain the teachings of the conquerors

> Are filled with doubts and apprehensions, like the
> Forders.
> Having fomented disagreement with those who recite the
> dharma,
> Those without faith moreover abandon the dharma.

And the *Eliminating Lax Discipline Sutra* says:

> Śhāripūtra, the sort of person who, drowning on the path of life clings to dispute and harms himself and others, the sort of person who is not a holy being, will completely fill this Jambudvīpa.

One should consider carefully the approach being taught in those scriptures and others like them. When the degenerate times have started up and those who show reverence for the teachings are mainly corrupting the key points of our own system of the supreme vehicle through a perverted understanding of the four reliances and counterfeit dharma has arisen, those treasuring this as the life of the Great Vehicle path will be rare indeed. Through reverence for the teachings of the Early Translation lineage vidyādharas, I saw and heard many precious authoritative statements of the lineage. And, due to the good fortune of receiving at the crown of my head the lotus feet of many authentic spiritual friends—the regent of Padmasaṃbhava and lord of conquerors Jampal Shonnu who was youthful Mañjuśhrī displaying himself as a man, and the all-knowing Dorje Ziji, and others, I who am immature in age and intellect have developed just a little knowledgeability in regard to this profound topic.

It is like this. This nice exposition of the meaning of the species residing as the nature of the dharmadhātu and that that has the mode of utterly non-dwelling unification free from all extremes, is the lion's roar. The *Sutra Petitioned by Brahma Viśheṣhachinti* says:

> Devaputra, the ones that express not being attached to any dharma at all are the lion's roar. The ones that express attachment are not the lion's roar, they are the fox's

> barking. The ones that teach the production of views are not the lion's roar.

And the *Great Nirvana Sutra* says:

> The lion's roar is the explanation that ascertains that all sentient beings have the nature of a buddha and that the tathāgatas forever abide and are unshifting.

And:

> Son of the family, many places explain that the topic is emptiness, but those should not be called "the lion's roar". What is proclaimed within circles of experts having prajñā should be called "the great lion's roar". That lion's roar is not explained as the fact that "all dharmas are impermanent, suffering, selfless, and entirely impure"; it is only explained as the tathāgata being permanent, blissful, self, and entirely pure.

Those and other sutras speak extensively about the lion's roar, using both example and meaning in order to illustrate it, so it should be understood from them.

Speaking straightforwardly in that way about our own path of sugata essence may cause some disagreement in others, but it is a presentation of the correct path, so others should not become upset by it. As is said in *Entering the Middle Way*:

> The work of composing the treatise was not done out of attachment to analysis and debate, it was done for complete liberation. If in explaining suchness, I have destroyed others' texts, there is no fault.

This approach also guards the dharma. The *King of Samadhis* says:

> What is "guarding the dharma"? It is connected with the fact that those who disparage the Buddha's dharma annihilate what accords with the dharma.

It also is holding the dharma, as mentioned in the *Sutra Petitioned by Gaganagañja*:

> Who has the character of the enlightenment of the Conqueror
> Wholly holds the character of dharma and
> Whoever fully knows this spotless limit
> Holds the qualities of all the buddhas.

The person who in that way has come to hold the dharma is grateful to the Buddha for what he has done and also attains immeasurable merit. This is because of what *Showing the Tathāgata's Great Compassion Sutra* says:

> It is like this: they approach because of the dharma of the Conqueror
> And they renounce because of the dharma, not material things.
> Thus someone who holds to the dharma of the Sugata
> Is grateful to all the buddhas for what they have done.

And it is because of what the *Sutra Petitioned by Gaganagañja* says:

> Although praised for tens of billions of aeons,
> There is no limit to the wisdom of the Buddha,
> And like that, the merit of the one who holds
> The holy dharma of the tathāgata cannot be measured.

❁ ❁ ❁

Due to this my knowledgeability of the textual tradition
Of the supreme vehicle has increased a little,
But who would rely on the words of me, a crazy monk,
Who is young in years and immature in training?

These days, the others follow after famous people.
They lack the intelligence to analyse what is and is not.
Most are completely agitated by the negativities of envy.
I know that it is not the time for eloquent explanations.

Still, by always respectfully making offerings to
The supreme guru and special deity on the lotus in my heart,
The words and meanings of the excellent texts
Dawn more and more clearly in the realm of insight.

At that time earnestly applying myself to becoming familiar with
elegant explanations,
Prolonged joy has arisen for a long time and in future lives
In other fields also, there will be a superior delight
In the Conqueror's way of dharma like the moon waxing.

Due to this story of the ultimate of the profound
Those with intelligence will find joy which is not like
The happiness when one has fallen into the extremes of becoming
and peace.
Therefore, this is a joyous feast for those of good fortune.

May the lion's roar of the supreme vehicle of unified appearance-
emptiness
That has abandoned strong clinging in its entirety,
Overwhelm the swarms of wild animals of wrong views
And resound throughout the ten directions as the essence of the
Conqueror's teaching.

The holder of the store of jewels of the three disciplines, the dharma brother named Guṇa said, "Write a complete explanation, whatever comes to mind, of 'Because the complete buddha kāya radiates' and the rest". At his urging, I, the monk Lodro Drimay, wrote this at Sharma. May virtue and excellence increase!

❁ ❁ ❁

We searched for the text of this composition amongst the texts of the lord guru, finding it after two full years, at which time we were to undertake the cutting of wood blocks. The person who previously urged the composition to be done came to meet us and together with the very knowledgeable Legpay Lodro urged us, "If you still need to do more, such as making additions, do whatever you need!" Therefore, some further wording was added to the original. All the points of the original together with the new additions were proofed during two days at the waxing moon of the Saga month in the Iron Rabbit year at the practice centre of Dudlay Namgyal Ling by Lodro Drimay Jampal Gyaypay Dorje.

MAṄGALAM

A Thorough Commentary to The Lion's Roar That is a Great Thousand Doses Of the Sugata Essence

by

Tony Duff

INTRODUCTION

The teaching of the Buddha hinges around the one point that anything living that has a mind has within it the potential to become a buddha. If they did not possess that potential, it would not be possible for them to become buddhas and the rest of the Buddhist teaching would be an interesting but useless philosophy. In fact, the Buddha would not have even bothered to teach if we did not have this potential. For us then, being certain about this potential and that it does exist in us is a central issue.

This potential is most generally called "buddha nature", meaning that we have the nature of buddha within us and because of that we can become buddhas. Of course, this begs the question of why we would bother to become buddhas even if we do have the potential to do so. Answering that question can take up a book in itself, so here it is enough to say that our mode of being is distorted because of a fundamental ignorance we have concerning our actual nature and, correspondingly, our existence as a whole is one of constant unsatisfactoriness. You would not be reading this book if you were not driven to find answers to the problems of life, so passing over that issue, the central question here is what buddha nature is and whether or not we really do have it in us.

Did the Buddha teach why the buddha nature exists in the mindstream of all sentient beings? Yes. His teaching on it was part of the complete set of teachings on the potential to become a buddha that he gave in his third and final set of teachings, called the final turning of the wheel of dharma. Did others also teach it? Yes, it was taught especially by the next buddha to be, Buddha Śhākyamuni's regent named Maitreya, and clarified by other great Buddhist masters of India.

The text here by Mipham starts by introducing the need to use our intelligence to develop certainty that we do have buddha nature. It continues by giving scriptural support for that, then applies reasoning to establish that what the scripture says is true. It ends by presenting very clearly what buddha nature is. By the end of the text, Mipham has not only given us a survey of the reasons for the existence of the buddha nature in all beings, but has also given us a complete presentation of the very profound teaching on the buddha nature that was originally given by the Buddha. It would be easy to read a precis of Mipham's text and think that it was a long dissertation on reasoning that was focussed on one issue within the overall teaching on buddha nature. However, it is essential to understand that his text also goes on to be a thorough presentation of the Buddha's extremely profound teaching on it.

To fathom the significance of that, it is necessary to know that there is what is called a common or ordinary understanding of buddha nature and an extraordinary, exceptionally profound understanding of it. The ordinary understanding is simply that buddha nature is like a seed of buddhahood that, if watered and nourished, will sprout and grow into full-blown buddhahood. That is a very simplistic, though extremely useful understanding for everyone to have that the Buddha presented early in his teachings. Later, during his final turning of the wheel of dharma, he gave a complete set of teachings on buddha nature that were taught from the exceptionally profound perspective that the buddha nature is actual buddhahood and that, rather than developing it in the way that one would develop a seed, all that has to be done is uncover it or, as Mipham says, transform it from its covered-over state to its pristine state of buddhahood that has always been existing in us.

Having clarified that, we can now point out that the uncommon, very profound teaching of buddha nature is the ultimate teaching of all of the sutras. Moreover, it has the same meaning as the extremely profound teachings of the tantras, including Mahāmudrā and Mahāti or Dzogchen, because the profound buddha nature is exactly the actual buddhahood that those higher teachings show.

There are many these days who want the profound non-dual teachings, especially of Mahāmudrā and Mahāti. I can see them putting aside this book just on hearing that it focusses on reasoning. However, theirs would be a grave mistake for the simple reason that this book does present the same ultimate, non-dual perspective as those very high tantric teachings, even if it does it from the slightly less direct approach of the sutras.

Everyone practising Buddhist paths has to accept that there is the potential for buddhahood in them—no-one would even begin to bother practising the path to enlightenment without that belief. In that regard, the common understanding of buddha nature works for everyone, regardless of the level at which they practise. However, for those practising the tantras and especially for those practising the extra-secret, unsurpassed level of Dzogchen, the uncommon understanding of the buddha nature—also called the sugata essence—shown by Mipham in this text is a necessity. In case you doubt that, here is what the great Dzogchen master Tenpa'i Wangchug said about Longchenpa's seminal text on Dzogchen called *Dharmadhātu Treasury*:

> "Dharmadhātu" in the title refers to the primal dhātu, the sugata essence.

In other words, the whole text of the *Dharmadhātu Treasury* is about none other than the profound meaning sugata essence. And he also said:

> Self-arising wisdom, the by nature completely pure sugata essence spontaneously-existing buddha, is the buddha at the beginning before all buddhas, so is also referred to in the *Rigpa Self-Shining Forth* as "the ancestor of all buddhas":
>
> > I am the ancestor of all buddhas.
> > In the prior condition when I do not exist,
> > There is no name of buddha to be.

If the *Rigpa Self-Shining Forth*, one of the seventeen root tantras of extra-secret unsurpassed Dzogchen, equates the potential for enlightenment—here named sugata essence—with the teachings of Dzogchen and then says that it is the ancestor of all buddhas using the special terminology of Dzogchen, you can be sure that the uncommon, extremely profound presentation of sugata essence is none other than the Dzogchen teaching, though expressed less directly. Therefore, the contents of Mipham's text are an essential part of every Dzogchen practitioner's understanding.

The Vocabulary of Buddha Nature

The buddha nature has been given many names over the centuries, by the Buddha himself to start with and by the great masters of India who wrote treatises on the Buddha's intent.

The buddha nature, garbha, gotra, dhatu, potential, and seed of a buddha

There are six terms commonly used to express buddha nature from the perspective of its being the seed of buddhahood.

1. Buddha nature

"Buddha nature" is the most generic term used to indicate the potential to become a buddha. It simply means that mind has in it the nature of a buddha.

Garbha or essence

The most commonly used term for the buddha nature is the Sanskrit "garbha", translated into Tibetan with "snying po". The term has several related meanings. It is used to mean "womb", a place from which something can be produced. It is also used to mean an internal space within which something resides. It is also used to mean an inner sanctuary for example of a temple, an inner sacred place where the most important work of the temple happens. It is also used to mean an essence existing within. When used to describe the buddha nature, it means a place internal to the mind that contains the precious essence of a buddha, a place which functions as an inner sanctum from which actual buddhahood can come. Given that we do not have a word with this rich set of associations in one English word, it would be preferable not to translate it. However, in order to have the text as much as possible in plain English, I have chosen to translate it as "essence", for example "sugata essence", "tathāgata essence", "buddha essence", and "the essence".

Dhatu of buddha

The next most common name for the buddha nature is the Sanskrit word "dhātu". This term has a very wide range of meanings in Sanskrit, so many that the Tibetans used three different words to translate it.

1. "Dhātu" translated into Tibetan with "dbyings" means a zone or space within which things can come into being. The term dharmadhātu is often used in Buddhism and is used in the teachings of buddha nature. The dharmadhātu is that zone within which dharmas or phenomena are born and exist. The term "dharmatā dhātu" is also used in the teachings of buddha nature to mean the fertile zone of dharmatā, which is the empty space that is our most fundamental nature. The term dhatū is used in other, similar ways in Mipham's text.

2. "Dhātu" translated into Tibetan with "khams" means the element from which something becomes full-blown and also the basic constituents of something. When used in that sense, it has been translated as "element" in this book. There are two different meanings of element that will be seen. One is "element" specifically meaning the element of buddhahood existing in all sentient beings. The other is the basic constituents or makeup of sentient beings—what sort of senses they have, what sort of consciousnesses of those senses they have, what sort of objects are known by the senses and consciousnesses, and the structures both gross and subtle they have, and so on.

There are other meanings of dhātu too but they are not used in this book.

Gotra or species

The other main term used for the buddha nature is the Sanskrit "gotra". It means that thing which, because it is of the same type or same family as something else, allows for that something else to be produced. In other words, because sentient beings have in them something of the same type as buddhahood, buddhahood is possible. Thus, this term is often translated as "family" or "lineage" in relation to the buddha nature, but Jamgon Kongtrul in one of his major works on buddha nature points out the meaning of "same type" is most important—the buddha nature is something that is the same type as buddhahood and therefore can give rise to it. In terms of the translations that have already been used the correct meaning would be "something of the same line or family". However, having thought this through and researched the Sanskrit meaning, the meaning of "gotra" in relation to the buddha nature is more like "species". The buddha species exists inside all sentient beings and therefore buddhahood is possible. In order to have the text in plain English, I have chosen to translate it as "the species", for example "the buddha species" and so on.

Sugata essence and tathagata essence

There are two principal names for the buddha nature in Sanskrit: "sugatagarbha" and "tathāgatagarbha". The two terms can be used interchangeably to refer to the buddha nature, however, each one conveys a particular sense and is used in a particular context.

The names sugata essence and tathāgata essence come from joining sugata and tathāgata with garbha, whose meaning has just been explained. Sugata essence and tathāgata essence mean that essential place within mind from which sugatas and tathāgatas respectively come.

Sugata is comprised of "su" and "gata". "Gata" means to go or to have gone. The prefix "su" is a general term that means anything and everything on the side of good experiences: happy, easy, comfortable, pleasant, nice, blissful, and all other such terms describing the good side of existence are wrapped up in this one term. Based on that, "sugata" conveys two meanings in one word: it means a person who goes in a pleasant, happy, easy, etcetera way and equally a person who has gone to a pleasant, happy, etcetera destination. Sugata is one of many terms for a buddha, but has the specific sense of a person who has gone on the Buddhist path which is considered to be a good and relatively easy spiritual path to travel compared to others and who has arrived at the happy, pleasant, and so on level of a completely enlightened person, a buddha. In short, it means "one who has gone happily to happiness", but that is clumsy so I have left it untranslated in here.

Tathāgata is comprised of "tathātā" and "gata". "Gata" again means to go or have gone. Tathātā means "as it is ness" and is used to indicate the situation of reality just exactly as it is. A tathāgata is a person who has completed the journey to enlightenment by having arrived at the situation of being completely in accord with reality just as it is. This has been translated into English as "thus gone one", but that is clumsy so I have left it untranslated in here.

The term tathāgata was and is frequently used in the Buddhist tradition to refer to our Buddha Śhākyamuni as an honorific form of address and likewise to all buddhas in general. The term sugata is not used as widely but is used in preference to tathāgata in certain contexts. One of those contexts is the set of teachings on the buddha nature or essence. In those teachings, a buddha is almost always referred to as a sugata and the buddha nature is almost always referred to as the sugata essence.

There is a reason for using sugata essence in preference to tathāgata essence, which is that sugata and sugata essence by association are very practical terms. They are used in teachings where there is a need to emphasize taking the journey to and actually arriving at enlightenment. The teachings on the buddha nature are all about the feasability of actually going on that journey and arriving at the ultimate relief of buddhahood, so the terms sugata and sugata essence are used to emphasize that point. It is important to understand that and to take these terms accordingly.

The Importance of the Teaching on Sugata Essence

When the sugata essence is transformed from being an essence of buddhahood it becomes the full-blown or manifest form of buddhahood. In other words—and this is a central issue in arguments about sugata essence that Mipham takes up at length—the essence of a buddha exists in all beings but that essence is not changed in order for it to become its fully manifest form but is simply transformed from its obscured form of buddhahood to totally unobscured buddhahood. It is not that the essence of a buddha is a precursor to buddhahood that is modified in a process of cause and effect that leads to it becoming actual buddha, but that the buddha essence simply has its actual entity of buddhahood revealed and made manifest.

That, in a short paragraph, is the gist of a large section of the arguments about sugata essence found in Mipham's text. The reason for the argument is that there were significant numbers of learned Buddhist teachers in Tibet who said that the essence was a precursor which through cause and effect type endeavours could be made into buddhahood. It can be understood that way but that is not a profound understanding of what the buddha essence actually is and how it becomes buddhahood for us.

Proving that the Sugata Essence Exists in All Sentient Beings

Next, there is the issue of proving that the sugata essence exists in the mindstreams of all sentient beings.

The Buddha stated repeatedly in his teachings on the sugata essence that it does exist in the mindstreams of all sentient beings. That the Buddha said so is sufficient for those who have sufficient trust in the Buddha's words to accept it as a fact. However, there are those who want reasons for that before they can completely trust in it.

At the time of the Buddha, the bodhisatva Maitreya had completed all ten levels of a bodhisatva. The Buddha gave the prophesy that Maitreya would be the next buddha. For that reason, anything that Maitreya says must be taken as authoritative statement. Later, Maitreya gave the Indian master Asaṅga many teachings that Asaṅga wrote down in a series of five treatises that became known as "The Five Dharmas of Maitreya". Of the five, the treatise called the *Great Vehicle Highest Continuum Treatise* is a complete teaching on sugata essence. Its title is a direct reference to sugata essence, because sugata essence is the highest type of mindstream that sentient beings possess. It is also called *Ratnagotravibhaṅga* meaning "distinguishing the precious species" where the precious species refers to the sugata essence, precious because again it is the highest type of mindstream within a sentient being's mindstream.

The *Highest Continuum* is one of the very important texts used in Tibetan Buddhist studies because it gives a final or ultimate presentation of sugata essence. The text consists of seven what it calls "vajra topics". The fourth vajra topic gives three reasons for why sugata essence exists in all sentient beings, then nine examples to demonstrate how it exists in them. These three reasons and nine examples are a very famous aspect of the treatise. The three reasons are given in a single four-line verse:

> Because the complete buddha's kāya radiates,
> Because suchness is without differentiation,
> And because the species exists, all bodied beings
> Perpetually have the essence of a buddha.

These three reasons have been understood in different ways by different Tibetan masters. Mipham's text in essence is a presentation of how the three reasons have been understood by learned Tibetans before him and how his Nyingma tradition understands them. By presenting the others' views and showing with reasoning how those views are faulty and then presenting his own tradition's view and showing with reasoning how it is correct, he does two things. Firstly, he gives a thorough explanation of the three reasons. Secondly, he presents the exceptionally profound teaching of the sugata essence which many learned masters of India and Tibet accept as being the Buddha's ultimate intent of the entire sutra teachings and also the intent of the tantras.

Mipham's text is laid out according to the form established in ancient India for treatises on dharma. It has a section of prefatory matter including the title, a line of prostration, and what is called the declaration of composition; the body of the text; and a section of concluding matter including colophons.

THE PREFATORY SECTION

THE TITLE

In the title, *Lion's Roar That is a Great Thousand Doses of the Sugata Essence*, "lion's roar" shows that this is a text about the ultimate teaching of the Buddha. When a lion comes into an area which other animals like foxes, jackals, tigers, and leopards have claimed as their territory and roars, all the other animals are overwhelmed and back down, leaving the lion in charge. None can compete with a lion when he roars and likewise, no other teacher and no lesser teaching, even of a buddha, can compete with the ultimate teaching of a buddha. The ultimate sutra teaching of the Buddha appears in a set of the sutras of the final turning of the wheel of dharma called the definitive meaning essence sutras[5]. Thus, the title begins by telling us that this book is about the ultimate teaching of Buddha, which is the teaching of the sugata essence.

Some people additionally explain that this text, with its complete set of scriptural supports and reasonings proving definitive meaning sugata essence is like the roar of a lion appearing in the midst of the many lesser explanations of sugata essence that were given over time in Tibet.

---

[5] Tib. nges don snying po'i mdo.

Finally, this text is a particular style of text called a "thousand doses"[6] text. This is an old term used to indicate a text that collects the many essential points of one or more vast texts on a subject into a single, smaller commentary, somewhat like a compendium of the main points of the text or texts. Moreover, it is a "great" thousand doses text because it includes the essence not of one or two sutras but of many sutras of both the middle and final turnings of the wheel of dharma.

The Prostration

Following the title, the text starts with "namo gurave" which is the correct Sanskrit for "prostration to the guru". The guru, where the basic meaning of guru is a teacher who has the knowledge needed to teach a student and the capability needed to carry the student along, is important at all levels of Buddhism, including at the level of the sugata essence teachings. It has been said:

> The guru is the embodiment of all the buddhas ...

The meaning is that gurus are the ambassadors of the Buddha who have learned the teachings and who pass them on to us in the times when a buddha is no longer available. Therefore, the text starts with a prostration to the guru. Here, "guru" includes both one's personal guru and the lineage gurus.

The Expression of Worship

The expression of worship shows what a text will be about and often highlights the main lineage teachers through whom the teaching on it has been passed down. The expression of worship can be a long piece of verse and possibly prose, but in this shorter text it is a single a four-line verse:

---

[6] Tib. stong thun.

In the primally stainless dharmatā of mind sits
The definitive meaning personified in the Warrior
Mañjuśhrī
Whose sharp sword of ascertaining logic continuously
Severs the total stupidity that weaves the web of
becoming[7].

The first line states the subject of the text. It is about "the primally stainless dharmatā of mind", which is the "definitive meaning" sugata essence taught by the Buddha in the final turning of the wheel of dharma.

The term "dharmatā" is used widely throughout this text, so it is important to understand it correctly from the beginning. It is a general term meaning the most basic property of something, for example the dharmatā of water is that it is wet and of fire is that it is hot. Our most basic quality as sentient beings, our dharmatā, is the definitive meaning sugata essence. For us, the stuff of dualistic mind acts as dirt or "stains" that obscure it from view. However, from the first or "primally", those stains do not affect and so taint or create a fault in the sugata essence itself. Thus our dharmatā or basic property is primally stainless wisdom in the form of the definitive meaning sugata essence.

That dharmatā of mind is the actual sugata essence, so the teaching here concerns the final or definitive meaning itself. Definitive meaning teaching straightforwardly and directly points out the definitive truth of any situation. Compare that with provisional teaching that shows a meaning that is not the final or definitive thing but leads towards the actual thing or definitive meaning itself shown by definitive meaning teaching.

The definitive meaning sugata essence is the actual buddha mind pointed out by the definitive meaning teaching on it that was given

---

7 "Becoming" is another name for samsara; see the glossary for more.

by the Buddha in the final turning of the wheel of dharma. One person who has transformed that definitive meaning sugata essence so that it is fully manifest buddhahood is Mañjuśhrī. Thus the definitive meaning sugata essence is personified in Mañjuśhrī. Of many buddhas, Mañjuśhrī is mentioned here because he is closely associated with the intelligence to know things correctly, which fits with this text's focus on correct reasoning. Moreover, definitive meaning sugata essence is brought to us through the particular form of Mañjuśhrī called Warrior Mañjuśhrī because he has the assured confidence of a brave warrior needed to proclaim the lion's roar of sugata essence.

Generally speaking, there are three ways to know whether something is true or not. We can rely on direct sight of something with our senses, we can understand it through correct reasoning, and we can accept the words of those who are in a position to make authoritative statements about it. If we are talking about very profound matters such as definitive meaning sugata essence, then we will not be able to validate it directly with our senses. Therefore, in the Buddhist tradition it is said that we can know the truth or otherwise of matters such as definitive meaning sugata essence by relying on the statements of the buddhas and great masters of the tradition and by relying on correct reasoning.

Mañjuśhrī wields a sharp sword in his right hand symbolizing the use of correct reasoning or logic to ascertain any matter under consideration, in this case the definitive meaning sugata essence. His sword continuously and completely severs the total stupidity—meaning having no knowledge of or being very obscured about reality—of sentient beings that weaves the web of becoming and traps sentient beings within it.

In what ways are sentient beings stupefied in regard to reality? In the study of valid cognition, seven kinds of rational mind are mentioned in connection with having a correctly cognizing mind. Three of them are rational minds that are not correctly cognizing: rational mind with no understanding, wrong understanding, and doubt. Warrior Mañjuśhrī's sharp sword continuously uses correct logic to cut through those minds in order to arrive at a rational mind that is a correct understanding.[8]

With the use of Mañjuśhrī's sharp sword of logic, we sentient beings can develop a correct understanding of the sugata essence within us. Through that we become confident of the presence within us of a sugata essence and are motivated to practise the path to buddhahood, eventually becoming buddhas ourselves. Thus, the use of correct reasoning at the beginning is an important step in making our escape from the web of "becoming" into emancipation. "Becoming" is another word for samsara, one that points out that sentient beings, due to the forces of karma and affliction, are constantly becoming or changing into something else with no control over it. When sentient beings practise the path and become buddhas, they enter the realm of changeless reality and have no more becoming.

---

[8] For rational mind, see the glossary.

THE BODY OF THE TEXT

Now Mipham shifts to prose and begins the body of the text. The prose begins with "Now I will give the actual explanation", a standard device used in Tibetan to show that the author has now shifted from the prefatory material to the body of the text. It has the sense "Now, in regard to this prefatory material, what we actually have to talk about is this".

Introduction: The Need to Establish the Meaning of a Sugata Essence Using Scripture and Reasoning

The text says:

> The essence of the speech of all the conquerors gone in the three times, the centre of their minds, the single central issue amongst all the teachings of the sutras and tantras, is only this all-pervasive sugata essence ...

"Conqueror" is one of many names for a buddha, with the particular sense of being someone who has conquered the four māras[9]. "The conquerors gone in the three times" means all of the buddhas that

[9] For māra, see the glossary.

ever will be: those who have gone to buddhahood in the past and present and those who will go to buddhahood in the future.

The very essence of what all of them teach, the most central issue for every one of them when teaching the dharma to their followers, is the sugata essence that pervades all sentient beings. It is the most central issue for all of them because understanding the sugata essence and then bringing it into manifestation is the one and only way to attain buddhahood. Because of teaching it, ordinary beings can become sugatas or buddhas. You might think, "Yes, but there are other ways to reach buddhahood, for example by practising other sutra teachings such as emptiness or by practising the tantras". In fact, sugata essence is the ultimate teaching of the sutras so, in the end, everyone who wants enlightenment through the sutras will have to practise it. Similarly, the profound meaning sugata essence of the sutras is exactly what is practised in the tantras such as Mahāmudrā and Mahāti. Therefore, this statement about sugata essence is correct.

The text continues:

> This approach is so profound that it was said that even the mighty lords of the tenth level, like trying to see a form in the darkness of night, have difficulty in realizing it just as it is, let alone ordinary people.

The Buddha taught that this teaching of the sugata essence that is the dharmatā of sentient being's minds is so profound that it is very difficult—just like trying to see something clearly at night without any extra lighting—to realize even for the mighty lords among bodhisatvas who have mastered the tenth bodhisatva level. Note that the term "mighty lords of the tenth level"[10] does not mean "the great bodhisatvas dwelling on the ten bodhisatva levels" nor does it mean "the great bodhisatvas dwelling on the tenth level" but refers

---

[10] Tib. sa bcu'i dbang phyug.

specifically to those bodhisatvas who have reached the tenth level, trained in it, and mastered it. Bodhisatvas who have reached that level of training are the most advanced of all bodhisatvas, being one step away from complete buddhahood. Buddha Śhākyamuni had disciples who were at this level, for example the bodhisatvas Maitreya, Mañjuśhrī, and Samantabhadra. If bodhisatvas at even that level of spiritual development have trouble understanding the definitive meaning sugata essence, then why even mention how difficult it would be for us ordinary beings to do so!

"**Moreover, when the teacher, the sugata, spoke ...**" The text moves on to explain that the Buddha taught sugata essence from two different angles but that actual, definitive meaning sugata essence has those two unified, not separate. It explains that some people have mistaken what definitive meaning sugata essence is because of that. Then it points out that there have been others fortunate enough to receive the profound instructions on it that accord with the Buddha's actual teaching on it, and it is through their way of talking about it that Mipham will explain it in the rest of the text.

Sometimes the Buddha taught the sugata essence from the perspective of its entity[11] meaning what it is at root. In Buddhism in general it is regarded that what anything is at root is emptiness, so to say that he taught it from the perspective of the entity of the sugata essence means that he focussed on its empty aspect, which corresponds to the teachings he gave in the middle turning of the wheel, for example, in the Prajñāpāramitā Sutras. Those sutras talk only about phenomena, including the sugata essence, from the perspective of their emptiness.

---

[11] Tib. ngo bo. See entity in the glossary.

Sometimes the Buddha taught the sugata essence from the perspective of its entity's nature[12]. The entity of something is what it actually is at root and the entity's nature is how that entity comes out. Note that the entity and nature of something are different and should not be confused as being the same. Teaching from the perspective of the nature of the sugata essence corresponds to the teachings given in the definitive meaning essence sutras that were taught in the final turning of the wheel. At that time, the Buddha taught the luminosity nature of the empty entity. It is crucial to understand that luminosity is a metaphor for knowing something; the entity of mind might be empty but it has a nature of being illuminative, of being luminosity that makes what it knows visible. Moreover, luminosity has all the good qualities of buddhahood—a buddha's ten strengths, four fearlessnesses, eighteen unmixed qualities, and so on, which are summed up as the "kāyas and wisdoms"—primordially present in it. Therefore, because a sugata essence exists in all sentient beings, those good qualities of buddhahood also exist in sentient beings.

Although the Buddha taught sugata essence from those two perspectives, his definitive teaching on it was that it has to be understood not as the emptiness aspect and not as the luminosity aspect but as those two aspects completely unified. Another way to say that is that he taught it as the inseparability of the two truths. This teaching of a sugata essence that is emptiness and luminosity or emptiness and appearance indivisible from each other is more than profound, exceedingly profound.

Historically, there have been people who, because of the profundity involved, have become afraid of and not trusted in this definitive meaning teaching. Due to their lack of trust, some learned teachers in Tibet asserted the view that sugata essence does not have an empty entity and in doing so fell into the extreme of permanence. They had such a strong view of the luminosity nature that they lost the empty

---

[12] Tib. rang bzhin.

aspect to a greater or lesser degree and in that way fell into a view of permanence or eternalism in relation to the sugata essence. Others, also due to their lack of trust, held that the sugata essence is a mere, bare emptiness, where the term "bare" means "by itself alone". They had such a strong view of the empty entity that they lost the luminosity aspect and in that way fell into a view of nihilism in relation to the sugata essence; one of the consequences and great faults of their view is that it is then not possible to posit a sugata essence that has the good qualities of a buddha.

Those are the two main types of mistake that happened in Tibet in relation to sugata essence. One way to look at them is that the first is overstatement, which can also be called exaggeration, involving the claim that something that does not exist does exist. The second is understatement or denial; a person who asserts that sugata essence is a mere blank emptiness is thereby denying the presence of the kāyas and wisdoms—meaning the buddha qualities as a whole—that primordially do exist in sugata essence.

The actuality of all dharmas is that they never depart from being the union of appearance—the luminosity aspect of mind—and emptiness, but not understanding that, some people grasped at the luminous aspect and others at the empty aspect, corresponding to the two principle extremes of permanence and nihilism.

The people who advocated those positions were very learned and would bolster their positions with much logical argument. The noise that happened in Tibet as they attempted to establish their own positions that they so dearly wanted to prove as the correct position and went about refuting the views of others was tremendous, like the crashing of a turbulent ocean. When you know all the details of the history involved, you will understand that this is not hyperbole. Therefore, to have a text like this from Mipham that correctly shows the meaning of sugata essence through the use of authoritative statements of both the Buddha and other masters of the tradition and through correct reasonings is essential.

Not everyone made those mistakes. Many very fortunate people in Tibet had the guru's foremost instructions on sugata essence—and there are now people both non-Tibetan and Tibetan who have them today—that explain that sugata essence is both emptiness and luminosity unified. These special instructions are like a most refined nectar of teaching that correctly shows sugata essence, and that nectar has seeped into their hearts[13]. People like these come to trust in the teaching of the inseparability of emptiness and luminosity, so for them any extreme views they might have had that fell on the sides of appearance or emptiness have collapsed and in that way they do not have faulty views of the sugata essence present in their minds. These people are the ones who see things as they really are, so Mipham will now write about how they would talk about sugata essence using the correct view of it that has been passed to them by the lineage in foremost instructions about the matter.

"Generally speaking the word of the tathāgata ..." Mipham goes on to explain that the first step towards correctly understanding any of the Buddha's teaching, including sugata essence, is to understand and use correct reasoning. Generally speaking, the words of a tathāgata—someone who has gone *gata* to being completely in accord with how things actually are *tathātā*—that is, a buddha, come from knowledge which is only ever valid cognition. Dharmakīrti, one of the great Indian experts on correct reasoning and valid cognition said in his *Complete Commentary on Valid Cognition* that valid cognition by definition is a non-deceptive understanding and a valid cognizer is a non-deceptive mind having the valid cognition. Accordingly, the buddha word is only ever non-deceptive[14].

As mentioned earlier, we say in Buddhism that the way to establish whether something is correct or not is to use "scripture and

---

[13] For foremost instructions see the glossary.

[14] Tib. mi slu ba. This is an important term in the topic of valid cognition.

reasoning". We need to clarify here what "scripture" means. The Sanskrit term is "agama" and its Tibetan equivalent is "lung". This has generally been translated into English with "scripture", but that is not the meaning. This term means something that has been said by someone who truly knows the matter and whose words therefore are "authoritative statement". When authoritative statement is written down, it is referred to in religious contexts as scripture but the actual meaning intended is "authoritative statement". For readability, this term has been translated as "scripture" in this book, but when you see "scripture", you must understand that it means authentic statements usually made verbally but which also may have been recorded in writing. This is a very important point because this term is used to imply validity of what has been said, not whether it has been recorded as scripture.

Generally speaking, all the words of the Buddha, the tathāgata, are correct and non-deceptive, so become authoritative statements which are "pure", meaning that they correctly state the situation, and which will withstand whatever reasoning are brought against them. However, we cannot afford to put aside analysis of them that would make us certain of their meaning and simply have faith in what has been said. Rather, it is essential that we investigate such statements or scriptures with reasoning to assess with certainty whether or not they are valid and non-deceptive.

In order to do such an investigation or analysis as it is called, there are what are called "the three analysers". It is said that the application of these three analysers can "completely purify" scripture, meaning that if the scripture withstands analysis with them, we will become certain that the scripture is "pure", meaning free of all faults. That certainty then leads to trust in the scripture, which is the desired goal.

The three types of analysis are: valid cognition using direct perception, valid cognition using inference, and valid cognition using scripture. Direct perception is the best of the three, inference next best, and scripture the least best.

We ordinary beings can rely on direct perception in some cases, but because of our general state of delusion that is not always possible. For example, a buddha can see everything, including the tiniest atoms in direct perception, but we can only see gross physical matter in direct perception. You might say, "There is a flower because I see it with my eyes" and you and others would accept that as proof that there was a flower because of your having directly seen it with your eyes. However, you might say, "There are no atoms because I do not see them with my eyes". That would be a direct perception of the eye but it would not be a valid cognition because your ordinary human eyes do not have the capacity to see atoms directly. A buddha on the other hand would say, "There are atoms, I see them directly with my mind" and that would be a direct perception that could not be refuted because a buddha's mind by definition is all-knowing. Thus, direct perception is the best type of valid cognition, but there is the further distinction that there are degrees of capacity of direct perception and that also has to be taken into account.

Inference is the next best way to have valid cognition. We humans are fortunate to have a rational mind that has the capacity to use inferential logic to validly know something. However, rational mind has to be properly trained in the use of inferential reasoning for it to be able to perform correct inference, that is, for the inference to be a valid cognition. It is noteworthy that these days, with compulsory schooling for most humans, people are generally very capable of performing inferential reasoning, but that it is incorrect because they have not been trained to ensure that the process is seated in valid cognition. Most commonly, people have accumulated many concepts that they hold to be true but which they have never examined to see if they are true. They use those as the assumptions behind their inferential reasoning but their conclusions are frequently incorrect because their assumptions are incorrect. Therefore, a text like this one of Mipham's is exceptionally useful to Western dharma practitioners, regardless of their level of practice.

Scripture or statement is the least reliable of the three analysers simply because it is the words of another person. Scripture or statement can only be relied on if we are certain that the person making the statements has valid cognition himself. Therefore, in our Buddhist tradition, we first prove to ourselves that a buddha's knowing is only ever valid cognition, then after that we can refer to a buddha as someone who only ever has valid cognition and can accept what any buddha has said as valid. The Buddha himself said in a talk with the people of Kalama village, recorded in the *Kalama Sutra*, that we should not simply accept his word as true because of his having the name "buddha". He said that we should analyse what he has said thoroughly and then, if we find it to be true, we can be certain of its validity then trust it.

Why should we not just trust the scripture of the Buddha? Mipham points out that it is undeniable that, when all types of scripture—Buddhist and otherwise—are taken into account, there are both true and counterfeit scriptures and moreover, even for true scripture, some are provisional in meaning and some are definitive in meaning. Remember that "scripture" here means authoritative and hence true statement. "True scripture" is true authoritative statement. "Counterfeit scripture" is scripture that looks like true authoritative statement but is not. Early in his teaching the Buddha said, "The dharma spoken by a buddha is well-spoken" and explained that buddhas always gave good and correct explanations whereas the teachers of the other religions of his time gave false, or incorrect, or poorly reasoned, or unsuitable explanations. Therefore, whereas a buddha's authoritative statement is always true, other teachers' authoritative statement will be counterfeit. Then there is a second point that, even within the true scripture of the Buddha, some teachings are provisional in meaning and some definitive. For example, the scripture of the Lesser Vehicle and the scripture of the Great Vehicle are not in agreement in places, but both are true. The difference is that the first is mainly provisional scripture designed to lead the followers of the Lesser Vehicle on to the definitive scripture of the Great Vehicle. In short, we cannot avoid the fact that not everything said and written is true and even if something is true it could be provisional in meaning, therefore it is incumbent on us to use reasoning to establish what is true and what is not and then within what is true to establish what is provisional and what is definitive.

"In view of that, ordinary people …" Mipham moves on to explain the complete process of learning and validating our knowledge. The term "ordinary people" means those who are not spiritually advanced, those who are subject to the total stupidity mentioned in the verse at the beginning of the text. It actually means "individualized beings"—beings who, due to fundamental ignorance, have developed the sense of being an individual separate from everything else. "Individualized beings" stands in contrast to the term "noble ones"—those who have transcended that fundamental ignorance and thereby become spiritually superior to the ordinary individualized beings.

Individualized beings like us start out by learning about what we need to know in order to achieve our goals, whatever they might be, including travelling the path taught by the Buddha. In the standard process of learning we first listen to someone who knows about what we want to accomplish, then think through what we have understood from that in order to refine our understanding of it. Refining our understanding includes both removing incorrect ideas that we have about the subject matter as well as finding places where we have doubts and need to ask questions or do further research. This process of first hearing someone speak about what we want to learn and then correcting our understanding of it through contemplating what we have heard is referred to in Indian and Tibetan cultures as "cutting exaggeration by hearing and contemplating".

"Cutting exaggeration" in that way brings a clear and correct understanding of the subject matter in which you are interested. However, a further step is necessary. You need to become absolutely certain that what you have understood is correct. In the Indian and Tibetan systems of logic, that certainty is gained by applying what are called "the three analysers" or "three valid sources of knowledge" to the understanding that you have developed using hearing and contemplating. Then, based on that certainty, you will gain a deep-seated conviction or trust in your understanding. Trust is actually a type of faith; in Buddhism, it is considered to be the strongest of three kinds of faith, which are explained extensively in the book *Unending Auspiciousness, The Sutra of the Recollection of the Noble Three Jewels*. You must have that certainty and the trust that comes from it to be truly successful in your field of study or, in this case, spiritual journey. Aside from the foundation that it will give you for your own journey, it will also give you what is needed to successfully convince others of your understanding and defend yourself against arguments brought against you.

The text says, "A person who has not in that way achieved certainty in himself through the use of his own valid cognition will not be able to establish certainty in others who are arguing against him". It continues with, "Such a person is comparable to someone who is obscured in regard to flesh-eaters yet claims 'There is a flesh-eater in front of me'". This sentence uses a phrase found in Indian texts on valid cognition that means "obscured in regard to the object, as with a flesh-eating type of spirit"[15]. The phrase means that a certain type of object is not visible to an observer because of the observer's obscuration, for example, human beings are usually unable to see flesh-eating spirits, even when one is standing right in front of them. For example, do you see flesh-eating spirits around you? For most people the answer will be no. Because you are obscured in regard to flesh-eating spirits, you can only assert that you do not see any; you cannot assert with certainty that there are none present. Certainty is the key word here. The point being made is that, until you have investigated and validated what you have heard and contemplated to the point of certainty, you will not fully trust in your understanding for our own purposes nor will you be able to prevail in argument where your opponent is following correct reason.

---

[15] Tib. sha za bskal don.

"Therefore, experts take the approach ..." Therefore, those who are really learned, for example, the experts of Buddhist teaching, always speak in accord with correct logic. When they argue, because their arguments are always proved by correct reasoning and cannot be refuted, their opponents are naturally quieted and, at the same time, the others on their own side, the ones who follow the same system of tenets, will be exuberant with nothing able to detract from their exuberance. On the other hand, when argument is done with logic that cannot be proved by correct reasoning, no matter how many people are involved and no matter how much they embellish the argument with various reasons, their words can only become grounds for further argument against them, further argument that will spring up all over the place, like the little springs that appear everywhere in the flat and very wet valleys in the summertime of Tibet.

"For those reasons ..." Having explained in that way the need for correct reasoning, Mipham says that you enter into this, the tradition of the conquerors and their great sons such as Mañjuśhrī and the regent Guardian Maitreya, together with the lineages that arose from them such as those of Nāgārjuna and Asaṅga, all of which follow correct reasoning that is in accord with what actually is and cannot be disturbed by the arguments of sophists. Sophists[16] translates a term that literally means "people caught up in discursive thinking only".

Having turned to that tradition and its lineages, you must use correct reasoning to examine and validate what the tradition says. To do so, you have to start by being honest about the reasoning and the conclusions it leads to. To do that, you give up all attachment to any assumption or conclusion, then follow correct reasoning and see where it leads you without attachment to the outcome. These are just a few words but they contain the essence of how to use reasoning

---

[16] Tib. rtog ge ba.

in order to come to a correct conclusion. Most people in the world simply do not have the courage to be honest with their reasoning. They are usually so attached to their beliefs and opinions that, even if correct reasoning leads them to a certain conclusion, they will not accept it. Mipham's words in this one sentence are few but they go right to the heart of why most people cannot get their reasoning straight and then, not trusting in what is actually the case, trust in ideas and beliefs that only lead into the miseries of samsaric existence.

With that sort of honest and correct assessment as your basis, you can examine and evaluate the teachings about the sugata essence in order to find out what can and cannot be proved to be the actual teaching of sugata essence taught by the Buddha. When you do that, you find that the two types of view about it that were laid out earlier as being extreme views—of those who overstate the sugata essence as being not empty of an entity and therefore truly existent and permanent and of those who understate it as being a cut-off emptiness[17], meaning that it has no relation to anything else and is therefore without the good qualities that the luminosity aspect has—are not in any way provable as the actual teaching of sugata essence. You will find in the process that those who proclaim these two views do not have any correct reasonings to prove that theirs is the correct view of sugata essence and you will also find that the reasonings they use to prove their views are undermined by the correct reasonings that you will apply with your honest approach to argument.

In that way you will find that the view of a sugata essence whose entity is empty and whose nature primordially has the good qualities of buddhahood in its luminosity, and which exists as the element of a buddha in the mindstreams of sentient beings, is a view that can be

---

[17] Tib. phyang chad. The term "cut-off emptiness" or "cut-off empty condition" is used throughout this book. It means a bare empty condition that goes no further than itself and so has no relation to anything outside the empty condition. It is the same as what is called a "bare emptiness".

proved with correct reasoning and cannot be undermined by correct reasoning at all.[18]

That completes Mipham's introduction. Now he moves on to the actual explanation of the reasons that prove sugata essence exists in the minds of all migrators[19]. As is done in logical argument, he starts by posing the question that is to be investigated.

Posing The Question

Mipham asks, "What is the proof of the existence of the element, sugata essence, in the mindstream of migrators?"

This is a key question because if beings did not have sugata essence, they could not become sugatas, buddhas. In that case, any and all efforts made to practise the Buddha's teaching would be a waste of time. Nāgārjuna makes this point in his *In Praise of Dharmadhātu* when he says:

> If the element exists, by doing the work
> You will see the pure form of the purest of gold.
> If the element does not exist, you might do the work,
> But it will end in only hardship being produced.

As explained earlier "the element" translates the Sanskrit "dhātu", which is one of several names for sugata essence. "Dhātu" has many meanings in Sanskrit, two of which are widely used in the sugata

---

[18] Tib. gnod pa. The term "undermined" is used to mean refuted by correct logic and refers to the situation where a refutation has been made that successfully faults an argument. For example, if there is a cup of tea and you say that there is a cup of tea, nobody could fault that with correct argument. However, if there is a cup of water and you say that there is a cup of tea, a correct argument could be used to refute that or to undermine your statement.

[19] For migrators, see the glossary.

essence teachings. This has been discussed in the introduction to the commentary but is re-visited here for the sake of clarity:

1. "Dhātu", translated into Tibetan with "dbyings" means a zone or region of space that is a source for something, like a garden bed is the zone or region within which flowers grow and appear. The dhātu here is the dhātu of dharmadhātu, which literally means the zone or region of space in which dharmas, phenomena, arise. It is also used alone to indicate any expanse of space, for example the dhātu of space itself and the dhātu of the sky. Dhātu with this meaning is often used in Mipham's text and to ensure that its meaning is not confused with the second meaning of dhātu also used widely in this text, it has not been translated but left as "dhātu".

2. "Dhātu", translated into Tibetan with "khams" means a basic constituent, a basic element of something. In the sugata essence teachings, it is one of several names for the sugata essence. It is the "element" of buddhahood found in the mindstream of every migrator. To ensure that its meaning is not confused with the first meaning of dhātu, it has been translated as "the element".

Giving The Answer

The bulk of Mipham's text is taken up answering the question just posed. He answers it in three sections: first the views of early Tibetans are presented and refuted; then the correct view, according to Mipham's own Nyingma tradition is presented and explained; then some specific wrong views of sugata essence are refuted. This section that constitutes the bulk of Mipham's text uses much reasoning but does not descend into mere polemic. In it, Mipham skilfully uses reasoning not only to validate his understanding of what the Buddha taught concerning the sugata essence but to guide his audience into a deepening understanding of the sugata essence. There are two main ways that the Buddha presented the sugata essence, a common and easy to understand way and a profound and very difficult to understand way. By the end of his answers to the question posed, Mipham has provided us first with a very clear understanding of the common approach and then with a very clear understanding of the profound teaching of the definitive meaning sugata essence.

To prove the existence of a sugata essence in the mindstreams of sentient beings we can use two of the three analysers described earlier: scripture and reasoning. First we will consider the scripture that can be used for the purpose.

Among the sutras of the Buddha there are Great Vehicle sutras of the final turning of the wheel that teach sugata essence and are considered to be the very essence of the Buddha's entire sutra teaching. Then, among all the masters who came after the Buddha and clarified the meaning of those essence sutras the two main ones have been Nāgārjuna and Asaṅga. Nāgārjuna wrote extensively about the sugata essence in his *In Praise of Dharmadhātu*. Asaṅga received extensive instruction on the meaning of the final turning of the wheel of dharma from Maitreya in person then recorded what he heard in the form of five important texts called the "Five Dharmas of Maitreya". Of the five, the one called the *Great Vehicle Treatise on the Highest Continuum* talks only about sugata essence and is universally regarded as definitive meaning teaching on it.

Mipham chooses the *Highest Continuum* as the scriptural authority for answering the question just posed. The *Highest Continuum* is comprised of what it calls "seven vajra topics". Of them, the fourth vajra topic presents the existence of a sugata essence in all sentient beings using three reasons and nine examples. The three reasons are presented in this verse:

> Because the complete buddha's kāya radiates,
> Because suchness is without differentiation,
> And because the species exists, all bodied beings
> Perpetually have the essence of a buddha.

The verse is a logical argument in the form of a syllogism. A syllogism is comprised of a subject, a thesis about the subject, and one or more reasons to prove the thesis. Here, the subject is sugata essence and the thesis to be proved is that "all bodied beings perpetually have the essence of a buddha". Three reasons are given to prove the thesis: "because the complete buddha's kāya radiates", "because suchness is without differentiation", and "because the species exists". Bodied beings here is simply a synonym for sentient beings.

The verse is the authoritative statement of Maitreya heard in person by Asaṅga and recorded by him in the *Highest Continuum* scripture. However, and as Mipham pointed out in his introductory material, we should not just accept this scripture simply because it is the words of Maitreya but should first investigate it with correct reasoning to establish a correct understanding of what it says, then develop certainty and trust in that understanding. Therefore, Mipham now uses reasoning to establish the meaning of the verse. The analysis is done under three main headings: a presentation and refutation of others' view of the meaning; a presentation of Mipham's own Nyingma tradition's view of the meaning; and a section in which he dispenses with three mistaken views about the nature of sugata essence.

1. The Presentations of Other Traditions

This section begins with a brief explanation of the way that early Tibetans understood the three reasons given in the verse from the *Highest Continuum* then gives an extensive refutation of that.

There was an initial spread of Buddhism in Tibet that started in the seventh century C.E. with King Songtsen Gampo and Thumi Sambhota and was later strongly developed by Śhantarakṣhita and Padmasambhava and their disciples. That spread of Buddhism in Tibet was almost destroyed late in the ninth century by King Langdarma. Following that there was a second spread of Buddhism in

Tibet that started early in the eleventh century C.E. The tradition that developed during the first spread later became known as the Nyingma, meaning "the early ones". Two major traditions appeared during the beginning of the second spread—Sakya and Kagyu. Later in the second spread, a smaller though important tradition called the Jonang appeared and later still in the second spread one more major tradition—the Gelug—appeared.

Thus, when Mipham says "early Tibetans" he does not mean Tibetan masters of the Nyingma tradition—that is his own tradition and he will present it later. By "early Tibetans" he means Tibetan masters who appeared during the beginning and first few centuries of the second spread, a period that lasted officially for one hundred years. These were masters who had a close connection with the Indian tradition, many of them having gone down to India and obtained the teachings there and then returned. They were people of a formative time who were strongly engaged with translating Indian Buddhist works and trying to establish their meaning once again in Tibet.

Mipham says nothing of it, but anyone well-versed in the views of this early time in the second spread will know about the various, distinct positions that the early masters of the time took in regard to emptiness and the meaning of sugata essence. A few of the translators and masters involved were people such as the great translator Ngog Loden Sherab, Tsalpa Chokyi and his eight great disciples called "the eight great lions", Drolungpa Loden Jungnay, Jachen Rolwa, Tolung Jamarwa, Shang Tsepongwa, Chakyi Lama, Go Lotsāwa, Zu and Tsan, and many others.

1.1. Presenting the Positions of Early Tibetans

"Early Tibetans explained ..." In this paragraph Mipham gives a summation of how early Tibetans understood the meaning of the three reasons given in the *Highest Continuum*. An extensive treatment of their understanding would show differences of opinion among them about this, but if we were to sum up the main opinions of the time, it comes out as Mipham presents it.

1. The first reason is "because the complete buddha's kāya radiates". The words "complete buddha" or in Sanskrit "saṃbuddha" are used to indicate a buddha of the unsurpassed type. The sutras of the Great Vehicle explain that the arhat buddhas of the Lesser Vehicle are not complete buddhas, that complete buddhas are the buddhas who, through journeying in the Great Vehicle, attain unsurpassed truly complete enlightenment. Then, the word "kāya" is an abbreviation of "dharmakāya". Thus this first reason has to be understood as "because the complete buddha's dharmakāya radiates".

The early Tibetans explained just above understood that to mean that "a truly complete buddha's wisdom dharmakāya pervades all objects", where objects includes all knowable objects, animate and inanimate.

2. The second reason is "because suchness is without differentiation". The term "suchness" is tathātā in Sanskrit and de bzhin nyid in Tibetan. It is similar to the Tibetan "de kho na nyid" which is used a few times in this text to mean "just that-ness". The early Tibetans took suchness to be the mere emptiness of the non-affirming negation type. For them, it did not refer to the primordial unity of appearance and emptiness in which the emptiness is not a non-affirming negation type of emptiness. Of these early Tibetans, Tsalpa Chokyi Sengge was very learned. He said that all dharmas, meaning phenomena or what can be known by mind, are without true existence[20] and that the actuality of this lack of true existence is merely emptiness, an emptiness that is a non-affirming negation, which is why Maitreya said, "because suchness is without differentiation". Tsalpa Chokyi Sengge says that that non-affirming negation emptiness is the species of a buddha.

3. The third reason is "because the species exists". The early Tibetans understood this to mean that all sentient beings can become buddhas. As explained earlier, "the species" means something of the

---

[20] Tib. bden med.

same type or species. Thus, if there actually is something of the same type or species as buddhahood existing in the mindstream, then a sugata essence exists in the mindstreams of all sentient beings. This uses the proof of the reverse logic that if buddhas exist, the species of buddhahood necessarily exists in the mindstream of sentient beings.

Mipham ends the current paragraph by pointing out that the early Tibetans explained the meaning of these three reasons with just a few words about each but in doing so did not arrive at and directly show the essential meaning of this verse from the *Highest Continuum*. Several of them wrote long commentaries on the *Highest Continuum* but, when they got to this verse, they did not go on at length about the three reasons. Rather, they briefly explained the meaning as just shown and in doing so did not bring out the real meaning contained in the words of the verse.

1.2. Refuting the Positions of Early Tibetans

Mipham now refutes the understanding of the early Tibetans. He does this in two main parts: a refutation of their understanding of the first reason and the second reason. He does not refute their understanding of the third reason because he basically agrees with their understanding of it.

1.2.1. The first reason

"Merely that the dharmakāya pervades all objects …" The early Tibetans said the first reason means simply that "the buddha's dharmakāya wisdom radiates" throughout or pervades all objects or knowables, therefore sentient beings can become enlightened. Their reasoning is that a buddha's dharmakāya includes wisdom which, by definition, knows everything, including not only its own appearances but—and this is important here—also everything that appears as part of others' appearances. Therefore, it radiates throughout or pervades all knowables. However, there is the problem that, if that is so, an actual buddha's wisdom is within us sentient beings and we should be enlightened because of it, but we are not. Therefore, Mipham says, "Because of seeing that the dharmakāya of one's own mindstream has not become manifest at present, one has doubts about this", where this means their understanding of the first reason. Later, when Mipham explains the more subtle understanding of his own Nyingma tradition, you will see how "the dharmakāya radiates" should be taken.

1.2.2. The second reason

"The meaning of the species is not found at all in mere assessed emptiness ..." begins a long presentation and refutation of others' views of the second reason that continues all the way to the end of the current main section "The Presentations of Other Traditions".

This section starts with a refutation of the view of the early Tibetans as explained above, but moves on to refutations of the views of Tibetans later in the second spread, such as the Gelugpas, Sakyas, and Jonangs. It contains a substantial amount of argument that cannot be fully understood without a good practical knowledge of the tenets of those various traditions.

Mipham starts by making a headline observation that covers this entire section: "The meaning of the species is not found at all in mere assessed emptiness". There is a classification of emptiness into what is called "assessed emptiness" and "un-assessed emptiness"[21]. Assessed emptiness is emptiness as assessed by dualistic, rational mind; in other words, it is what we ordinary beings think emptiness is, not the fact of what it actually is known in direct perception. If we cultivate the path of dharma, then at the point when we have completed the third of the five paths[22], the path of seeing, we will have become noble ones having a direct perception of emptiness.

---

[21] Tib. stong pa rnam grangs yin pa, stong pa rnam grangs ma yin pa respectively.

[22] For five paths, see the glossary.

That emptiness in direct perception is what is called "un-assessed emptiness"; it is the fact of emptiness as opposed to a rational-mind-based concept about it.

Mipham does not say it directly, but there are second and third headline observations for this entire section. The second headline observation concerns the classification of phenomena into "un-compounded" and "compounded". Uncompounded phenomena are those not created by causes and conditions and compounded phenomena are those created or compounded by causes and conditions. An important point here is that the two are mutually exclusive, that is, something uncompounded can never be compounded and vice versa. A second important point is that whatever is uncompounded is devoid of the ability to perform a function, for example, it cannot produce a cause-and-effect type of result, whereas whatever is compounded can produce a cause-and-effect result.

The third headline observation for this entire section is that there are two types of negation in logic: non-affirming negation and affirming negation. The former is negation in which, something having been negated, there is no possibility of something being established in its place, so it is sometimes referred to as an absolute negation. For example, if you believe that you have a self that truly exists and you investigate that with logic, you can arrive at a kind of blankness in which the truly existent type of self has been negated with nothing else established in its place. The latter is a negation in which one thing is negated but it is still possible for something else to be established; for example, you can say that something is not white, but that does not rule out its being another colour, such as black.

A non-affirming negation emptiness is one in which there is just nothing, in which everything has been negated. The Nyingmas usually regard this as a conceptually-known or assessed type of emptiness. The fact of sugata essence meaning the actual sugata essence known in direct perception has an emptiness aspect that is un-assessed. Thus, for Mipham, the understanding of the earlier

Tibetans that the suchness in the second reason "because suchness is without differentiation" is an emptiness of the non-affirming negation type has the problem that a non-affirming negation type of emptiness has to be an assessed emptiness and if it is an assessed emptiness, then there is no actual sugata essence because the actual sugata essence has to be an un-assessed emptiness.

To return to the current paragraph "The meaning of the species ..." Mipham proceeds by examining the commonly used example for how the sugata essence, the species, becomes full-blown or manifest buddhahood. The early Tibetans said: "the species is like a seed which shifts status to being a sprout, with the species having none at all of the good qualities of a buddha at present but, after it has been taken hold of by the condition of the path, having them from the very beginning". In other words, the early Tibetans claim that the seed is merely emptiness and no more, so has no buddha qualities present in it now, but that cultivation of the dharma path will be the condition needed for the seed to become a result in which the buddha qualities were not created by the path but were there from the beginning. Mipham finds two faults with this. First, they claim the seed to be an emptiness of true existence of the non-affirming negation type, something which is uncompounded, but it follows from that that the seed would have no ability to perform a function such as producing a result. Second, while it is true conventionally speaking that a seed can produce a result by transforming into a sprout, there is still the problem that this seed having been claimed to be without true existence, could never turn into the dharmakāya of a buddha having all the good qualities of buddhahood.

You might think that if someone joins the seed of buddhahood, sugata essence, with the necessary causes and conditions for the development of the qualities of buddhahood by cultivating the dharma path, then, like a seed that is watered and nourished becomes a sprout, that person will become a buddha. However, that would entail the sugata essence, which is uncompounded by definition, becoming compounded because of being produced by cause and effect, which is impossible. Therefore, according to the way that the early Tibetans understood this second reason, there would be no connection between the uncompounded seed and compounded result, meaning that the buddha qualities did not end up having been there from the beginning as they say but were produced by cause and effect. The conclusion is that the good qualities of buddhahood could not be developed in a sugata essence of the type they are asserting, so their understanding of this second reason is totally untenable.

To say it another way, the example used by the early Tibetans to establish their understanding is that of a seed which, conventionally speaking, is able to transform into a sprout. However, in the fact of reality as opposed to dualistic convention, their non-affirming negation type of lack of true existence in a seed could never transform into the sprout of sugata essence having the good qualities of buddhahood, and on top of that, the good qualities of buddha are not compounded, they are uncompounded so, even though they say that the conditions of the path produce buddhahood with primordially existing qualities, such a thing is not possible.

⁂

Starting with "Furthermore, proving the possibility …" and going down to the end of this whole section, Mipham is still addressing what the early Tibetans of the second spread said about the second reason but also addresses what some later, but still early generations of Tibetans, said about it.

"Furthermore, proving the possibility …" brings the views of Tsongkhapa of the fourteenth century and his Gelugpa lineage into the discussion. Their views caused some deep problems within Tibet, exacerbated by the fact that their lineage in later centuries went out of their way to destroy Nyingma and Kagyu monasteries and teachings. After that, Mipham brings in the voices of the Jonang and Sakya followers, whose presentations, if properly made, he says are correct. In that way, he covers how some of the main voices of the later generations of early Tibetans viewed the sugata essence. Mipham does not mention the Kagyu anywhere in his presentations and refutations of others views because the Kagyu view of the sugata essence is the same as for the Nyingma.

"Furthermore, the proof that it is possible to become a buddha by a key point of being empty of true existence also is just spouting unexamined ideas". This especially addresses Tsongkhapa and his followers who laid great emphasis on finding emptiness using the key point of emptiness of true existence. Tsongkhapa came up with a way of emphasizing the middle turning of the wheel, whose main subject is emptiness, as the ultimate teaching of the Buddha and he especially focussed on referencing looking at "emptiness of true existence". Other traditions of Tibet mostly did not agree with him, either not agreeing with his "emptiness of true existence" approach or not agreeing with his claim that the Buddha's ultimate sutra teachings were in the middle turning, not the final turning of the wheel. Those who disagreed with the Gelugpa point of view summed up how the Gelugpas saw emptiness in a saying that became very popular. They said that for the Gelugpas "A vase is not empty of a vase; a vase is empty of true existence". Other Buddhist traditions of Tibet mostly asserted that a "vase is empty of a vase" which means that the concept of vase is gone but the superfactual truth of emptiness can still be there, whereas Tsongkhapa and his followers asserted that "a vase is empty of true existence", which, essentially speaking, is the non-affirming negation type of emptiness that cuts out all other possibilities and is still a conceptual understanding of emptiness, even if a very subtle one.

The words "true existence" and "true establishment" are a hallmark of Tsongkhapa's position that have long been a major ground for debate. Very extensive presentations of Tsongkhapa's way of asserting lack of true existence and Mipham's refutations of it that are related to a correct understanding of the sugata essence can be found in Mipham's sister text to this text, the *Lion's Roar Proclaiming Other Emptiness*.

Now, if mind truly existed, it would not be possible to become a buddha, because that mind would be fixed in its existence and therefore could not change. "It is true" means that there is no-one who would disagree with that. However, if it were without true establishment, that would mean that it was non-existent, and in that case even the idea that someone could become a buddha would simply disappear—"no ascertainment" means that no one would think of it any longer. Thus, it has to be agreed that all phenomena are without true existence, but then who could prove that any phenomenon at all—earth, stones, mountains, trees, ocean, and so forth as well as sentient beings—could become a buddha simply on that basis? Nobody could do that! In other words, to understand the second reason here as meaning simply that all phenomena are suchness or emptiness or lacking true existence could not be used by anyone to prove that sentient beings have a sugata essence.

Now Mipham pulls out another problem in general. "Positing the species only as the ability to abandon obscurations by referencing lack of true existence also is useless." Now he points out that Tsongkhapa and his followers themselves understand what he has just said because they do say "that it makes no sense only to reference emptiness to abandon the obscurations to knowledge, that following that there must be adornment with an infinite accumulation of merit". However, he points out to them that, even though they get that right, they then go and assert "sugata essence in relation to this sort of non-affirming negation", which, because of connecting suchness or emptiness or lack of true existence—as they would like to call it—with a non-affirming negation, renders their claim as to what the sugata essence is completely meaningless.

There is a small point in the last piece. "Referencing" or using concept to know something implies knowing it through dualistic mind, not non-dualistic wisdom. It is regarded that one of the faults of the Gelug tradition's presentation is that they do not get at a direct perception of emptiness but that they only dualistically reference or conceptualize emptiness with their "empty of true existence".

Continuing on, Mipham says that, because of doing it that way, your way of asserting sugata essence is meaningless. It becomes the ordinary species or the sugata essence that followers of the Lesser Vehicles of Buddhism accept, not the very profound presentation found in the final turning sutras of the Great Vehicle. And he says, moreover, because of doing it that way, your way of asserting sugata essence cannot establish that sentient beings could become buddhas, and gives reasons for that. To start with, everyone agrees that all-knowing wisdom will arise after the obscurations to knowledge have been abandoned but your approach cannot prove that. Why not? Because a non-affirming negation sugata essence has no knowing in it, it is a blankness, which means that, even when it has gone from being the sugata essence to a fully manifest buddha, the fully manifest buddha would not have any factor of knowing in it! Note that the word "species" was used here to emphasize that if the species at the earlier time has no factor of knowing, then what comes later, being exactly the same species also could have no knowing.

With "**if you are enamoured of that**" Mipham says to them, if you are so enamoured of that conventional presentation of sugata essence, why don't you just keep that part and drop the problematic part, which is your connecting sugata essence with a non-affirming negation emptiness?

In the conventional approach to the sugata essence that they are using, it is understood that the seeds of threefold knowledge, love, and capacity—a formula that sums up all of the good qualities of a realized buddha—have existed from beginningless time in the mindstreams of all sentient beings because of the way that uncompassionate beings such as carnivorous animals, and so forth, are not kind to others but are kind to their own offspring and do recognize and react accordingly to those who help and harm them. It is understood that sentient beings' development of the knowledge, love, and capacity of a buddha is small, but that if they address them using the path of emancipation, those good qualities will be freed from obstructions to them and will increase steadily until they become their full-blown form in a buddha who has them. That view of sugata essence would at least work for people wanting to practise the path, so Mipham says clearly that it would be much better to have just that view and not take the next step of mixing it with a non-affirming negation suchness or emptiness, which becomes very problematic.

According to the conventional approach to the sugata essence that was just under discussion, the cause creating those good qualities of a buddha has to be the fruition. It follows on from that that the cause which for the people who he is talking about is a momentary and compounded thing—the moments of compound, dualistic mind that they assert are the cause—must be the creator. But lo and behold, they put all of that, which would at least work conventionally, aside and insist on asserting the cause as a non-thing which by definition is uncompounded and therefore could not be a creator of anything. That is very weird!

"One person who thinks that way, further thinks ..." Before going on, note that the terms dharmin and dharmatā are about to be used. It is essential to read the entry in the glossary "dharmin and dharmatā" now, before proceeding.

This paragraph says that there might be someone who generally accepts what has been covered so far, but who wants to refine it a little. This person says that all knowables being without true existence could not be claimed as the species, that only what is mind in nature being without true existence would be acceptable as the species. But his position of the mind being without true existence retains the problem that such a species could not perform the function of producing something in cause and effect mode. Mipham then cleverly turns the argument back on him and says, "Well, it is true that a dharmin mind could do the function of creating further minds, such as those having the buddha qualities, in a conventional understanding. But in that case you and your people would not need the uncompounded, lack of true existence species that you so strongly insist on, so why not just drop that sort of presentation?!"

In other words, even with the point made that the species only needs to be understood in relation to mind, not in relation to every knowable, it would be better for them to stay with the conventional part of their presentation in which dualistic mind could be the cause that produces the result of buddhahood than to also accept an uncompounded thing, a non-affirming negation emptiness, as the cause because their uncompounded cause could not produce a result. Their position has not been well thought out. It seems that their overall presentation does not require the use of the uncompounded aspect, so they should abandon it!

"If there is a group who thinks 'We are not ..." This paragraph moves on to another group of people entirely who think, "Unlike the people who were being discussed above, we are not positing this on the basis of a separated two truths; we assert the species as the actual fact that is the inseparability of the luminosity of the dharmin mind and the emptiness of the dharmatā". This is in reference to later generations of the early Tibetans such as the Jonangs and Sakyas, who thought mainly in terms of the unity of the luminosity of mind and emptiness. Mipham says that such a position is completely in accord with scripture and reasoning *if* the dharmin mind that they are talking about is non-dualistic wisdom, not dualistic consciousness. Mipham's own position is one in which the two truths are not separate items because the luminosity aspect of the mind—which is the dharmin or dharma-possessing awareness—and emptiness—which is its dharmatā—are inseparable. There, "luminosity aspect of mind" means the unobscured luminosity of wisdom, not the obscured luminosity of dualistic mind. For him, that is how sugata essence sits in reality, so that is how the species has to be known, and if the group currently being looked at also thinks that way, well then, their presentation is completely in accord with scripture and reasoning.

Of the two related items, consciousness and wisdom, if you accept wisdom, which is unchanging and not compounded by causes and conditions, for the species, then that is very much how it is, because that is fully established by the scripture of the Buddha and by correct reasoning. However, if—and now he is going back to Tsongkhapa and others like him—you have your mind set on the dharmin to be unified with the empty condition as momentary consciousness then think that "this gradually shifts in status to being buddha", that is useless! It is useless because your claim has the consequence that the species, the sugata essence, would be both compounded and uncompounded. With that sort of view, you have an uncompounded factor which has no capability to produce what is needed—the result of a buddha with all of the needed buddha qualities—so the species becomes a mere mentally imputed species, not the actual species. And, with that sort of view, you have a compounded factor that has become the fully characterized[23] species able to produce a result, which means that the intent of the Great Vehicle sutras, all of which maintain that the naturally present species is the uncompounded dharmadhātu, has been totally lost.

Maitreya said in the *Highest Continuum*, that the sugata essence could be seen as being a naturally present species and a developed species:

> That species should be known as twofold:
> Like a treasure and a tree with fruit,
> That which is naturally present without beginning
> And the highest that has been fully accomplished.

The naturally present species has existed from the beginning, primordially, and that is the factual sugata essence. According to all the Great Vehicle sutras and the tantras too, the naturally present species is the uncompounded dharmadhātu. The developed species is simply a name for the naturally present species after the accumulations have

---

[23] Skt. lākṣhaṇika, Tib mtshan nyid pa. "Fully characterized" means the actual one, not an incorrect version of it that will not have all the characteristics of the actual one.

been amassed, the stains have been cleared away, and buddhahood has been realized. The developed species is by definition compounded. It is a name for the naturally present species at buddhahood but by itself is an imprecise understanding of what the species actually is.

"Thus, while your mind cannot let go of a species …" Mipham continues by saying that, in effect, these people do not understand how the naturally present species and developed species should be understood. They have become stuck on the idea of a compounded, cause and effect type of species—the developed species—yet verbally claim that the species must be the uncompounded dharmadhātu—the naturally present species. That shows a major contradiction within their overall presentation that comes from not having understood how the two aspects of the naturally present species and the developed species should be understood. It should be noted that in reality—and I have seen this myself having studied with the Gelugpa tradition for many years—these people fall very strongly on the side of a compounded buddhahood explained in terms of the cause and effect developed species; they focus on that, though they do also say that the uncompounded dharmadhātu is the actual sugata essence. Nevertheless, as pointed out in the previous paragraph, their overall presentation ends up having both compounded and uncompounded aspects with the faults that come from that, and as pointed out in this paragraph, there is a fundamental contradiction in their presentation.

They just cannot let go of a species that is posited in cause and effect terms because of thinking that developing the dualistic mind is what brings the good qualities of buddhahood. However, the developed species in that case is not the naturally present species, it is just something created by causes and conditions. All in all, the way that they present their view puts on display a fundamental contradiction in it. Following on from that, we are talking about the unchanging dharmadhātu being claimed as the buddha species, so the first thing that has to be done is to identify what it is to which the name "dharmadhātu" has been given. In accordance with the sutras of the

Great Vehicle and the tantras too, it has to be identified as unassessed superfactual truth, the great unity of the superfactual and fictional two truths, the fact of the Middle Way that does not dwell in any extreme whatsoever. Those three names all point at the same thing—the actual fact of dharmadhātu, another name for which is "the naturally present species". Given that the dharmadhātu is the naturally present species and has been identified as uncompounded, we understand that the naturally present species also is uncompounded.

Now for those—and he is still talking about Tsongkhapa and his lineage, though it could be anyone with the same view—who do not identify the dharmadhātu as such but accept just the assessed superfactual truth as sugata essence, it is as though they are looking at a group of monkeys in the forest but due to their confusion are thinking that they are in the very amazing god realm called the Heaven of the Thirty-Three amongst the gods of that heaven. As a result of their confusion they take what is not dharmadhātu for dharmadhātu then assert that as the species of buddha. Taking a species like that as their reference in meditation, they claim that they are meditating on Prajñāpāramitā and claim that their meditation is the cause of the svabhāvikakāya, and so on. In fact what is happening is that they are referencing a mistaken understanding of the species which becomes what they think is correct meditation on Prajñāpāramitā and then, with that, they think that their Prajñāpāramitā meditation will be the cause of the svabhāvikakāya—the kāya of emptiness of an actual buddha. It is true that a correct Prajñāpāramitā meditation is the cause of the svabhāvikakāya, but they are meditating on consciousness, which is assessed superfactual truth, and that cannot become the svabhāvikakāya! The Great Vehicle sutras spoken by the Buddha establish that the framework of classifications that these people have in that way built up as the basis for their path has resulted in an invented path that seems like, but is not, the path of the Great Vehicle. It is true to say that because the Great Vehicle sutras of the Buddha do say that a Prajñāpāramitā path that only takes the assessed superfactual truth into account is a counterfeit Prajñāpāramitā path. Why does Mipham focus on Prajñāpāramitā here? It is because Tsongkhapa and his lineage in particular have insisted that the Prajñāpāramitā sutras of the middle turning are where the Buddha's definitive meaning teaching is to be found and their view and meditation revolves around that.

"The fact of the dhātu that is the unity of the two truths ..." Well then, what is the unassessed dharmadhātu, the actual thing that the word "dharmadhātu" points toward? It is that dhātu or zone that is the unification of superfactual and fictional truths, removed from all the webs of elaboration made by dualistic mind. How is it seen? It is not seen by the dualistic mind that sees this shore of samsara but is seen by personal self-knowing, the wisdom of the noble ones, that sees the other shore, nirvana. That sort of dharmadhātu is called "the complete purity nature dharmadhātu" and "emptiness". You can name it in many ways, but all names for it point to the one fact, the fact of the fully-characterized buddha species, the sugata essence.

At the time of sentient beings, it is the sugata essence covered by affliction and at the time of buddhahood it is the svabhāvikakāya having the two purities. The two purities are the natural, primordial purity that is the entity of the sugata essence and the purity of its having been freed of the adventitious[24] stains that is acquired on the attainment of buddhahood. It is just like there is the entity of the sky, what it actually is, which is an entity primordially pure of anything other than the sky itself, and there is today's sky when it has been cleared of adventitious coverings such as clouds, pollution, fog, and so on. To say that someone has the two purities means that buddhahood has been accomplished for that person on the basis of the naturally present species: the person has the complete purity nature of the dharmadhātu or naturally present species that primordially exists and also has the purity of having had all the coverings removed from that naturally present species. The purity of the naturally

---

[24] For adventitious, see the glossary.

present species exists for everyone but that does not mean that all of them are buddhas. It is a person who has the two purities who is a buddha.

In sum, all the Great Vehicle sutras and commentaries on their intent talk like this, so there is nothing else to do but accept that, which includes the understanding that the naturally present species is uncompounded.

Mipham says, "Given that it has to be uncompounded, your position that the naturally present species by its very nature does the work of producing a result and then does the work of stopping itself is unacceptable. Therefore, you cannot do other than accept that the qualities of the dharmakāya are a disconnected result." A disconnected result is one of the five kinds of result mentioned in the *Treasury of Abhidharma*. It is defined as "cessation through analysis", is realized by means of prajñā, and "only the noble ones have realized its nature through personal self-knowing". How an uncompounded fruition can have a cause is a problem within Buddhist philosophy.

"That that is so was taught by the regent ..." means "everything that has been explained in the last few paragraphs about the buddha essence is not something that my tradition has invented but was explained by the great masters of India who correctly knew the Buddha's teaching, and by Maitreya and Nāgārjuna in particular." Mipham says that it is that way and because of that it was taught that way by the Buddha's regent Maitreya, the great being who had completed the tenth level of the bodhisatvas, in the *Highest Continuum*, and moreover was clearly taught by the glorious guardian noble one Nāgārjuna in his *In Praise of Dharmadhātu*. Therefore, Mipham says, our tradition follows the texts of the two great charioteers Nāgārjuna of the profound tradition and Maitreya of the vast tradition and asserts the uncompounded dharmadhātu as the species. Because of that, he says, we assert that the uncompounded dharmadhātu is the actuality of all phenomena, so its entity is primordially without birth and without cessation, meaning that it is empty of dualistic phenomena. And at the same time, we assert that it has the buddha qualities because it is present in the personage of inseparable appearance-emptiness. Because of those two points, the view of our tradition does not fall into any extremes.

"This is how it is." Mipham ends this whole section with a clear statement of how the sugata essence must be understood. First, he makes the point that compounded things might appear initially to arise and finally to cease but are not established as they appear because they are products of confusion, thus the innate disposition or the inner character of the dharmadhātu primordially is never shrouded by that confusion. Therefore, the dharmadhātu is primordially pure in that it is primordially free of cause-and-effect samsara. Second, he makes the point that at the same time as the dharmadhātu is primordially free of cause and effect samsara, it has the appearances of the nature, in the spontaneously-existing unoutflowed luminosity, and has them without meeting and parting. Those two points combined into one key point is the way that the sugata essence has to be identified.

The no meeting and parting mentioned can be understood through this statement in the *Heart Sutra*:

> There is no freedom from impurity; there is no decrease and no increase …

In other words, it means that, no matter how the dharmadhātu was previously, that is how it is right now and that is how it always will be, which is why the *Highest Continuum* says:

> Just as it was before, so it is later—
> The unchanging dharmatā.

That completes Mipham's explanation of the ways that the three reasons were presented by very early and somewhat later learned Tibetans and his refutations of their presentations of the first two reasons.

2. Stating our own Tradition

In this section, Mipham presents how his own Nyingma tradition views the three reasons.

2.1. The First Reason

"The meaning of the first line of the verse 'because the complete buddha's kāya radiates' is as follows." A truly complete buddha's ultimate kāya, the dharmakāya, has qualities that are unending like space is unending. The qualities of the dharmakāya primordially exist in the continuum of an ordinary person who has the fetters of the obscurations but at that time they are obscured by the obscurations and are not manifest. Later, by cultivating the path, the obscurations are cleared away and the primordially existing qualities of the dharmakāya radiate or become evident or become manifest. Because of that it is established that sugata essence exists now in the mindstreams of sentient beings.

There are two ways that this proof is accepted to work—an ordinary way and an extraordinary way.

2.1.1. The ordinary way

"The ordinary way is as follows." If a sentient being who has manifested the wisdom dharmakāya exists, it is necessarily the case that a species that makes becoming a buddha possible exists in that being's mind, and, if a species definitely does not exist that would not be tenable.

The species is known to exist because that being has become a buddha, and, conversely, if a species for that definitely did not exist, there would not be sentient beings who became buddhas. The proof is done here first by means of what is called the forward pervasion and then by what is called the reverse pervasion. For instance: "if something is compounded, it necessarily is impermanent, for example a vase" is the forward pervasion and "if something is permanent, it is necessarily not compounded, for example space", is the reverse pervasion. In this case, the forward pervasion is that, if there is someone who has manifested the wisdom dharmakāya, it shows that the ability to become a buddha necessarily exists in all sentient beings, as for example with Buddha Śhākyamuni. The reverse pervasion is that, if the species does not exist, then the ability to become a buddha necessarily does not exist, as for example with a rock—in other words, such a thing would not be tenable.

This is supported by scripture—what *In Praise of Dharmadhātu* says fits with that:

> If the element exists, by doing the work
> You will see the pure form of the purest of gold.
> If the element does not exist, you might do the work,
> But it will end in only hardship being produced.

If gold exists in a stone and you do the work of purifying it, finally you will see the gold. There was a type of gold called "sa le bram" in Indian culture; it was the purest type of gold, which is what is referred to with "purest of gold". It is an analogy for sugata essence, the purest of minds. However, if gold does not exist within mineral ore, no matter how much you work on that mineral ore, it will only give rise to hardship.

2.1.2. The extraordinary way

"The extraordinary way is as follows." You might think, "The proof just shown, using the example that crops can grow in a field, establishes simply that this mind of ours is a cause that can become buddha. But how is a species that has the distinction of primordially having the good qualities of a buddha proved?" That too is proved by scripture and reasoning, which establish that the buddha bhagavats, the ones having the wisdom kāya whose personage has been utterly distinguished as uncompounded do not have a compounded, impermanent nature.

"Thus, for scripture ..." How is it established by scripture? It is said in the *Nirvana Sutra* that:

> For a monk with perfect discipline it would be easier to become a Forder[25] or even die than to say about the uncompounded Tathāgata that "The Tathāgata is compounded".

and so on, a total of three quotes from that sutra are given. Now the factor merely of non-affirming negation does not make nirvana possible, so the same scripture says:

> Whenever what is called "the emptiness of emptiness" is sought, nothing at all is found. Such "nothing at all" exists even for the naked ascetics, but emancipation is not like that.

Such "nothing at all" is not so special—even the naked ascetics, the Nigrantha Jains, have that sort of thing. Emancipation comes with realizing the actuality of things not with realizing that sort of nothing at all. It comes from realizing a freedom from elaboration, not from dwelling in an extreme type of emptiness. Some say that dwelling in nothing whatever—non-existence of the pair existent and non-existent—is emptiness that leads to emancipation but the Buddha says that that is not so.

Moreover, the Prajñāpāramitā *Vajra Cutter Sutra* says:

> Those who see me as form,
> Those who know me as sound,
> Have entered a path which is wrong.
> Those beings do not see me.
>
> The buddhas are viewed as dharmatā,
> The guides as the dharmakāya.

---

[25] For Forder, see the glossary. Here it means followers in general of religions other than Buddhism.

> The dharmatā is not to be known so
> It cannot be known by consciousness.

As for dharmatā and dharmakāya, dharmatā is mainly the empty aspect, freedom from elaboration, and dharmakāya is the wisdom aspect. Mentioning the two here shows the unity of emptiness and wisdom. The dharmatā of all dharmas is emptiness and cannot be known by dualistic rational mind. Therefore, the Buddha's wisdom dharmakāya can never be cognized by dualistic rational mind. It cannot be an object of sentient being's consciousness. True emptiness is not within reach of samsaric mind. This point is shown in those and many other sutras, though the Great Vehicle sutras of definitive meaning teach it more extensively than any others.

Altogether, those quotations mean a tathāgata is to be viewed as the dharmakāya and that is permanent. The buddha essence must be the same so it follows that the buddha essence must have had the good qualities of a buddha existing within it primordially. Thus the extraordinary understanding is proved by scripture.

"And then for reasoning, there is the following." The thesis here is primarily established through the use of reverse pervasion. If that ultimate result of being equal in taste due to being non-dual with the primal dharmadhātu, all-knowing wisdom, is impermanent due to being newly compounded by causes and conditions, then it has the faults of these and other consequences:

- it would not be self-arising wisdom;
- the pain of change would not have been abandoned;
- it would have a factor of ceasing and arising again and again;
- being destructible by its very nature, it would be deceptive;
- it would not be a lasting refuge because as soon as it arose, it would cease;
- it would dwell for a short while only, whenever the assembly of causes for it was complete;

- it would not have gone into equal taste with all phenomena;
- it would not have gone beyond all extremes;
- the arising, dwelling, ceasing, and so on that are the nature of mental mind—of something compounded—would not have ceased ("nature of mental mind" is connected with the debate between the Great and Lesser Vehicles—the Great Vehicle says that the nature of mental mind still exists in the continuum of an arhat and therefore the path of the arhat does not lead to the unsurpassed complete enlightenment);
- it would not be under its own control but would be under the control of other, the formatives[26];
- and so on.

To proclaim that all-knowing wisdom is impermanent brings the great mistake of seeing the vajra kāya, the indestructible dharma, as impermanent which then leads to a vast array of faults such as those just listed. Therefore, we should reject this bad path and see the non-dual wisdom kāya as having the excellences of being uncompounded and permanent. Note that this kind of "permanent" is the "great permanent" which is beyond the duality of impermanence and permanence.

"If you think "Uncompounded wisdom is impossible …" Someone might think that it is not possible to establish uncompounded wisdom with merely the reasoning that is based on the ordinary perceptions of the beings of this shore, samsara, because a common basis for consciousness and permanence is impossible, but that sort of thinking is useless, meaningless. Why? Generally speaking, it is

---

[26] Tib. 'du byed. The formatives are the contents of the fourth aggregate. Their name is usually translated as "the formations" but that is incorrect. They are the causes that form future states of cause and effect samsara for sentient beings, they are not the resulting formations or future states of samsara.

necessarily the case that the short-lived moments of consciousness that know objects are impermanent, but wisdom in which awareness and what it knows are one taste has a vajra or indestructible nature like space pervading space, so is not like that impermanent consciousness.

"Output" in this paragraph means the output that comes from something, like sound comes from a speaker. Wisdom has its own natural output or self-output which is not created by karmic cause and effect. The self-output of that wisdom, output that is not compounded by causes and conditions, is the output of unchanging luminosity in which all the knowable phenomena of samsara and nirvana are comprehended all at once. Being comprehended all at once is somewhat like drinking a cup of tea in one gulp—nothing is left out and all of it is taken in or known at once. The nature of that wisdom is that it is primordially unborn and unceasing because of which it is established through the use of a knowing awareness that does analysis of the ultimate.

A reasoning awareness that examines for or does analysis of the ultimate is not available only to the noble ones for we ordinary people can have it too. The knowing awareness here means a reasoning awareness that directly perceives what it is examining; this is available only to the noble ones. We can have an assessed version of their un-assessed awareness. For example, all the reasonings of the Middle Way are reasoning awarenesses using an assessed approach to develop a correct view of the un-assessed superfactual truth. They are referred to as reasonings that analyse the ultimate but they are not the wisdom of noble ones which are knowing awarenesses that analyse the ultimate directly. The reasoning awarenesses of ordinary beings here in samsara are consciousnesses, not wisdom, and as such they do not directly see the ultimate. The actual view of the un-assessed superfactual truth happens in the wisdom of the noble ones, which here is called a knowing awareness.

Therefore, wisdom like that in which knower and knowable are one taste is the "great uncompounded" of not dwelling in either of the extremes of compounded and uncompounded. Anything that dwells in either the extreme of being compounded or the extreme of being uncompounded is not "the great uncompounded". In other words, "great uncompounded" means the circumstance that has gone beyond both compounded and uncompounded. The great permanence is beyond both permanence and impermanence. Similarly, the great purity is that purity beyond purity and impurity, the great self is that self beyond both self and non-self, and the great awareness is that vajra awareness beyond both knower and knowable.

"That being so, wisdom like that ..." The "great uncompounded" is not at all like a bare non-thing. And then, if we consider things and non-things in general, all of them are knowable phenomena and all knowable phenomena are interdependent arisings. There are two interdependent arisings. One is interdependent arising of being produced in dependence on something[27], meaning that in dependence on one thing, something else arises; all such interdependent arisings are substantial things. The other is interdependent arising of being imputed in dependence[28]: in dependence on existence, the name non-existence is imputed; in dependence on large, something small is imputed; in dependence on something small, we impute something large. Right and left, front and back, happy and sad, and so on all are like that. Similarly, when something exists, one imputes non-existence. Non-things do not arise as substances due to interdependent arising but are only imputed. Thus, analysis done in terms of the authentic on both things and non-things shows that they are compounded, accumulated, fictional, and deceptive. Sugata essence is the dharmatā of all things and non-things, the great uncompounded, non-deceptive situation.

---

[27] Tib. brten nas skyes pa'i rten 'brel.

[28] Tib. brten nas btags pa'i rten 'brel.

What Nāgārjuna said in the *Root Prajñā* fits with that. He said that the nature or way things are of anything is not newly created by causes and conditions, that the nature of things does not depend on something else. You can also say it the other way around, that that nature is not artificial and does not depend on causes and conditions; in short, it is not compounded. He also says that thing and non-thing are compounded—both thing and non-thing are grasped as objects of dualistic mind, therefore they are compounded—whereas nirvana or true emancipation is uncompounded.

That is the end of the extraordinary proof by reasoning.

——— ◆◆◆ ———

Now Mipham explains the nature of the dharmakāya and how it is present in sentient beings as the sugata essence.

"That that ultimate dharmakāya wisdom ..." Ultimate actuality, the wisdom of buddha's dharmakāya, has the nature of pervading all becoming—meaning samsara— and peace—meaning nirvana. It has the nature of being the great equality. It has the nature of being uncompounded. It has the nature of being the unchanging superfactual truth. That is established both by the scriptures of the Great Vehicle sutras of definitive meaning of the Buddha and by the valid reasoning that analyses the ultimate actuality. Such wisdom of the buddha's dharmakāya exists now in the mindstream of all sentient beings who then are able to manifest it in the future.

Buddhas have manifested that wisdom by freeing themselves of the adventitious stains and sentient beings have not manifested it because they have not done so. If you consider the actual situation, things as they are, then there is no difference of bad earlier when someone is a sentient being and good later when the person has become a buddha. Why? Because the unchanging dharmatā has the nature of not being compounded by causes and conditions. In regard to that, the *Highest Continuum* says:

> How it was before, so it is later.
> It is the unchanging dharmatā.

How it was before at the time of being a sentient being, so it is later at the time of being a buddha—the entity of the dharmatā is not different, it is the unchanging dharmatā. This can also be understood as "How the dharmatā, emptiness, was before, so it is later". The Buddha said in one of the Great Vehicle Prajñāpāramitā sutras:

> Whether the tathāgata comes to this world or not,
> whether he teaches the dharma or not, the dharmatā of
> dharmas always exists without faults.

And the *Highest Continuum* also says:

> That which is mind's nature, luminosity,
> Is like space without change;
> The adventitious stains of passion, and so on come from
>   conceiving the not authentic
> Do not change it into affliction.

Here is what that verse is saying. The nature of mind, the dharmatā of mind, is luminous. That never changes—like space it is unchanging by nature. You might ask, "How is it with all sentient beings?" For them, due to conceiving of the not authentic there is grasping at a self. From that as a cause arises desire, anger, ignorance, delusion, pride, envy, and so forth—in short, the afflictions—all of which are adventitious stains. Those stains cover the unchanging dharmatā and make it obscured, but they never mix with the entity of the dharmatā, so it always remains clear of them and pure. In other words, the afflictions put a cover over it but no more than that.

All the phenomena of the three realms of samsara are momentary, changing, unstable, and impermanent. Although all of them appear to make shifts into something else within that state of dharmatā, the completely pure essence of mind that is primordially pure, sugata essence, remains unchanging, for example like space. The text here mentions "without shift and change". Shift and change is a phrase used to refer to the shifts in time and the changes that come with them in the dualistic world. For example, in our dualistic world, we always speak in reference to time and the change that occurs with it; we have past, present, and future and the things of our world are always shifting and changing throughout those three times. Being without shift and change is usually referred to, as is being done here, in order to make the point that the dharmatā is simply outside the world of time and the changes that occur with it. You must understand this, which the Buddha said not just once but again and again, and not just a little but extensively, in the Great Vehicle sutras and the secret mantra Vajra Vehicle tantras.

In the same way, the dharmadhātu, uncompounded by causes and conditions and naturally luminous has never been covered by confusion but is naturally completely pure. In the self-output that is emptiness in union with luminosity are the good qualities of buddhahood—the ten powers, four fearlessnesses, eighteen unmixed qualities, and so on of a buddha. For example, the *Ornament of Manifest Realizations* says:

> There are the qualities of twenty-one sections of unoutflowed dharmas. They are the qualities of the Buddha's dharmakāya". The qualities of the fruition dharmakāya exist inseparable from it, like the sun and its light rays.

The *Highest Continuum* says the same thing too:

> The element is empty of that which has the characteristic
> Of being separable, the adventitious.
> It is not empty of that which has the characteristic
> Of being not separable, the unsurpassable dharmas.

Here is a paraphrase of this exceptionally famous and much-quoted verse. "That which possesses the characteristic of being separable from the element, the sugata essence, is the fictional, adventitious stains. Because they can be separated away from the element, the element is empty or void of them. Thus, even though they cover it, they never shroud it, never taint it. On the other hand, the qualities that exist within the entity of the element possess the characteristic of being not separable from it. These are the unsurpassable buddha dharmas or buddha qualities—the ten powers and so forth, mentioned above. These good qualities always have and always will exist in the entity of the element, the sugata essence, so it is is not empty of them".

The remainder of the current paragraph is a commentary on that verse. What is the cause of all the faults of three-realmed samsara? All of them come from a confused mind that clings to a self of persons and self of dharmas. Yet that confused mind does not shroud—meaning in this context cover over and mix with—the primordial nature, luminosity, but is present on the empty luminosity like clouds scudding across the surface of the sky. The faults of clinging to those two selves are adventitious, meaning that they are not part of the element, sugata essence and, because of that, the entity of the element, sugata essence, is empty of those faults, not shrouded by them. The element sugata essence in having no relation to being spoiled by confusion is luminous by its own nature and is not empty of the buddha qualities that are not separable from the self-arising wisdom that has engaged the just-that-ness of all phenomena. Here just thatness[29] means what is, only or just that and no more or less. It is a generic term that can be used to refer to anything and which here is being used to refer to superfactual truth. The reason for that is that the buddha qualities are inseparable from the entity of sugata essence. Thus the sugata essence is like a luminous sun and its rays: if there is sun, there are rays; it is not that you have the sun and then have to add the rays newly. In the same way, whenever sugata essence itself exists, its good qualities spontaneously exist as well.

---

[29] Tib. de kho na nyid. The meaning of this was mentioned earlier.

"If the naturally present species like that is established as" the entity of the dharmakāya uncompounded by causes and conditions and primordially possessing the buddha qualities, then, because it makes becoming buddha possible, the wisdom dharmakāya must exist free from decrement and increment in the mindstreams of all sentient beings. Here, without decrement and increment means an absence of faults that, previously present, have decreased and an absence of good qualities that, previously not present, have increased.

If a person cultivates the path, it is established by reasoning of the force of the thing[30] that it is possible to become a buddha. The reasoning of the force of the thing is one of the most important types of inferential reasoning. It is used to establish that something is so by applying the test of whether the thing in question is actually the way that is has been proposed to be. Thus, through the *force of* what *the thing* itself is, we correctly know whether the proposal is true or not. For example, it is said that "fire is hot". One way to determine whether that is true or not is to look at the qualities of fire. If we find that one of those qualities is "hot" then the statement is proved to be true by the force of the hotness itself being present.

The reasoning of the force of the thing has two valid cognizers associated with it—direct perception and inference. Fictional truth and superfactual truth each have these two valid cognizers, making four valid cognizers for it. The direct perception of fictional truth is actually seeing a glass as a glass. The inference of fictional truth is for example inferring that people are talking from hearing their voices. The direct perception of superfactual truth is the noble ones' realization that all phenomena are empty; we ordinary people do not know that in direct perception, only the noble ones do. However, we ordinary people have the inference of superfactual truth. Those are the ways of the reasoning of the force of the thing.

---

[30] For "the reasoning of the force of the thing" see the glossary.

It is established by the reasoning of the force of the thing that a person who cultivates the path can become a buddha. The dharmakāya at the time of buddhahood that is seen to come from cultivating the path is uncompounded so could not possibly have been newly compounded by causes and conditions. Therefore, it is established by reasoning that the dharmakāya is right now seated in the mindstreams of all sentient beings as the entity itself of buddhahood.

What has been established here is that the first of the three reasons "because the complete buddha's dharmakāya radiates" is a valid reason for "all sentient beings perpetually having the essence of buddha". The way that it has been established is through the reasoning of the force of the thing. Mipham's view is that the first of the three reasons means that the dharmakāya of a complete buddha with its primordially existing qualities exists, without decrease or increase, in the mindstreams of ordinary beings because it is proven by the reasoning of the force of the thing that the dharmakāya of a complete buddha existing as an essence without need of being changed one day radiates and becomes evident or manifest as buddhahood.

Mipham's understanding of "radiate" in the first of the three reasons is very different from that of the others whose positions were presented and refuted in the previous section. They make it out, generally speaking, as meaning that the dharmakāya pervades all objects whereas he makes it out to mean that the dharmakāya one day becomes visible or evident or manifest, which itself shows by the force of the thing that it must have been there to begin with.

Others who came early in the second spread accepted that the buddha qualities exist in all sentient beings, but in a different way to what Mipham's tradition—and the Kagyu, too—assert. For example, Ngog Lotsāwa Loden Sherab, Tsalpa Chokyi Sengge, and others asserted sugata essence mainly as emptiness of true existence, a non-affirming negation. Later, the very learned Tibetan Sakya Paṇḍita asserted in his *Distinguishing the Three Vows* that the sugata essence is provisional meaning, not definitive meaning. Dolpopa Sherab Gyaltsen and others of the Jonang tradition asserted sugata essence to be definitive meaning but permanent, so they did not have the union of the dhātu of emptiness and the spontaneously-existing luminosity. Later still, Tsongkhapa in the *dgongs pa rab gsal*, a commentary on *Entering the Middle Way*, said that sugata essence is provisional in meaning, though his way of presenting that was different from that of Sakya Paṇḍita.

Addressing the views of Tibetans early in the second spread who thought that the dharmakāya of the perfect buddha was just emptiness, Mipham said that non-affirming negation emptiness of itself is not sufficient to prove that beings could become buddhas. Some complained, saying that their position was that it is mere emptiness together with luminosity. They said that the aspect of luminosity was just an aspect of samsaric mind and that developing that mind was what gradually brought one to buddhahood. However, Mipham said that that too was no reason for becoming a buddha because something compounded cannot become a buddha, which is uncompounded.

At this point, Mipham has explained his tradition's view of "because the complete buddha's kāya radiates", by saying that the species is the uncompounded dharmatā and that the uncompounded is not mere emptiness but primordially possesses spontaneous good qualities, like the sun and its light rays. In his approach of unified appearance and emptiness, the spontaneously-existing good qualities that are primordially present are established and moreover are established as being inseparable from the entity of sugata essence. Thus, whether in appearance they are manifest or not, in other words, whether one appears as a sentient being or a buddha, the good qualities of buddhahood exist in an inseparable mode, and without decrease or increase.

Mipham's treating the term "radiate" to mean that what has existed primordially comes out, manifests, is not just Mipham's idea but is taught in the definitive meaning sutras. The Buddha said that, due to the fact that the good qualities have existed from the beginning, a person who cultivates the path will become a buddha. Now if those good qualities were not spontaneously present from the beginning, but were compounded qualities produced through cause and effect, there is the consequence that they would not be lasting. If they are spontaneously existing, then someone like Milarepa, who did not study philosophy, could cultivate the path and suddenly be able to sing songs of the profound meaning of the sutras and tantras because of the knowledge needed to do so existing spontaneously and primordially in him.

Thus, what Mipham explains is quite different from the other traditions mentioned, though it is the same as what the Kagyu tradition explains. However, everyone in the end has to follow what the very great Indian masters Nāgārjuna and Asaṅga had to say about this. For that, one also has to rely on scripture and reasoning. If you study and actually understand Mipham's Nyingma tradition concerning this, you will see that it does not fall into any extremes. It stays in the middle, pointing out what actually is.

"Some people having pondered what was just said think 'If it is seated right now ..." In the paragraph just explained, Mipham has ended by saying that dharmakāya as the cause is seated right now as the entity of a buddha in all sentient beings. Mipham's statement fits with the logic found in the very profound definitive meaning final turning sutras. This logic is not available in the ordinary teachings of Buddhism, therefore people who have not been trained in the definitive meaning final turning sutras but only trained in the lesser teachings of Buddhism can easily become confused about Mipham's statement. They will try to apply logic according to what they have been taught in which case Mipham's statement seems to them to be problematic. For example, some might think, "If a buddha's dharmakāya is actually present now in sentient beings, the all-knowing wisdom of that dharmakāya would have to dispel the obscurations of sentient being but that does not happen, therefore your claim, Mipham, must be wrong". Some other people think that Mipham is using what is called "the reasoning of the result existing in the cause", which will be explained just below. However, these and other arguments like them do not apply because the definitive meaning sutras use a different sort of logic to prove that "it is seated right now as the entity of a buddha". That logic is called "the synchronisation or not of the way things are and the way things appear". As just explained, that logic is not known in the ordinary sutra teachings, so it will require explanation. Before doing that, we'll go on to explain the reasoning of the result existing in the cause.

Using a lesser type of logic called the result existing in the cause, Mipham's claim that the result, the all-knowing wisdom of the dharmakāya, is existing right now in sentient beings as the cause, means that if you kill a sentient being, you would kill a buddha, but that is not the case. Therefore, the others say that Mipham's claim is wrong. As another example of the result existing in the cause, there is the argument that eating food is eating excrement, an argument that Dharmakīrti put forth in his *Complete Commentary on Valid Cognition*, when refuting the Hindu school called the "Saṃkhya" meaning Enumerators. That school classifies all knowables into twenty-five suchnesses, which it distills down to two principal ones. The first principal one, which has an entity of knowing, is connected with the self and is permanent. The second principal one is very vast and common to all knowables—it is matter, not consciousness. From the second one come twenty-three dharmas that transform or evolve; all are impermanent and on ceasing return again to the second principal one. In that case both the cause and result are always there in the principal one. Thus, for the Enumerators, the real or main cause of all knowables, all dharmas, is the second principal one and within that the result also already exists in addition to the cause. The Enumerators believe that the result is newly produced, but that there is not anything that did not exist previously and is newly produced, rather, that everything exists primordially within the principal one and becomes manifest. To refute their position, Dharmakīrti said that if in addition to cause the result exists, then both would have to be visible at the same time. That would mean that when we eat food we are eating the excrement that is the result of having digested the food, too, which we obviously are not. Again, the others here say that Mipham's claim is wrong.

"They might not be to blame for their doubts ..." As explained above, Mipham points out that these people cannot be blamed for thinking that way on hearing his explanation of the sugata essence because they have not been trained in the logic of the very profound, definitive-meaning sutras. Nevertheless, the kinds of reasoning that they are using do not apply. Therefore, Mipham now shows how the dharmakāya can be existing right now as the entity of buddhahood in sentient beings without them needing to be manifest buddhas because of it, and so on.

This is done with what is called the synchronisation and non-synchronisation of the way things are and appear. There can be dharmakāya present in sentient beings right now as a cause because, although it is there, the sentient beings having it also have confusion which is a non-synchronisation of the way things are and appear, so do not have it manifest as such. However, at the time of buddhahood, the exact same dharmakāya is now manifest due to the way things are and the way they appear having been synchronised. In this logic, the practise of the path has not newly created a buddha's dharmakāya with all of the good qualities of buddhahood in it, but has synchronised the way things are and the way that they appear so that what was originally there but obscured is now present without the obscurations. This understanding is contained in the very famous passage from *Highest Continuum* that Mipham has quoted just above as he has been developing the view of a dharmakāya existing right now in sentient beings:

> The element is empty of that which has the characteristic
> Of being separable, the adventitious.

It is not empty of that which has the characteristic
Of being not separable, the unsurpassable dharmas.

You could rephrase that to say that the dharmakāya always has and always will be there just as it is. However, when it comes out as this mind of ours of adventitious confusion that together with its object is named "samsara", it does know just as it is the dharmatā that exists in us. This confused situation is similar to being asleep and, due solely to the dualistic mental consciousness, having dreams in which limitless appearances of body and external objects and consciousnesses knowing them—eye and so on—arise and when they do, having a dualistic mind that believes that there are external perceived objects and an internal perceiving subject that are two different things. That dualistic mental consciousness knows its own dualistic situation and all that goes with it, but it is incapable of knowing its actual mode of being, which is that the dualistic grasped at objects and grasping consciousness do not actually exist. It is a case of confusion in which the way things are and the way they appear are not synchronised or not in tune or not consistent with each other. It is like perceived objects and perceiving subjects seeming to be there in a dream when in fact they are nothing more than the confusion of the sleeping mind.

It is important to understand that, while the dualistic mental consciousness is operating without knowing its actual mode of being, it has not changed to something other than the actuality underlying the confusion. This is like all knowable dharmas being empty but just the fact that they are does not mean that all sentient beings realize that. It is like sentient beings are buddhas by nature but just the fact that they are does not mean that they necessarily become manifest complete buddhas. The key point here is that the mind can be confused without its underlying actuality having changed, in other words, that there can be confusion in which the way things are and the way they appear are not in harmony or not in line or not synchronised with each other. That is how Mipham's tradition can present the entity of dharmakāya being in all sentient beings without it being the result existing in the cause.

The logic of the synchronisation or not of the way things are and the way they appear has two conventional valid cognizers connected with it: the valid cognizer that sees this shore of impurity[31] which is the valid cognizer of us ordinary sentient beings and the valid cognizer that looks at purity[32] which is the sight of the noble ones. This is saying that we ordinary beings here on the samsaric side of things see impurity, samsara. With that, we are not capable of seeing purity, the far shore or nirvana side, whereas the noble beings, with their realization of a direct perception of un-assessed emptiness, can see it. These two types of valid cognition are presented in connection with the synchronisation and non-synchronisation of the way things are and the way they appear. We, as beings living in the non-synchronisation of the way things are and appear, have the sight only of this shore, samsara. As such we cannot definitively say that the sugata essence does not exist in us as the entity of the dharmakāya. However, the noble ones, living in the synchronisation of the way things are and appear, have the valid cognition of seeing the other shore, the side of purity. They can say definitively whether the sugata essence exists in us as the entity of the dharmakāya. Regarding this, Guardian Maitreya said that we ordinary beings are like children with very limited minds but that we could grow up, develop our minds, and overcome that limitation.

Generally speaking, Mipham's tradition does not accept the view of compounded cause and effect production of a result in regard to the sugata essence. For him, the sugata essence is a primordial purity in which both buddha and sentient being are inseparable. The primordial purity in which both buddha and sentient being are inseparable is the way things are that is seen by the noble ones but

---

[31] Tib. ma dag tshu rol mthong ba'i tshad ma.

[32] Tib. dag pa gzigs pa'i tshad ma.

not by us. If buddha and sentient being were a matter of cause and effect, they would be two separate items, which is how it appears to us who see this shore of impurity, where the way things are has been obscured. When you have completely abandoned the obscurations, you will have gone to the other shore, the side of purity, nirvana, and for you the way things are and appear will be synchronised.

The way things are is the view of the ground, but it is not enough to understand that view conceptually, it is necessary to cultivate the path in order to remove the obscurations so that you can see the view of things as they are in direct perception. Adjunct to seeing that view, the good qualities of buddhahood will arise precisely because they exist in you now as the dharmatā causal dharmakāya. Finally, when all the obscurations have been abandoned, you will have manifested all of the good qualities of buddhahood. In short, as the way things are and the way they appear become more synchronised, the buddha qualities become more apparent until, when the way things are and appear have become inseparable, buddhahood has become fully manifest.

Samsaric mind and the wisdom of the buddha essence are not the same. The first is a dharmin, the second is its dharmatā. The dharmin of samsaric mind is classed as fictional and the dharmatā of the essence's wisdom is classed as superfact. Mipham's tradition shows that from the standpoint that buddhas and sentient beings are the way things are and the way things appear respectively. The buddha side with the essence's wisdom is demonstrated by speaking of the way things are and the sentient being side, with the dharmin of confused dualistic mind, is demonstrated by speaking of the way things appear. The logic involved is not the same as the logic that the people who have not been trained in the meaning of the definitive meaning understand and try to apply to this. They are looking at the fictional side alone, they are not including, as they need to, both superfact—the way things are—and the fictional—the way things appear. Mipham concludes by saying that there is no problem here at all, it is just that their type of logic is very different from ours.

To summarise, Mipham's tradition explains that sentient beings have the entity of dharmakāya in them right now. That can happen because there is what is called "the confusion of the non-synchronisation of what is actually the case and what appears to be the case". The sugata essence does exist as the entity of the dharmakāya because that is the actual situation but the confused mind at that time is confused so does not see the dharmakāya for what it actually is. Thus, there is always the actual dharmakāya of a buddha in sentient beings as the cause and manifesting it through cultivating the path is simply a matter of re-synchronising the actual situation and how it appears. This synchronisation and non-synchronisation of the way things are and the way they appear is a crucial point in understanding the profound meaning of the definitive meaning sutras of the final turning of the wheel. This matter is dealt with in the *Other Emptiness, Entering Wisdom Beyond Emptiness of Self* and *Lion's Roar Proclaiming Other Emptiness* books cited earlier and they should be read carefully in order to understand this type of reasoning.

"**This first reason proves …**" This is the last paragraph of this section on the first of the three reasons. It says that this first of the three reasons proves, using the argument of the dharmakāya at the time of fruition radiating or being obviously manifest, that the species at the time of the cause, at the time of being a sentient being, exists primordially possessing the good qualities. In the way things are there is no distinction of cause earlier at the time of being a sentient being and result later at the time of fruition. However, in the way things appear, which is the situation of being confused and obscured, it is necessary to posit cause and effect, therefore, the cause is proved from the result, which is called "the reasoning of reliance on the result".

The reasoning of reliance on the result is one of a set of four reasons. The Buddha in the Great Vehicle sutras, for example in the *Definitely Unravelling the Intent Sutra*, and the great Indian masters in their treatises on the Buddha word, for example Asaṅga in the *Compendium of Abhidharma*, taught these four reasonings[33]: 1) the reasoning of the cause doing its work; 2) the reasoning of the reliance on the result; 3) the reasoning that is established through acceptability; and 4) the reasoning of the dharmatā entity, where "dharmatā entity" means the property of something, what it is actually like.

"Because the complete buddha's dharmakāya radiates" uses the reasoning of reliance on the result. It is like understanding that, in reliance on there being smoke, there must be fire. This reasoning is applicable here because it is a fact that there are beings who have become buddhas, for instance Śhākyamuni Buddha.

That completes Mipham's explanation of his own tradition's understanding of Guardian Maitreya's first reason, "because the complete buddha's dharmakāya radiates".

2.2. The Second Reason

The meaning of the second line of the verse "because suchness is without differentiation" is as follows.

"**All dharmas of samsara and nirvana are**" inseparable from their dharmatā, suchness, where suchness is not a mere emptiness but is understood to be the great actuality of emptiness that is primally luminous. In this great wisdom of primordial luminosity, all dharmas of samsara—becoming—and of nirvana—peace—are not differentiated as separate items apart from their actuality, emptiness, and so are of one taste with it. With that, samsara is not regarded as bad and nirvana as good, rather, whatever is samsara is nirvana and whatever is nirvana is samsara because in the dharmatā actuality they are inseparable and of one taste. Therefore, that buddhas are pure and sentient beings are impure are only names given within fictional

[33] The Tibetan for these is: 1) rgyu bya ba byed pa'i rigs pa; 2) 'bras bu ltos pa'i rigs pa; 3) 'thad par 'grub pa'i rigs pa; and 4) ngo bo chos nyid kyi rigs pa.

truth; in superfactual truth the two are inseparable. The reasoning here is the equality of becoming and peace, the inseparability of samsara and nirvana.

The appearance of sentient beings is, like an illusion created by a magician, a manifestation created by adventitious confusion. All these seeming sentient beings appear yet without wavering in the slightest from actuality, the dharmatā of superfactual truth. That is established by the fourth of the four reasonings listed above, the reasoning of dharmatā. Note again that dharmatā in "the reasoning of dharmatā entity" has the meaning of "the basic quality of whatever thing it is that is being examined". Because of the reasoning of dharmatā, it is definitely ascertained that all sentient beings have the essence of buddhahood. Not only is it ascertained by reasoning but it is also ascertained by scripture: in the Great Vehicle sutras the Buddha taught that all dharmas primally are luminosity, primally are nirvana free from all suffering, and primally are of the nature of manifest buddha.

"You might think, 'Well, as you said …" Here, someone says to Mipham, "Well, this sounds like what you yourself have already criticized as incorrect when you were previously refuting the views of others—the earlier Tibetans. If the existence of the buddha species in all sentient beings is proved by merely the fact that dharmatā, suchness, is without differentiation, there is the consequence that the species exists even in earth, rocks, mountains, lakes, and the like, that is, in all material things." Mipham replies that the argument about that has already been presented. All dharmas, all knowables are pervaded by emptiness and are without differentiation in the emptiness. If you accept that all that is pervaded by emptiness is pervaded by the nature of buddhahood, you must accept that everything—the externally known dharmas and the internal mind knowing them, too—has the nature of buddhahood as well.

Mipham replies that his reasoning does not have that sort of fault. He says that what is to be established in this discussion is what is called the "species element, sugata essence", which is something connected with mind, not with anything else. He says that it is the cause for buddhahood which is turned into the result of buddhahood by cultivating a path that removes the obscurations to reveal the intelligence that knows the actual situation of all knowables. When the species is posited in that way, given that there is no practising of the path of sugata essence in relation to anything that is not mind—earth, stones, rocks, lakes, and so forth—then, even though we do conventionally designate that all things—mind and matter—are without differentiation in dharmatā suchness, it is not necessary to posit the species in relation to all of them, only in relation to what is mind.

Mipham continues his reply by pointing out that it is due to mind that material things appear, it is not that mind arises due to the external phenomena of material things, something which is illustrated by and to be understood through the example of the appearances of a dream and the awareness at that time. When you are dreaming, you experience happiness, sorrow, and so on that seem definitely to exist, but on waking from the dream, you understand that all of it was your own mind, and the material things and awarenesses knowing them appear due to mind.

Thus, mind is the creator of the entirety of the three realms of samsara, something which the Buddha himself said in the *Ten Levels Sutra* contained in the *Avataṃsaka* collection of Great Vehicle sutras:

> Sons of the conqueror, all the three realms are just mind.

The Buddha also spoke about this extensively in the *Descent into Laṅgka Sutra*. By understanding that this mind that makes the three realms has seated in it, like water has wetness, the dharmatā sugata essence having a nature of un-outflowed, superfactual virtue, you can understand that the appearances of samsara and nirvana are simply the plays of consciousness and wisdom respectively, so do not need to be different, separate items. At the time of samsara, there is the play of consciousness, and at the time of nirvana, there is the play of wisdom. Therefore, one does not need to separate samsara and nirvana. It has been most strongly proclaimed in the sutras that in the fact of the authentic, in the fact of dharmadhātu, all appearances never waver in the slightest from the state of dharmatā, primordial enlightenment, so never depart from the nature of the primordial enlightenment. Therefore, one has to accept that that is so. For example, one of the six Mother Prajñāpāramitā texts, the *Verse Summary Prajñāpāramitā* says:

> The purity of form is to be known as the purity of
> fruition.
> The purities of fruition and form will be the purity of all-
> knowing.
> The purities of all-knowing, fruition, and form
> Are analogous to the realm of space—not differentiable,
> not divisible.

Whatever form arises at the time of the cause when one is not a buddha is primordially pure, a purity which is the same as the purity at the time of the fruition when one has become a buddha. Thus, if you exhaust the stains of the element's perceiving subject that knows and become a buddha, it will be pure of perceived objects without exception, none remaining. The purities of all-knowing, fruition, and form are analogous to the realm of space, not differentiable—there is no distinction of good and bad in those purities and they cannot be separated by mind.

When the buddha nature, dharmatā wisdom, is gradually freed of obscurations, actuality becomes more and more purified until, when it has been freed from even the tiniest of obscurations, the greatest thing to be realized has been realized and that is buddhahood. When the obscurations of the internal perceiving subject, the element sugata essence, have been removed, automatically there will, without exception, be no more impurity of external perceived objects remaining. For example, an eye disease can cause you to see outer objects unclearly, in other words, they will not be pure. If the disease is removed, the distortions of vision produced by the disease also and automatically will be removed. The floaters mentioned in the text are a particular disease of the aqueous humor of the eye in which one sees what seem to be filaments floating around in space. If the floaters heal, the appearance of what seems to be things floating out in front simply stops. In other words, the mention of floaters here means "mistaken beliefs that there is something there when there is not".

"You might think, 'Yes, but when one person becomes a buddha …" You might think, "Yes, but when one person becomes a buddha, all of impurity's appearances will cease", but it is not so. Each person has his own appearances produced by his own obscurations, causing him to be obscured in his own particular way, and then not seeing the purity of things-as-they-are of external objects. That is why even though one person becoming completely pure by becoming a buddha does not mean that all the others automatically become the same.

"You might think, 'Yes, but at the level of a buddha …" This paragraph goes on to say that you might think, "Well then, if that is so, at the level of buddhahood where the actuality of things as they are and the appearance of things as they appear always are synchronised, does a buddha have all these impure appearances or not? If he has them, all dharmas would not be manifest, complete buddhahood, and if he does not have them, it would not be possible that he would know the paths that beings constantly travel and the rest". If a buddha has them, the consequence would be that all dharmas would not be manifest, complete buddhahood, meaning that the buddha would not actually be completely enlightened with respect to all dharmas. If a buddha does not have them, it would not be possible that he would know the paths that sentient beings constantly travel in samsara, and the rest—which would mean that he would not have a tathāgata's ten strengths that include the sixth strength of knowing all the paths within samsara that sentient beings are constantly travelling, where they lead, and which should be taken and which should not. Mipham's reply to that is that a buddha's all-knowing wisdom knows effortlessly and spontaneously everything that exists—all the dharmas of samsara and nirvana—within the state of their being equal taste with the buddha's all-knowing wisdom. All knowable dharmas are only seen as the great purity by a buddha in his own perspective and yet at the same time and without losing that in the slightest, a buddha is seeing all of appearances of all of the beings of the six migrator's realms as they individually experience them. This type of seeing happens because a buddha has exhausted all the obscurations of dualistic perceiving subject and perceived object.

The term dharmin here means the dualistically known objects of sentient beings and you could also say that it means the fictional. A buddha sees all of the many dharmins of sentient beings all at once but without any merging of them, meaning each one is starkly known, without mix-up or blurring. A buddha is not like us samsaric beings for whom all the dharmins are mixed together in our conceptual consciousness. For example, if you say, "India", everybody thinks of India as mixture of concepts about India. A buddha's all-knowing knows each person, each language, each region in India, all of them, but knows each one individually without mixing them together. The wisdom of equal taste does not arise newly earlier and so also does not cease at some point later. Thus, being free from arising and ceasing, it is uncompounded. This is the great all-knowing wisdom that sees the nature of the uncompounded. The bodhisatvas who dwell on the ten bodhisatva levels have difficulty in thinking about this all-knowing wisdom of a buddha, let alone the ordinary people whose minds can only understand it through discursive thought.

That wisdom simultaneously sees all dharmas and dharmins, happiness and sorrow, within one taste, but that does not mean that there is happiness and suffering within it because all-knowing wisdom sees universal purity within which everything is only pure—there is nothing impure. However, a buddha also knows the impure appearances of the fictional, of the six realms of migrator beings. For example, it is like a person with extra-sensory perceptions who is awake in the same room as someone having very horrible dreams.

That person knows all of what the other one is dreaming and experiencing but is not affected by it and could even laugh at the absurdity of it.

"Sees them all at once" in the current paragraph refers to the fact that a buddha sees both the universal purity and the impure appearances all at once. The ultimate valid cognizer that sees purity is all-knowing wisdom and there is no valid cognizer higher than that. That is spoken of in the bodhisatva sutras, the sutras of the Great Vehicle:

> All dharmas being the same in equality
> Is realized as such by self-arising.
> Therefore, the authentic manifest buddhas,
> The tathāgatas, have the same way of seeing.

The first line points out the actuality of all dharmas, that they are the same in equality. The second line says that the wisdom of the sugata essence when it is still an essence knows all dharmas as such. The third line sets out the situation when wisdom of the sugata essence is no longer an essence but fruition wisdom. The person who has achieved that fruition has reached the authentic situation of having become a manifest buddha. On the fourth line, tathāgata is another name for a manifest buddha, so is it not redundant to mention tathāgata here? Tathāgata is deliberately put here because it means "one who has arrived at how it actually is". All of those who have arrived at how it actually is necessarily see what is, which is that same equality of all dharmas mentioned on the first two lines.

Then there is another quote from the bodhisatva sutras:

> By knowing the mind which is naturally luminous accordingly, it is because of that that by means of the prajñā that has one moment of mind there is what is called "unsurpassed, truly complete enlightenment, manifest complete buddahood".

The sugata essence in mind has to be understood not merely to be empty but to have a luminous nature, a wisdom nature, in which all phenomena are known to be of equal taste yet at the same time and without loss of that knowledge in the slightest are known individually, without mixup, and all at once. When that buddha essence is known for what it is through the use of prajñā, then precisely because of what it was as the untransformed sugata essence, it has become the fruition state of the sugata essence which is none other than what we call "unsurpassed, truly complete enlightenment, manifest complete buddahood". Here, the phrase "prajñā that has one moment of mind" is used to indicate that it is a prajñā not merely seeing the emptiness aspect of dharmadhātu but also seeing all appearing phenomena, all compounded things, within the unchanging dharmadhātu. In short, it is that sort of prajñā seeing the essence of wisdom possessing mind for what it actually is that results in the essence species becoming the manifest species of buddhahood.

In accord with that, the master Chandrakīrti says in *Entering the Middle Way*:

> The sky is not differentiated in different vessels and
> Likewise compounded things are not differentiated in
> suchness because of which
> Having made them known as one taste in the authentic,
> You of excellent knowledge know knowables by the
> instant.

"You" in this verse is the Buddha. The verse praises the Buddha's wisdom knowing, explaining how it is of two types: the wisdom that knows how phenomena actually are and the wisdom that knows phenomena as they appear. The first three lines concern the first type of knowing and the fourth line concerns the second type of knowing. For the first wisdom, no matter what vessels you fill with water—porcelain cups, wooden cups, and so forth—the image of the sky in the different vessels is not differentiated. Similarly, although for a dharmin type of awareness compounded things will be differentiated as this, that, and the other, for a dharmatā wisdom awareness compounded phenomena will be undifferentiated, all of them being known as one-taste in the space-like authentic situation of the dharmatā. The Buddha, having done the work of treading the path and so having obtained the first type of knowing—that all compounded things are one taste in the authentic—will also know, because of his excellent knowledge's second type of knowing, all compounded things individually, without mixup, and all at once. The verse is written in the sequence that it is because the wisdom knowing how it is for phenomena is the cause of the wisdom of extent; if a buddha did not have the realization of how it is for phenomena, there could be no wisdom knowing them in their extent.

Mipham now explains his overall position that has been backed up by those quotations and concludes his presentation of the second reason according to his own Nyingma tradition.

The great wisdom that is non-dual with the dharmadhātu pervades all dharmas or knowables and sees all of them effortlessly at once, like for example on a full moon day the moon and all of the stars arise simultaneously in a clean ocean. A buddha's wisdom pervades all knowables all at once by the instant, but a buddha's wisdom also sees all of them within the state of the complete pacification, meaning the non-existence, of the discursive thought of ordinary people. From what cause does such seeing arise? The two obscurations are exhausted by means of the path, then the dharmatā of the primordial self-arising luminosity wisdom that exists in the ground will have been manifested exactly as it was in the ground. That that is so is known by force of its having become manifest as it actually is in buddhas, so if you rely on a correct reasoning of dharmatā—the fourth of the four reasonings explained earlier in this commentary—used in an ultimate analysis, you will acquire an irreversible trust that this wisdom sugata essence exists.

Otherwise, if you evaluate this with some other, less far-reaching kind of mind, you will see many rubbishy contradictions and concepts:

- you will prove that there is no wisdom at the level of the buddha or that, even if it does exist, it is equivalent to the ordinary dualistic mind that changes;
- you will assert that a buddha does not see the makeup of sentient beings or alternatively that a buddha has impurity's appearances;
- you will not be able to prove that the knowledges of nature and extent have entities of equal taste;
- and so on.

With "less far-reaching mind" and "rubbishy" Mipham is referring to the fact that, within the circles of Tibetan learned ones, there had been a great deal of discursive thought and contradictory logic expressed in the form of all sorts of small-minded argument that only served to obscure this matter.

Thus this second of the three reasons is not proved merely by the actuality of the thing, emptiness. It is proved by the fourth of the four reasonings explained earlier, the "reasoning of dharmatā, the entity". That reasoning of dharmatā, the entity, does apply here in that self-existing wisdom exists primordially, its entity being the uncompounded nature of equal taste and that whoever sees things as they are does manifest the result exactly in accordance with that. There are no distinctions within its entity which is undifferentiable and if you realize that, that is buddhahood, which is why Guardian Maitreya said, "the species of a buddha exists in sentient beings because suchness is without differentiation".

2.3. The Third Reason

"The meaning of the third line of the verse 'because the species exists' is as follows." "All sentient beings" is the subject of the syllogism. "The species of being able to become a buddha exists in all sentient beings" is the thesis to be proved. The reasons that make the proof are that "it is established that the adventitious stains can be abandoned" and "it is established that the dharmakāya primordially having the good qualities exists in all beings without difference".

"If there is a species that in that way can become a buddha existing in all sentient beings", it is ascertained that those bodied beings have the essence of a buddha because in their buddha phase the dharmakāya of a buddha also is established as an uncompounded entity so, from the aspect of the entity, there is no difference of bad earlier and good later.

"By means of this third reason, one knows that the result" that can be manifested is created from a cause which is the ability to become a buddha, which is the reasoning of the cause doing its work, another of the four reasons[34]. In this case, it is not that the mere existence of a cause means that a result is produced. The result here is established as coming from the cause in dependence on a collection of causes. If all the causes are complete, then a result will be produced. How many causes are needed? When all that are required are complete, the result will be produced. This is so because of three key points. Firstly, the dharmatā suchness species is unchanging; there is no proof that it changes and if it did change it would not be the dharmatā. Secondly, when the result is manifested, there is no good or bad in the dharmatā entity between earlier when it was not realized and later when it was realized. Thirdly, no matter how long the adventitious stains have persisted, they can always be separated and removed, so it is impossible for the species to become spent, losing its ability to become buddha.

"That causal species that exists is no different in entity ..." This paragraph says that there is no difference in entity between that causal species that exists spoken of above and a buddha's dharmakāya at the time of the fruition. And if the dharmakāya of the time of the result

---

[34] Skt. kṛituakarana, Tib. bya ba byed pa. Each consciousness, faculty, and so on performs its own individual work and cannot do the work of another consciousness. For example, when an eye consciousness arises, it is able to do the work of seeing a visual form but is not able to hear a sound, and a barley seed is able to produce barley, but not able to produce corn.

exists, it must also at the time of a sentient being exist without increase and decrease. And although we designate them one as the earlier cause and the other as the later result, in the fact of actuality they are of one taste in the entity of the unchanging, space-like dharmadhātu. Those three reasonings prove that all sentient beings are possessors of the tathāgata essence, which is due to the correct reasoning of presence by the force of the thing.

That is the path of the correct reasoning of presence by force of the thing. How do you prove the existence of sugata essence by this reasoning given that you cannot see it? The reasoning by force of the thing has proof both by direct perception and by inference and it has both of those both for us ordinary beings and for noble ones; in other words, there are four possibilities altogether. The first two are fictional force of the thing and the remaining two are superfactual force of the thing. We ordinary beings cannot completely establish sugata essence by direct perception of our senses because, as explained earlier in the commentary, we ordinary beings have only the valid cognizers that see this shore, impurity. We can infer the far shore of purity but cannot completely prove its existence until we have the valid cognizers that go with the sight of the other shore, purity, which are not acquired until we become noble ones.

The term "thing" is, generally speaking, one of a pair of items—things and non-things[35]. Texts on valid cognition define a "thing" as that which can be taken as an object of mind. Thus, the reasoning of the force of the thing is a reasoning that works by the fact that the thing being referred to in the argument can be known as such through the senses. For example, when you know that the sky is blue, that is a valid reasoning by the force of the thing. If when the sky is covered with grey clouds you think that the sky is blue, that is not a

[35] Tib. dngos po, dngos med respectively.

valid reasoning by the force of the thing[36]. The argument here is proved by means of correct reasoning of presence by the force of the thing.

"By this reasoning that proves ..." By this reasoning discussed above that proves that the tathāgata essence exists in all sentient beings, ultimate emancipation, the tathāgata, and the actuality of all dharmas in superfact are not different, separate things. Here ultimate emancipation means final attainment of emancipation; the tathāgata is someone has realized the dharmatā just as it is; and the actuality of all dharmas is all dharmas in superfact. Moreover, if one knows that they arise due to the causal tathāgata essence, then ultimately they are established as a single, ultimate vehicle. There are many different enumerations of vehicles for buddhahood: one, two, three, nine, and more. In the end, they all come down to being one ultimate vehicle, which is the vehicle of tathāgata essence as just explained.

On the other hand, the systems of those who get the meaning of the Great Vehicle back to front saying that sugata essence does not exist in the makeup of sentient beings, does not exist at the time of buddhahood, does not possess the good qualities at the time of the cause but newly has them at the time of the result, and so on speculate endlessly over the reasoning that establishes a single, ultimate vehicle. The systems of those people have endless amounts of discursive thought concerning the reasoning that establishes one ultimate vehicle and so end up not correctly establishing anything concerning this. For that reason, those interested in the topics of the supreme vehicle must acquire a mind that has thoroughly mastered the subject matter being presented, this topic of sugata essence.

---

[36] The long names for this are "dngos po stobs kyis zhugs pa'i rigs pa" meaning reasoning that has entered by the force of the thing and "dngos pa stobs las byung ba'i rigs pa" meaning the reasoning that has arisen due to the force of the thing. The abbreviated name is "dngos stobs rigs pa" reasoning of force of the thing.

"What we have posited above, the existence of an element ..." The existence of the element posited above that at the time of sentient beings primordially has the good qualities is a profound topic of the inconceivable. It is a profound topic concerning the way things are that is outside the range of concept, due to which the Buddha instructed his four retinues, "Trust in my words concerning this and you will not be deceived. In this case you must trust me because it will be very difficult to understand by your own intellectual capacity". In that way, the Buddha taught sugata essence as the ultimate of profound topics. Therefore, it is the ultimate knowable and as such does not fit into the sophists' limited intellects. They argue about this topic of sugata essence back and forth and around and around yet can never come to a correct understanding because all of their arguments are based in discursive thought. They endlessly dissect topics such as "mind that is a common basis for buddhas and sentient beings" but get nowhere because their capacity to understand these matters is limited only to a conceptual understanding based in conventions, an understanding that is disconnected from the inconceivable convention-free reality that it is. This has been spoken of like this in the *Definitely Unravelling the Intent Sutra*:

> The character of the formative realms and superfact
> Is a character free of same or different.
> Those who comprehend them anyway as same or different
> Have engaged them not in accord with how they are.

Paraphrased, the verse is saying, "The characteristic of the realm of formatives—meaning fictional truth—and of superfactual truth is beyond same and different. Someone who, despite that, comprehends them as same or different has engaged them or is understanding them improperly or incorrectly", which is what the sophists do.

Mipham explains the verse like this. Both mind's dharmatā—the dhātu of the entity of sugata essence—and the mind which is a dharmin should not be accepted as either the same or different. The two have not departed from—meaning are always within—the fact of dharmatā, the way things are, but that does not contradict them looked at from the way things appear in which confused sentient beings are possible. On top of that, any other way of asserting this will end up having faults in whatever reasoning is presented, for example, one would have to accept no emancipation or that a confused sentient being is not possible, and so on. However, because there is non-synchronisation of the way things are and the way they appear, it is proved that it is possible for confused sentient beings to exist and proved that by entering the path they abandon confusion then become buddhas.

"The reasoning of superfactual analysis establishes ..." The reasoning of superfactual analysis establishes that all dharmas are empty in entity. However, establishing in that way that they are empty does not negate the good qualities of the sugata essence. Why not? The sugata essence has an empty entity but also has in its own entity all the unsurpassable qualities of a buddha, as was explained earlier and backed with quotations from the *Highest Continuum*. "Because that one maintained verbally" refers to Guardian Maitreya whose teachings on synchronisation and non-synchronisation form the basis for the immediately preceding paragraph of the text. He —Maitreya—maintained it to be that way and explained it verbally to Asaṅga who then wrote it down. Because that is how sugata essence has been taught, the meaning taught by the Buddha in the middle turning of the three turnings of the wheel of dharma, that all the dharmas both of total affliction—of three-realmed samsara—and complete purification—of nirvana—are empty also is established here in this definitive meaning teaching of the sugata essence.

Nevertheless, the buddha essence that Mipham is presenting was taught in the definitive meaning sutras with the extra feature that the emptiness has a nature of kāyas and wisdoms, a nature which the sugata essence has constantly, without coming and going. This sort of buddha essence that Mipham is presenting is the one that is the intent of the definitive meaning sutras of the final turning. From that approach alone this type of buddha essence is special compared to the tathāgata essence mentioned in the middle wheel, which is spoken of only in terms of its emptiness. Therefore the sutras and commentaries on their intent commend the meaning of the final turning as supreme.

However, note that not all sutras of the final turning are regarded as supreme; only the definitive meaning sutras that teach the essence are regarded as such. The Buddha taught it for example in the *Sutra Petitioned by King Dharaṇeśhvara* using the example of cleaning a jewel, where it says:

> Son of the family, it is like this. For example, there is a skilled jeweller who knows the craft of jewellery well. Of the various types of precious jewel, he has taken a precious jewel which is completely dirty. He wets it with a penetrating, chemical salt solution then thoroughly cleans it with a hair cloth and in that way gives it a thorough cleaning. He does not stop his efforts at just that, either. Beyond that, to clean it he wets it with a penetrating decoction then thoroughly cleans it with a woollen flannel and in that way gives it a thorough cleaning. He does not stop his efforts at just that, either. Beyond that, to clean it he also wets it with a strong chemical liquid then thoroughly cleans it with a fine cotton cloth and in that way thoroughly cleans it. Thoroughly cleansed and free of encrustation, it is now called "an excellent type of Lapis Lazuli".
>
> Son of the family, in the same way, the tathāgata, knowing the element of totally impure sentient beings, uses the story of renunciation which is about impermanence, suffering, lack of self, and impurity to arouse disenchantment in those sentient beings who like cyclic existence and to get them into the taming that goes with the noble dharma. The tathāgata does not stop his efforts at just that much, either. Beyond that, he uses the story of emptiness, signlessness, and wishlessness to make them realize the mode of a tathāgata. The tathāgata does not stop his

> efforts at just that much, either. Beyond that, he uses the story of the non-regressing wheel and the story of the three spheres of total purity to make those sentient beings who have the cause of varying natures enter the tathā gata's place.

"That being so, both the emptiness taught ..." This paragraph points out that, from the foregoing, it has to be that the emptiness taught in the middle turning and the kāyas and wisdoms taught in the last turning are known as unified appearance-emptiness. The issue of which of the sutras of the middle and final wheels is definitive in meaning should be understood only in the way that all-knowing Longchen Rabjam maintained, which is that both wheels can be definitive meaning, without need of eliminative differentiation.

Eliminative differentiation is the use of logic to determine which of two things something should be. In this process, one is differentiated as the one that is the case with the result that the other is necessarily eliminated. Which of the middle and final wheels is provisional and which definitive in meaning is usually decided using eliminative differentiation, with the result that one has to be provisional and one definitive. However, Longchenpa says that it does not have to be that way, that both middle and final wheels could be decided on as definitive meaning. The Kagyus also decide which of the sutras of the middle and final turnings are provisional and definitive in meaning by assigning the second turning sutras as non-ultimate definitive meaning and the final turning sutras as ultimate definitive meaning, which is a variation on Longchenpa's approach.

Longchenpa's approach has the effect that sutras of the middle and final turnings can be definitive meaning. If so, sugata essence can be defined as unified emptiness-appearance. That then means that sugata essence also fits with the meaning of causal tantra. Due to all of that, we end up with a sugata essence in which all the instructions of sutra and tantra are combined so that all of the teachings of the Buddha are reduced to the single key point of a sugata essence as taught in the definitive meaning sutras of the final turning. Together with this, it becomes very clear that the pair Nāgārjuna and Asaṅga are in fact of one mind in regard to this ultimate meaning, as can be seen from Nāgārjuna's *In Praise of Dharmadhātu*, *Enlightenment Mind Commentary*, and so on and Asaṅga's *Highest Continuum Commentary*, and so on. It is usually said that Nāgārjuna was the great champion of the meaning taught in the middle turning Prajñāpāramitā sutras and that Asaṅga was the great champion of the meaning taught in the final turning sutras. It can seem that they did not agree, which has the potential for making someone doubtful over what the Buddha was actually teaching. However, by clarifying that there is a final turning sugata essence that includes the meanings of emptiness and appearance as taught in the sutras and the unified emptiness-appearance taught in the tantras, this apparent difference between the two masters is resolved.

Master Nāgārjuna also said that sort of thing:

> The sutras that show emptiness,
> As many as were taught by the conqueror,
> All turn away the afflictions
> But do not degrade the element.

He said the same sort of thing because any of the discourses of the Buddha that showed emptiness always did so in a way that turned away samsaric mind but did not undermine in any way the element sugata essence and so did not undermine the presence of the buddha qualities.

In accordance with what Nāgārjuna has said, the result to be accomplished through analysis with superfactual analysis is a sugata essence that has both empty and appearing aspects unified, not a sugata essence in which the necessary empty aspect somehow degrades or removes the appearing aspect containing the good qualities of a buddha. Thus superfactual analysis properly done leads to the actual fact of the vajra-like—meaning indestructible—inseparable ultimate truth, which is the dharmadhātu that is invincible in the face of the sophist's type of mind. Sophists' arguments are entirely based in discursive thought whereas the fact of dharmatā dharmadhātu is inconceivable, beyond the reach of their thought and arguments. Therefore, Mipham says, our sugata essence is invincible, cannot be defeated by them, because there is no basis in it by which their arguments could attack and overwhelm it.

"Now, I will explain how the element is seated ..." Mipham will now show how the element is seated in the mindstreams of those sentient beings. From the standpoint of actuality's own entity, all dharmas are contained within the space of that dharmatā, that actuality, and given that the dharmatā's own entity has no birth and cessation in it, all dharmas are residing in equality. Thus in actuality the element has no good and bad of samsara and nirvana, and so on, and there are no factors of this shore and that shore, self and other, greater and smaller, and so on, and there are none of the distinctions of earlier and later times, and so on. Thus that actuality, that sugata essence, is the single unique sphere of dharmadhātu, without shift and change.

"It is like that in actuality, but" if we do this in terms of confusion's adventitious appearances, it is that appearances of the objects of body and mind of three-realmed samsara shine forth and then, although at this point dharmatā's nature is not being seen, the dharmatā is not non-existent—it is there without moving in the slightest away from its own nature. Thus, the dharmatā of mind that, like that, has been enclosed by adventitious stains is not visible, nevertheless it is present there in the centre or pith of that enclosure in the manner of an essence or garbha, so it is spoken of as a "gotra" meaning "species" or "garbha" meaning essence. It has been taught that it should be understood through its illustration by the nine examples of a treasure under the earth, and so forth in the same vajra topic in which the three reasons are taught in the *Highest Continuum*. Furthermore, the element is defined in relation to the degree to which the adventitious stains have been removed as having three phases: impure, pure and impure, and utterly completely pure, though there is no such distinction in the element's own entity. It is as the *Highest Continuum* says in part 1, verse 27:

> Because the wisdom of the buddha has entered the mass of sentient beings,
> That stainless nature is non-dual and
> That, the species of buddha, is accurately designated as the fruition,
> So it is said that all migrators have the essence of a buddha.

And the same text says:

> This is the nature dharmakāya,
> Suchness, and the species ...

And the same text in part 1, verse 47 says:

> According to the sequence impure,
> Pure and impure, and utterly completely pure,
> The names "sentient being,
> Bodhisatva, and tathāgata" are given.

Those three quotations all show that there are three main phases for the element: as a sentient being who has not started the path, as one who has started the path, and as one who has completed the path.

Mipham has completed his explanation of how sugata essence sits in the mindstreams of all sentient beings. In the next paragraph he talks about what it will be like for someone whose understanding of how sugata essence is seated in the mindstreams of all sentient beings is not like that.

"For someone who does not understand it that way ..." Such a person will have various problems when he tries to establish his own ideas about it using reasoning. When he presents his idea of "sugata essence", his mind has an idea of it as something which, like Juniper sitting in a basin—Juniper sitting in a basin is a dense matrix of leaves and branches within which it is hard to see anything clearly—is somewhere or other in the cage of the five aggregates, an imprecise idea that will be clearer or murkier depending on his level of confusion. That imprecision will be carried over into his efforts at negating others' ideas and establishing his own, which can only end up with others crying aloud, "Oh no!" when they see how his idea is not in line with the intended meaning of the Great Vehicle. For that reason, it is pointless to broadcast this account of the buddha essence in the places of close-minded sophists who have not trained their minds in the Great Vehicle.

This account says that the profound is not to be taught to the immature—those who have not been properly trained and prepared for it—and not to the Forders because they are not suitable vessels for hearing this profound dharma. Forders here also means followers in general of religions other than Buddhism[37]. It was because of them that the Buddha taught dharma starting with no self, impermanence, and so forth. And it is also not to be taught to them because it must be proved by reasoning, but, as explained earlier, these are ordinary beings who will not be able to prove it with their seeing of this shore only, so if it is explained to them, they will bring it down with their ordinary logic into a topic of over- and under-statement only. They will not be able to apply reasoning that will see it for what it is and in doing so will lose its meaning.

"A person's mind should be trained first ..." Mipham says that in order for someone to be able to understand this profound sugata

---

[37] For Forder, see the glossary. Here again it means followers in general of religions other than Buddhism.

essence, his mind should first be trained in the tenets of the lower Buddhist schools, such as the Śhrāvaka and Pratyekabuddha vehicles. Following that, the person needs to gain an outstanding level of certainty in the meaning of un-assessed great emptiness through studying the sutras of the second turning of the wheel. When he has gained that, if he is gradually taught the story of sugata essence according to the definitive meaning sutras of the final turning of the wheel, he will come to trust the primal situation, the primordial reality seated in us sentient beings as sugata essence.

"Thus it is said that …" This paragraph completes the whole section on the Nyingma understanding of the view. Appropriately, it ends this section on the note that the use of reasoning to gain the certainty of a correct understanding of sugata essence is not enough. It is then necessary to practise the path and transform the element sugata essence into manifest buddhahood.

In view of what has been explained above, there is the standard Buddhist saying that, "Though the path is completely pure, it cannot be established by reasoning, it has to be realized in direct experience". In other words, as is always taught when Buddhism is correctly expressed, it is not enough just to use your rational dualistic mind to establish that there is the wisdom of a buddha in you, you have to do the next step of practising the path in order to reveal that wisdom beyond thought to yourself. Prior to using the path to purify the stains of sugata essence in order to arrive at manifest wisdom, you first have to expose the stupidity of those who think, "If it does not become a path of the seeing of this shore, then it is not a valid path". That means that you first have to see the mistake of those of lesser understanding, those who are stuck in the belief that the exercise of reason can in the end provide all answers—logicians, sophists, philosophers, and so on. Once you have clearly understood that, you have to learn the practical matters of how to practise the path, and finally you have to get on with the practice and do it until you have become expert in the key points of the path. As explained earlier, when you have gained sight of the other shore, purity, you will have seen that wisdom for yourself and will not need inferential logic to prove its existence. You will see it in direct perception.

3. Dispensing with some Mistaken Positions

It has been said already that sugata essence as explained in the final turning sutras is very profound, the most profound of the teachings given by the Buddha in sutra and equivalent to the final meaning of the tantras. Because of the profundity of the teaching it is very easy to go astray on certain points of how sugata essence should be viewed and end up misunderstanding the deep meaning of it. Three such ways of going astray are dispensed with in this section, though the final effect is to clarify the definitive meaning sugata essence taught in the final turning even further.

The three views dispensed with in this section are: that the sugata essence in not being empty is truly established; that the sugata essence is empty but is a cut-off empty condition; and that the wisdom that resides in the sugata essence and is manifested from it is, due to being called impermanent, taken to be compounded.

3.1. Dispensing with the View that the Element in Being Not Empty is Truly Established

Some, because of certain things that the Buddha taught in the final turning of the wheel, claim that sugata essence is not empty and as such is truly established. The Gelugpa tradition following Tsong-khapa in particular made this claim, citing the Buddha's teaching of sugata essence as permanent, stable, and eternal. Those words of the Buddha sound very much like the view of the Forders, where Forders does not mean followers in general of religions other than Buddhism but means followers of religions other than Buddhism who believed in an eternal self, such as the mainstream Hindu schools of the time.

The *Descent Into Laṅgka Sutra* is one of the sutras of the final turning of the wheel. The first piece quoted from it here is:

> The bodhisatva Mahāmati asked the Bhagavat ... the bodhisatva mahāsattvas who arise in the future and the present should not strongly cling to a self.

In this piece, Mahāmati points out that the works, meaning texts, of the Forder schools—specifically meaning the non-Buddhist schools who have a view of a permanent self—use the words "permanent, stable, and eternal" in their teaching of a permanent self. He also points out that their texts explain that the permanent self is without good qualities. Mahāmati asks whether that means that the Buddha's teaching on sugata essence, which also teaches sugata essence as "permanent, stable, and eternal" and as possessing the good qualities of enlightenment, is the same as their teachings on a self or not. The Buddha says that his teaching is not the same as theirs. He clarifies that he first taught the tathāgata essence in the middle turning using the words of that turning that specifically show the emptiness of phenomena, for example, he used the words "the three doors of complete emancipation—emptiness, signlessness, and wishlessness", and "nirvana not dwelling in any extreme", and "the unborn, unceasing emptiness that is the entity of all phenomena" to describe the tathāgata essence. He first taught the tathāgata essence that way in order to tame Forders—where Forders means followers in general of religions other than Buddhism—and others with a lesser level of understanding in a way that would gradually introduce them to the extremely profound meaning of tathāgata essence that he later showed in the final turning of the wheel, where he mostly referred to it as sugata essence. In showing phenomena as empty, he did explain a cut-off emptiness as a domain or place for a practitioner's mind to focus on during a meditation in which there is no discursive thinking. By teaching that way, he could bring the disciples in and gradually show them the really profound meaning of emptiness in the final turning. There, he showed wisdom, not mere emptiness, and that wisdom can be understood to be "permanent" and so on when correctly explained. However, that explanation of permanence is very different from that of the Forders who believed in an eternal self, such as the mainstream Hindu schools of the time. In short, the

Buddha himself did not deny teaching the sugata essence as permanent and so on, but also emphatically stated that the sugata essence was taught as emptiness in the second turning. Moreover, he ends this piece by saying "In regard to this Mahāmati, bodhisatva mahāsattvas now and in the future should not strongly cling to a self" which makes the matter crystal clear.

Then in the second quotation from that sutra, the Buddha instructed his audience:

> If something is not empty of self-entity, even though it might exist empty of other dharmas, that would not fulfill the function of emptiness.

This neatly gets to the point. From the quotations given earlier from the *Highest Continuum* and Asaṅga's commentary to it, the *Highest Continuum Commentary*, it is clear that there are two ways of defining "emptiness" of sugata essence. The first is that it is empty of a self as explained in the middle turning, which the Buddha has just verified for us. The second is that "it is empty of the adventitious stains which are separable from it", that is, it is empty of other, which is the profound meaning of emptiness taught in the final turning in relation to sugata essence. In this one sentence spoken by the Buddha himself, the two types of emptiness—emptiness of self and emptiness of other[38] are fully verified for sugata essence. This leads into a major discussion of empty of self and other which is beyond the scope of this book. However, this topic should be studied at this point and to do that there are two other books that should be read—firstly *Other Emptiness, Entering Wisdom Beyond Emptiness of Self* and secondly the *Lion's Roar Proclaiming Other Emptiness*. The quotation here also makes the point that the emptiness of self kind of emptiness taught at the level of the middle turning is not the highest approach to emptiness. It is an emptiness arrived at through negating one conceptually invented thing after another, which means that all of

---

[38] Tib. rang stong and zhan stong respectively.

them have to be eliminated using concept in order to complete the work of realizing all phenomena to be empty of a self, which is the approach of, for example, the *Heart Sutra* which says "No eye, no ear, no nose, no tongue ..." The highest kind of emptiness is the emptiness in which one goes into wisdom, which is empty of a self, but is by the mere fact of its presence, empty of everything other than wisdom. That is the non-conceptual approach to finding sugata essence to be empty and, given that sugata essence includes the dharmadhātu, it means that that also is the non-conceptual approach to finding all phenomena to be empty of a self.

The remaining two quotations from the same sutra make the point that anyone following the Buddha's teaching is to go beyond all elaborations, which is one definition of emptiness according to the middle turning.

"In line with the meaning of such scripture ..." Mipham now explains this matter. He says that with the use of reasoning at the level of conventions even, the sugata essence can be validated as having an empty entity that is mind's basic nature—dharmatā—and which can be said to be all-pervading, permanent, inconceivable, and shining forth without bias as every aspect of the good qualities of buddhahood. It would be quite wrong, given the explanations of the Buddha such as the ones just quoted, to take those words as meaning that sugata essence is not empty of a self-entity and therefore is a truly established thing. If it were truly established like that, then everything that it could be—the dharmatā of other dharmas, and so forth—would forever be impossible.

And then, putting reasoning at the level of convention aside and taking up reasoning that uses a valid cognizer at the level of superfactual analysis, the result to be accomplished of buddhahood that has been determined by such a valid cognizer could never be reached by anyone because in the aftermath of all dharmas having been analysed as lacking in true existence, the establishment of even a single truly established phenomenon does not remain, like darkness not remaining when there is light. A valid cognizer of conventional analysis also cannot establish true establishment, because for it there might be true establishment—meaning that the phenomenon being analysed is not non-existent—but merely by that that phenomenon cannot ever be established as not empty. In fact, phenomena have to be truly established or there would be no phenomena to be empty of self. Given that "not empty and hence truly established in the sense of being truly existent" cannot be established through either of the two valid cognizers, going after any proof of it would be like chasing a sky flower or some other imagined but totally non-existent thing, so attempting to prove it ends up in meaningless weariness. In other words, he is saying to these people, who include the people of Tsongkhapa's tradition who were known for pressing this point again and again from every angle possible, don't waste your time on chasing after this point with all of your clever logic, for if you use correct logic at either the conventional or superfactual levels, you cannot prove that sugata essence is not empty and will only be wearing yourself out if you continue to persist in your attempts to do so.

2. Dispensing with the View that the Element is A Cut-off Empty Condition

There are "**those who do not understand**" the type of reasoning used in connection with the dharmadhātu of unified appearance-emptiness and take a different approach to it. They take the species, dharmadhātu, and emptiness to be mere assessed superfactual truth, non-affirming negation, and make proofs that contradict the sutras and their commentarial texts that say that the sugata essence primordially possesses the good qualities of enlightenment.

The *Samādhi of Wisdom Mudrā Sutra* that explains that there will be people in generations after the Buddha who will position themselves as true followers of the dharma but who will in fact be making this kind of mistake. A first quotation from it says that these are people who will talk endlessly about everything being empty in what is merely an assessed emptiness way. They will say that that is the correct way to explain and understand the dharma when it is only a first step towards explaining and understanding the profound emptiness of wisdom.

A second quotation from it has the words "that reference we properly train in as emptiness" that show that they do not understand the profound emptiness because a reference is a dualistic way of understanding anything. The first two lines quoted indicate that those people understand only the emptiness taught in the midde turning of the wheel, the third line indicates that they understand it only conceptually, and the fourth line shows that the Buddha regards them as ones who will take away what is correct dharma, the profound understanding of an emptiness which is not cut off from appearance that was taught in the final turning.

A third quotation from that sutra says that anyone who is immature in their spiritual development and is focussed only on the cut-off emptiness of a non-affirming negation type of non-existence of phenomena due to thinking that that is the correct approach to emptiness will have a mind disturbed by concepts and will be bound in samsara because of it. The cut-off empty condition that some people believe is how sugata essence should be viewed is not a correct understanding of emptiness.

Next, a quotation from the *Verse Summary Prajñāpāramitā* says that a bodhisatva might have the thought that realizes "these five aggregates of mine are empty", but he is living the path while coursing in concept labels[39] rather than in a direct perception of the emptiness of the aggregates, so he is one who thinks he has faith in the true unborn emptiness but in fact does not. This illustrates a cut-off empty condition being mistaken for un-assessed emptiness. With this very well-known quote, the cut-off empty condition that some

---

[39] For concept labels, see the glossary.

people believe is how sugata essence should be viewed is proved by the Buddha's own words to be incorrect.

Next, the *King of Samādhis Sutra* says that someone who is expert in the view and meditation of the Buddhist path will not dwell in the extreme of believing that phenomena exist nor in the extreme of a cut-off empty condition in which phenomena are non-existent nor in somewhere between the two. Again, the cut-off empty condition that some people believe is how sugata essence should be viewed is, by the Buddha's own words, incorrect.

Next, the *Angulimālā Sutra* says:

> Oh my! There are two beings in this world who destroy the holy dharma. Both those who have the view of an extremely empty condition and those in the world who advocate a self destroy the holy dharma, ruining the holy dharma with their mouths.

The extremely empty condition referred to in that quotation is the cut-off empty condition. Again, the Buddha himself is saying that such an approach to emptiness is incorrect.

Then Nāgārjuna famously said:

> If one clings to emptiness, the antidote that pulls out all views, as a thing or non-thing, that is a view that is incurable.

A cut-off empty condition is a view that supposedly uproots and removes all dualistic views, but it is actually a case of clinging to a concept of emptiness, so is something that prevents the person who holds that view from ever being cured of holding to dualistic views. It is an highly undesirable, if not dangerous, approach to emptiness. The final quotation in this string of quotations takes that further by saying, "If you view empty and not empty with concepts then you have not gone beyond all dualistic references. All dualistic references, including the concept of a cut-off empty condition, must be abandoned".

"In other words, even if those people ..." Now Mipham gives a short explanation of the essence of what it means for those people to be involved with a cut-off empty condition. He does not go on at length about it because he explains it practically, not theoretically, in a way that is easy to understand. He says that, in other words, even if those people who hold to a cut-off empty condition as being real emptiness have done an examination using reasoning, there is the problem for them that the non-affirming negation used in their analysis by reasoning will have merely severed true establishment. Why? Because it involves a severance of that to be negated which has been merely imputed by a grasping consciousness that has dualistic thought. Therefore, they have stayed within dualistic mind with conceptual elaborations about emptiness and so have not arrived at actuality freed of exaggerations about it.

"The mere factor of emptiness of truth ..." Mipham sums up this second dispensing with wrong thoughts by pointing out that the mere factor of emptiness of truth that is the result of non-affirming negation is not the same as fully characterized dharmadhātu and actuality in which emptiness is not a cut-off blankness but is unified with appearance. He says that despite that, it can be useful for beginners to train their minds in this type of blank emptiness in which true existence has been eliminated as long as they do not take it as final but use it for a while as a step towards engaging the fully characterized actuality not merely of emptiness but of emptiness unified with appearance as explained for sugata essence wisdom. Mipham then quotes from a scripture to back that up. In the quotation, the bodhisatva who has the thought, "All compounds in becoming are impermanent. All compounds are suffering. All compounds are empty. All compounds are without self", would not be engaging the full meaning of actuality, only the lesser level taught in the middle turning. Nevertheless, the Buddha is recommending that bodhisatvas could take such an approach because it would lead to the most profound understanding of emptiness taught in the final turning in relation to sugata essence.

3.3. Dispensing with Wisdom in Being Impermanent Taken to be Compounded

The third dispensing with wrong views in relation to sugata essence is much longer than the first two because it not only dispenses with a wrong view about the wisdom that is manifested from ground sugata essence but becomes a platform from which Mipham can bring us to a clear statement about the correct view of sugata essence and wisdom before going on to conclude the text.

"You might wonder 'Ground sugata essence …" The all-knowing wisdom that is the result of the ground sugata essence having been made manifest was sometimes defined in sutra as permanent and sometimes as impermanent. Thus there can be the very valid doubt, "Is all-knowing wisdom that has been manifested permanent or impermanent?" And there is also the doubt, "How should this be taken given that the wisdom dharmakāya has been defined as uncompounded?"

"Conforming to the mind set …" Conforming to the mind set of those other disciples in the Buddha's retinues who had not reached the level of development at which they could see wisdom directly because of having transformed their sugata essence and for whom profound explanations of that wisdom would be difficult to understand or accept, the Buddha taught that all-knowing wisdom is impermanent. In regard to wisdom being explained and known to be impermanent, Dharmakīrti's *Complete Commentary on Valid Cognition* gives a very tersely stated verse which Mipham then explains:

> A valid cognizer of permanence does not exist
> Because of a valid cognizer knowing substantial existence,
> And because knowables are impermanent
> Their one also is impermanent.

In general, all-knowing wisdom has to be said to be impermanent because it arises from the path's causes such as the arousing of enlightenment mind, meditation on emptiness, and so forth. Because of that, it is not tenable to say that it arises without cause, and then all things produced from a cause are impermanent. On top of that, all-knowing wisdom has to be said to be impermanent because it is a direct perception valid cognizer of all dharmas. Given that a valid cognition can only be in relation to a non-deceptive mind—as explained in the introduction section of Mipham's text and this commentary to it—a valid cognizer that evaluates impermanent "things" must in accordance with that be a non-permanent valid cognizer, and that means that wisdom, knowing all of those things, must be an impermanent valid cognizer. In other words, because its object, the knowable, is impermanent, the valid cognizer that evaluates it also must be impermanent, arising as something having a succession of moments. On the other hand, if it were permanent, because it would be established by valid cognition as empty of the ability to perform a function, it would be ascertained to be empty of actions in their entirety of evaluating objects, and so on. Thus, it is totally untenable to say that all-knowing wisdom is permanent and thereby it is established as impermanent. Similarly, all things are designated as impermanent and all non-things as permanent, but there is no basis for it to be permanent, so a dharma that is a fully characterized permanent will not be found at all.

That explains why all-knowing wisdom was defined by the Buddha as impermanent. Mipham says that that approach of wisdom being impermanent had to be taught for the sake of the Forders, where Forders means followers in general of religions other than Buddhism, and for those followers of the Buddha who were in the common vehicle and therefore had not trained their minds in the approach taught in the final turning. That is true now as well; as Mipham explained earlier, beings have to be matured gradually, in an appropriate sequence, before they will be able to withstand hearing the most profound explanations of reality. In terms of this level of explanation in which all-knowing wisdom is said to be impermanent, there is no other way within the framework of dualistic consciousness, that is, in terms of the way things appear, to explain how all-knowing comes about.

"Despite that, from the point of view of wisdom …" Despite that explanation of wisdom being impermanent within the framework or point of view of dualistic consciousness, from the point of view of the all-knowing wisdom that is the result of entire transformation within sugata essence, all-knowing wisdom has to be established as permanent. In the end, that the knowables set out in the proof of impermanence given just above have momentary arising and ceasing and the perceiving subject wisdom also arises having a succession of moments, and so on—other such observations not taken up above—only appear that way in the appearances of those who have not entirely transformed the ground. In the fact of how things are that has been established in accordance with a direct perception of suchness, that being impermanent is known because of wisdom that knows all, but it is not the only way established; in that fact of how things are, there is no dharma at all that arises for even a single moment, and if that is the case why state the obvious, which is that the succession that starts at the time of such an arising, and so forth—its cessation and all other observations that can be made in relation to the arising—are not established? For example, a dream has from its own perspective various appearances with boundless time successions with an earlier beginning and later end and directions but they are not established as such.

Thus, when the fact of dharmatā …" Thus, when the fact at the time of ground sugata essence of dharmatā without birth and cessation has in accordance with what it is been entirely transformed into ultimate wisdom, that ultimate wisdom is the wisdom kāya of inseparable knower and knowable, and, even in the case of no transformation that comes with ordinary people who have not practised the path, mind's innate disposition—or we could call it the actual unified dharmatā that is naturally luminous—is changeless, because of which, given that there is no distinction of earlier and later, it is called, "the species which is present in the nature". Note that the words here "the species present in the nature" are slightly different from "the naturally present species". The former refers to the nature, sugata essence as the nature of sentient beings. The latter is saying that the species is naturally present in sentient beings, not something that has to be developed by them.

That all-knowing wisdom is changeless both before and after it has been transformed. The other situation of that which is not changeless, of that which has change, is the situation of the adventitious stains appearing on the surface of the all-knowing wisdom. These stains because they are only adventitious are separable from the all-knowing wisdom. In the phase when they have not been separated from it, they arise in a succession of momentary arisings and ceasings that appears in the form of the non-equality of samsara and nirvana, good and bad, and all the other dualistic pairs that appear at that time. And for those having such dualistic appearances that come with not having done the transformation, those appearances are undeniably non-deceptive. However, the dualistic phenomena that arise and cease are not established in the innate disposition of those sentient beings' minds. There, dharmas reside as the great equality within the state in which all factors of change of time and direction are all at once comprehended. Moreover, that great equality does exist as the object of the personal self-knowing wisdom of the noble ones. Moreover, it is not spoiled by change into the three times, thus it is designated using the convention "the great permanence", because it is something that exists but exists without the momentary arising and cessation.

"It is like this ..." To restate that more clearly, it is like this. All the knowables of time and direction, such as changeable things and non-changeable non-things like space, and so on, are included in that dharmatā in equal taste, but that dharmatā is not contained by any dharmins that have change, and so on. It is like the sky is a container of the clouds but the sky is not contained within the clouds.

"That being so, the dharmatā great equality ..." That being so, the dharmatā great equality and the dharmadhātu with its innate disposition of luminosity are present simultaneously in a single unique sphere of self-arising wisdom that naturally pervades all things. Now, at the time of sentient beings it has adventitious stains, so its own nature has not become manifest for them. However, through the power of the abandonments and realizations that happen in connection with the practise of the five paths that dispel the stains, that self-arising wisdom will be gained as the great wisdom in which knower and knowables are inseparable. When that happens, those sentient beings will have gained the great all-knowing wisdom that, while not having any of the discursive thinking of a dualistic mind, effortlessly—meaning without any efforts of dualistic conceptual mind—and spontaneously—meaning without the causality of cause and effect—knows that all awarenesses—because they are in fact unchanging self-arising wisdom—are of equal taste in the innate disposition of dharmatā.

"Now that approach will not lead ..." You might think that the approach just explained will lead to self-arising wisdom being born from causes, which would be a total contradiction in terms, for what is self-arising is by definition not born from causes. However, that is not the case. In the authentic, that is, in the state of things as they actually are, dharmakāya freed from the adventitious stains has been reached as the disconnected type of result explained earlier in this commentary. It might seem to be something newly arisen from causes, but in the end, it only appears that way in the case of the way things appear to sentient beings who have not done the transformation. On the other hand, in the fact of the authentic, the entity of the dharmakāya that is the dharmatā's nature has no birth and disintegration. According to the ultimate intent of the definitive meaning sutras of the profound that were taught in the final turning of the wheel, all dharmas primally are manifest buddhahood in equality or are from the beginning peaceful nirvana, or are luminosity by nature, and so on. These are the various ways that those sutras speak about the primal situation of dharmas. The profound understanding behind the use of such words can easily be mistaken by someone of lesser understanding to mean something other than the actual intent behind them. It has been said a few times already that words expressing the ultimate intent concern topics that even the bodhisatvas dwelling on the bodhisatva levels have difficulty contemplating. If that is so, why bother to try to express how difficult it would be for ordinary people to understand them correctly and to apply correct reasoning to them! Nevertheless, there is the possibility that, rather than having a deep comprehension of this whole subject of definitive meaning sugata essence, you might hear the explanations of the Buddha and great masters that commend it as equivalent to obtaining the prophecy of having become irreversible from buddhahood, then simply accept and trust in this as being actually the case and so simply devote—meaning dedicate yourself with faith—to it.

There is an important point here that appears in quotations in the next, concluding section. In the introduction to the text, Mipham said that it was not sufficient simply to have faith in the scriptures, that one needed to apply correct reasoning and develop faith in the authoritative statements that make up the scriptures. Here, he is saying that this subject of definitive meaning sugata essence is so profound that even the high level bodhisatvas have trouble understanding it, let alone us ordinary beings. Therefore, if you have some understanding of what he has explained about sugata essence in this text and if on top of that you already have faith or develop faith in the Buddha as someone who did correctly cognize all of the matters he then spoke of for our benefit, you might just accept what has been said, trust it as being so, and then have faith in it and devote, meaning to dedicate with faith, to that approach.

The Buddha himself proclaimed with the roar of a lion that orienting yourself with faith to this approach of definitive meaning sugata essence is equivalent to obtaining the prophesy of irreversibility from buddhahood. That prophesy is obtained when you have gone so far along the path to buddhahood that a buddha gives you in front of the surrounding audience of bodhisatvas the prophecy that you now will not fall back from attaining buddhahood at such and such time and place and with such and such name. Knowing these things and having faith in the Buddha, it is possible simply to accept his explanations of this very profound matter, orient yourself accordingly, and so reach a point in your development that you are now irreversibly on the path to buddhahood and that you will never fall back to lesser understandings, such as those of the middle turning, and take those as the definitive meaning.

"If in accordance with that ..." If in accordance with having developed faith in that approach of definitive meaning sugata essence you view the tathāgata's wisdom dharmakāya as permanent, merit will arise because of it. Here, "merit will arise" does not simply mean that you will make merit as is commonly spoken of in the Buddhist teachings, but means that you will become a more meritorious person altogether, someone who has advanced considerably because of it. This is backed up with one quotation from the *Sutra Called "Samādhi due to Miracles that Fully Ascertain Utter Peace"*, two quotations from the *Great Nirvana Sutra*, and a final quotation from sutra whose source is not named.

These quotations back up the point that, when one understands the thrust of the definitive meaning teachings, one understands that the right view to have of the tathāgata is permanence. In that sense, the various quotations here are an important conclusion to this section. However, there is also the point that the tathāgata—where tathāgata has to be understood as dharmakāya—is permanent and is the true refuge. As the last quote in the series of quotes here says:

> Viewing the kāya of the tathāgata as impermanent is not going for refuge at all and if the vajra kāya is viewed as impermanent, immeasurable disadvantages will arise.

And as the quote before it says:

> If someone assiduously works at the perception of permanence in regard to the inconceivable, that is the place of going for refuge.

There is a very complete explanation of the ordinary and ultimate ways of going for refuge in the book *Unending Auspiciousness, The Sutra of the Recollection of the Noble Three Jewels*. It would be helpful to read that to understand this point more clearly. Furthermore, there is an excellent treatment of this point in a very practical explanation of the meditation of sugata essence in *"Instructions for Practising the View of Other Emptiness" A Text of Oral Instructions by Jamgon Kongtrul.*

Mipham concludes this section by saying that, having understood what those sutras are saying about the tathāgata correctly being viewed as permanent and so on, it is necessary to bow to, meaning to respect, that as the meaning of the authentic, of reality.

THE CONCLUDING SECTION

"In that way, sugata essence's own entity …" In that way, sugata essence's own entity is free of all conceptual elaborations of existence and non-existence, eternalism and nihilism, and so on; it is the single unique sphere of the inseparable truths, equality. Within the state of that actuality, all dharmas of appearance and becoming, where becoming is another term for samsara, have become one taste, just thatness. As explained earlier, suchness is a term specifically used to indicate the suchness of reality whereas just thatness is a general term used to indicate exactly how it is with something. To see in accord with that just thatness is to see the fact of the authentic without removal and addition. It is to see reality without needing to add or subtract anything to make it reality.

When you see in that way, you are seeing with a mind separated from the subjective grasping consciousnesses that grasp at their perceived objects in their entirety and that is the mind that has the excellent view that realizes superfact. There is a quotation from *Showing the Dharmas Conducive to Enlightenment Sutra* that can be hard to understand because of the wording:

> Mañjuśhrī, the one who, in regard to all dharmas being non-dual in being without not being equal, sees them without duality has the correct view.

It says that, given that all dharmas are non-dual because they are only equality in the space of wisdom, the person whose mind sees them without the duality of a grasping consciousness and grasped at object is the person who is seeing all dharmas correctly.

Then there is a quotation from the *Sutra Petitioned by Gaganagañja*:

> There is things and non-things consciousness
> And what is residing in the authentic limit.
> Those expert in the view do not grasp
> Things and non-things.

This says, "There is both consciousness that has things and non-things for its objects and wisdom that is residing in the other possibility, the authentic. Those who are expert in the view of the authentic do not rely on consciousness with its grasper that has grasped at things and non-things. They rely on wisdom, because that is the one that sees the authentic, just as it is."

Then there is a quotation from the bodhisatva sutras which says:

> In superfact, in face of the noble ones' prajñā and wisdom, any dharmas to be thoroughly known, or abandoned, or meditated on, or made manifest are not present at all.

This says, "In superfact, in the view of the noble ones' prajñā and wisdom that is operating, there are none at all of the dharmas to be thoroughly known because they are part of the path or to be abandoned by the path, or to be cultivated by meditating on them, or to be made manifest because they are a desired result of practising the path."

"Nevertheless, in the case of …" That is so in superfact, nevertheless, in the case of making good distinctions using the valid cognizer of conventional analysis:

- you know what is true as true such as knowing the path of the noble ones to be non-deceptive;

- you know what is not true as not true, such as knowing that advocating liberation by meditating on a self is a wrong view;
- you know what is impermanent as impermanent, such as knowing that all compounded things are momentary;
- you know what is permanent as permanent, such as knowing that sugata essence, self-arising wisdom, is always unchanging; and you know what is non-existent as non-existent, such as knowing that the self and the appearances of grasped-at and grasper are not established by nature;
- you know what is existent as existent, such as knowing the way things appear of interdependent origination is non-deceptive cause and effect and knowing that the dharmatā sugata essence with the good qualities spontaneously present naturally exists in all sentient beings;
- and so forth.

That is the style in which conventional prajñā that is not twisted conventionally apprehends the mode of things. It is a non-twisted or correct prajñā, so if you use your mind to engage whatever it is that is to be known through the use of such prajñā, you will in that way attain vast good qualities, because such prajñā is a root of virtue that has no delusion.

"Using that style of correctly understanding ..." Using that style of correctly understanding the matter at hand through the use of a correct prajñā, the sutras teach many dharmas generally and specifically. Especially, even though there is no self of a person, they refer to sugata essence which is beyond both the elaborations of self and non-self as "the great self", "the great permanence", and so on. In that way they teach it as having the supreme good qualities of having gone to the other shore. Thus they speak of it as being purity, bliss, permanence, and self. Therefore, sugata essence exists as the changeless good qualities of the peaceful, cool, perfect, ultimate, great non-abiding nirvana, the great nirvana of not abiding in any of duality's extremes whatsoever. The Buddha, in order to ensure that we did know that it exists in that way said at the time of his passing into nirvana as recorded in the *Nirvana Sutra*:

> What is called "self" is any dharma that is permanent in the authentic. That which has become an owner that is unchanging and unshifting is called a "self".

"Owner" is a term that in this case means something that is master of the situation. The definitive meaning sugata essence with its empty dharmatā and nature of wisdom having all the good qualities is exactly the owner of the being of all beings—those who have transformed it and become buddhas, those who have only partially transformed it and are bodhisatvas, and those who have not transformed it at all and therefore are ordinary sentient beings.

As a small anecdote, I remember being the translator for one well-known Tibetan tulku at a retreat in the United States in the 1990's. The one hundred or so students there were nearly all from a Theravadin community called Spirit Rock. The Tibetan tulku was teaching highest level Dzogchen, in which the explanation of the mind is exactly as just described, using the words "having a self". The audience almost went beserk; they had so strongly come to believe that there is "anatman"—no self as described in their Lesser Vehicle teachings—that they just could not stomach these words explaining that there was a self. It took some of them several years to get over it. This was an intensely practical demonstration of the truth of the explanations that this topic is so profound that it should not be mentioned to people in the common vehicles (which includes the Theravada vehicle) because they will not be able to accept it or will defy it somehow. It was also a vivid demonstration of the truth of the explanations that the real meaning of the Buddhist path is not to dwell in any extreme, such as those of existence and non-existence.

This is the end of the main part of Mipham's explanation. The explanation is filled with much reasoning and uses the technical vocabulary of Buddhism, making it hard for some to follow. Still, the text as a whole tells a story of a sugata essence that is not a mere intellectual exercise. For example, as with the anecdote just shared, I have found repeatedly throughout my life as a translator and teacher of Buddhism, that what seem to be nebulous statements about this and that and the other turn out to be very true when circumstances suddenly come together that allow these matters to surface. Therefore, I would encourage the reader not to be weighed down by the details in here but to read carefully and think and not merely pass off what is said in here because it seems trite or traditional or somehow removed from your own "way that things appear".

Above all, remember that you do have what we call wisdom. It does not mean that we have the ability to be "wise", it means that we have this most fundamental knowing in our being that only knows without duality, that only knows in a mode which is the final refuge for all of us. "As it was before, so it is later" and if you have done enough meditation and received enough oral instructions on this wisdom that is unchanging, you will start to notice in your life that although what appears to you is a constant flux, in fact there is an odd-at-first experience of nothing having changed from moment to moment.

——— ◆◆◆ ———

"Having heard the explanation …" Mipham starts his final remarks by saying that, having heard the explanation of this profound sugata essence given above, even just accepting what has been said on faith and then orienting yourself accordingly will produce immeasurable benefits. It is as the *Highest Continuum* says in chapter 5, verses 2 to 4, which has been paraphrased here for the sake of providing a commentary:

> The intelligent one who accepts this object which is
> known fully only to the conquerors
> Thereby becomes a vessel suitable to develop the buddha
> qualities.

In doing so he delights in the inconceivable qualities of buddhahood and so
His merit surpasses the merits of all sentient beings.

For example, there is someone who in pursuit of enlightenment decorates every day the dharma kings—the buddhas—with gold and gems
Numerous as the atoms in the buddha fields by offering the gold and gems to them.
In comparison, if someone else hears some words from this *Highest Continuum* text and having heard them moreover has devotion to it,
He will gain much greater merit than what came from the generosity.

For example, an intelligent person wanting unsurpassed enlightenment during a period of many aeons even
Works effortlessly to keep stainless discipline of body, speech, and mind.
In comparison, if someone else hears some words from this *Highest Continuum* text and having heard them moreover has devotion to it,
He will gain much greater merit than what came from the discipline.

For example, there is someone whose meditative absorption that has been engaged in so as to remove his own fire of afflictions of the three becomings—the three realms of samsara—
Has developed to the point that it has reached the level of the absorption of the form realm abodes of the gods in general and Brahma in particular. He then uses that absorption as a method for cultivating shiftless complete enlightenment.
In comparison, if someone else hears some words from this *Highest Continuum* text and having heard them moreover has devotion to it,

> He will attain much greater merit than what came from
> developing and using the absorption.

This teaching on sugata essence has a profundity and depth that are difficult to fathom, so if you have come to some understanding of it and with that have devotion to it, even that much will be very meaningful. After all, this teaching is the lion's roar of the irreversible teaching of definitive meaning sugata essence, the very essence of the supreme vehicle that shows the story of sugata essence. As explained earlier, this is the final teaching of the Buddha, the true roar of the lion of the Śhākya clan, the buddha known as Śhākyamuni. It is not just another teaching for it causes irreversibility in those who hear and at least partially comprehend it—it causes them to graduate to the place in their spiritual journey from which they never turn back from its meaning and revert to having their main faith in a lesser teaching of the Buddha.

This teaching is of the utmost profundity, so it is difficult for those of little previous training and inferior intellect to have devotion to it. As the *Compendium of the Tathāgata Sutra* says:, "This wisdom of mine is doubted by those of immature mind. Therefore, they do not do the transformation of the definitive meaning sugata essence and manifest it as wisdom. Instead, like an arrow shot into the sky, they fall back, retreating into the lesser teachings. They do not reach the irreversible lion's roar sugata essence".

Following that there are two more quotations that explain that those of bad character cause this kind of dharma to be left behind. A third quotation from the *Eliminating Lax Discipline Sutra* makes it clear that in the centuries following the Buddha's time, more and more people will appear who will not assist the dharma but cause harm to themselves and others:

> The sort of person who, drowning on the path of life
> clings to dispute and harms himself and others, the sort of

> person who is not a holy being, will completely fill this Jambudvīpa.

"One should consider carefully the approach ..." One should consider carefully the approach being taught in those scriptures and others like them. When the degenerate times have started up and those who show reverence for the teachings are mainly corrupting the key points of our own Nyingma system of the supreme vehicle through a perverted understanding of the four reliances[40] and counterfeit dharma has arisen, those treasuring this teaching of definitive meaning sugata essence as the very life of the Great Vehicle path will be rare indeed.

Due to my own reverence for the teachings of the Nyingma tradition whose texts contain the earliest teachings and translations of the Buddha Word in Tibet and for the lineage vidyādharas or knowledge holders of that tradition, I have seen and heard many precious authoritative statements of the lineage. In particular, due to the good fortune of receiving at the crown of my head the lotus feet of many authentic spiritual friends—the regent of Padmasaṃbhava and lord of conquerors Jampal Shonnu who was youthful Mañjuśhrī displaying himself as a man, and the all-knowing Dorje Ziji, and others, I who am immature in age and intellect have developed just a little knowledgeability[41] in regard to this profound topic.

"It is like this." This nice exposition of the meaning of the species residing as the nature of dharmadhātu and that has the mode of utterly non-dwelling unification free from all extremes, is the lion's roar. The *Sutra Petitioned by Brahma Viśheṣhachinti* says:

> Devaputra, the discourses of mine that express not being attached to any dharma at all, that express not dwelling in

---

[40] For the four reliances, see the glossary.

[41] For knowledgability, see the glossary.

> any extreme at all, are the lion's roar. The discourses that express attachment are not the lion's roar, they are the fox's barking. The discourses that teach the production of views are not the lion's roar.

And the *Great Nirvana Sutra* says:

> The lion's roar is the explanation that ascertains that all sentient beings have the nature of a buddha and that the tathāgatas remain forever and are without shift in the three times.

And another sutra says:

> Son of the family, in many places it is explained that the topic is emptiness, but those should not be called "the lion's roar". What is proclaimed within circles of experts having prajñā should be called "the great lion's roar". That lion's roar is not explained as the fact that "all dharmas are impermanent, suffering, selfless, and entirely impure"; it is only explained as the tathāgata being permanent, blissful, self, and entirely pure.

Those and other sutras speak extensively about the lion's roar, using both example and meaning, in order to illustrate it, so it should be understood from them.

Mipham says that speaking straightforwardly in that way about his own Nyingma tradition's path of the sugata essence may cause some disagreement in others—and historically speaking it did—but it is a presentation of the correct path, so others should not become upset by it. As is said in *Entering the Middle Way*:

> The work of composing the treatise was not done out of attachment to analysis and debate, it was done for complete emancipation. If in explaining suchness, I have destroyed others' texts, there is no fault.

Then he says that this same straightforward approach also guards the dharma. The *King of Samadhis* says:

> What is "guarding the dharma"? It is connected with the fact that those who disparage the buddha's dharma annihilate what accords with the dharma.

The same approach is also to be holding the dharma, as mentioned in the *Sutra Petitioned by Gaganagañja*:

> Who has the character of the enlightenment of the
> Conqueror
> Wholly holds the character of dharma and
> Whoever fully knows this spotless limit
> Holds the qualities of all the buddhas.

The person who in that way has taken hold of the dharma is grateful to the Buddha for what he has done and also attains immeasurable merit. This is so because of what *Showing the Tathāgata's Great Compassion Sutra* says:, "It is like this: in their ordinary lives they first approach because of hearing the dharma of the Conqueror. After that, they renounce samsara and leave the worldly life on account of the dharma, not on account of material things. Because of that, someone who holds to the dharma of the Sugata is grateful to all the buddhas for what they have done". And it is also so because of what the *Sutra Petitioned by Gaganagañja* says, "Although someone praises the wisdom of a buddha, trying to express a praise for every one of its good qualities, that person's work is not done even after tens of billions of aeons, because there is no limit to the wisdom of the Buddha. Correspondingly, the merit of someone who holds the holy dharma of the tathāgata cannot be measured".

Now, the only thing left for Mipham to do is to provide the verses of poetry that are usually written at the end of a composition in order to give the author room to sum up in an eloquent way what he has on his mind. Mipham's poetry, paraphrased goes as follows.

Due to composing this text, my own knowledgeability—
knowledge of a subject combined with the ability to express that knowledge clearly to others—of the textual tradition
Of the supreme Great Vehicle has increased a little,
But who would rely on the words of me, a mad monk,
Who is young in years and immature in training?

These days, I see that others follow after famous people.
They lack the intelligence to analyse what is and is not.
Worse, most of them are completely agitated by the negativities that come with envy.
When I see this state of affairs, I know that it is not the time for making eloquent explanations, for they will just be lost on these people.

Nevertheless, because of my always respectfully making offerings
To the supreme guru in the form of the special deity that is my main deity of practice seated on the lotus in my heart,
The words and meanings of the excellent texts
Dawn more and more clearly in the place of insight within my mind.

At that time I earnestly applied myself to becoming familiar with the many elegant explanations available in our tradition.
Because of that for me now prolonged joy has arisen in this life and because of that in future lives
In other fields—meaning other places in samsara or buddha fields within which bodhisatvas stay—there will be a superior delight
In the Conqueror's way of dharma, a superior delight that, like the moon, waxes ever brighter.

Due to this story of sugata essence, a story which is the ultimate
story of the profound,
Those with intelligence will find joy unlike the sort of happiness
Experienced when one has fallen into either of the extremes of
samsaric becoming or peaceful nirvana.
Therefore, this is a joyous feast for those of good fortune.

May the lion's roar of the supreme vehicle of unified appearance-
emptiness
That has abandoned strong clinging in its entirety,
Overwhelm the swarms of wild animals of wrong views
And resound throughout the ten directions as the essence of the
Conqueror's teaching.

For the colophon, Mipham wrote the following:

The holder of the store of jewels of the three disciplines, my dharma brother named Guṇa, also known as the first Jamgon Kongtrul, said, "Write a complete explanation in whatever words come to your mind of 'Because the complete buddha kāya radiates' and the other two reasons". At his urging, I, the monk Lodro Drimay, wrote this at Sharma. May virtue and excellence increase!

That is the end of the original composition by Mipham.

❁ ❁ ❁

A further colophon was added by the person who collected and published Mipham's works, giving a synopsis of events surrounding the publishing of the composition. It is as follows.

We searched for the text of this composition amongst the texts of the lord guru, finding it after two full years, at which time we were to undertake the cutting of wood blocks. The person who previously urged the composition to be done came to meet us and together with the very knowledgeable Legpay Lodro urged us, "If you still need to do more, such as making additions, do whatever you need!" Therefore, some further wording was added to the original. All the points of the original together with the new additions were proofed during two days at the waxing moon of the Saga month in the Iron Rabbit year at the practice centre of Dudlay Namgyal Ling by Lodro Drimay Jampal Gyaypay Dorje.

❁ ❁ ❁

As is often the case with Tibetan texts that are reprinted, some editions of the text have yet another colophon giving the names of people who contributed financially and otherwise to the reproduction of the text. There was no point in reproducing those here.

LIST OF TEXTS CITED

Aṅgulīmālā Sutra; Skt. aṅgulimāla sūtra. The "Sutra Taught for the Benefit of Aṅgulimāla" is one of the definitive meaning essence sutras of the final turning of the wheel.

Compendium of Abhidharma; Skt. abhidharmasamucchaya by Asaṅga.

Compendium of the Tathāgata Sutra; Skt: tathāgatasaṅgiti sūtra.

Complete Commentary on Valid Cognition, Skt. pramāṇavarttika, Tib. tshad ma rnam 'grel, the extensive commentary on the subject of valid cognition written by Dharmakīrti. Included in the Translated Treatises.

Complete Explanation of Enlightenment Mind; Skt. bodhicittavivaraṇa, Tib. byang sems rnam bshad, by Nāgārjuna.

Definitely Unravelling the Intent Sutra; Skt. saṃdhinirmocana sutra, a Great Vehicle sutra of the final turning of the wheel regarded as one of the four main Mind Only sutras. A translation into English is available.

Descent into Laṅgka Sutra; see *Noble One, Descent into Laṅgka Sutra*

Dgongs pa rab gsal by Tsongkhapa.

Dharmadhātu Treasury; Tib. chos dbyings mdzod, by Longchen Rabjam. An electronic version of the whole text with reader software is available from Padma Karpo Translation Committee.

Distinguishing the Three Vows; Tib. sdom gsum rab dbye, by Sakya Paṇḍita.

Eliminating Lax Discipline Sutra; Tib. tshul 'chal tshar gcod pa'i mdo.

Enlightenment Mind Commentary; see *Complete Explanation of Enlightenment Mind*.

Entering the Middle Way; Skt. madhyamakāvātara by Chandrakīrti, a text that presents the ten levels of the bodhisatvas with a very long explanation of the Middle Way Consequence view according to Nāgārjuna's system. Included in the *Translated Treatises*. An electronic version of the whole text with reader software is available from Padma Karpo Translation Committee.

Great Nirvana Sutra; Skt. mahāparinirvāṇa sūtra, a Great Vehicle Sutra that is one of the definitive-meaning, profound sutras of the Other Emptiness system.

Great Vehicle Highest Continuum Treatise; Skt. mahāyānottaratantra śhāstra; one of the Five Dharmas of Maitreya. Some feel that the Sanskrit name given is an invention and that the text was actually called "ratnagotravibhāṅga", "Distinguishing The Precious Species". A translation into English is available. An electronic version of the whole text with reader software is available from Padma Karpo Translation Committee.

Heart Sutra; Skt. prajñāpāramitā hṛidaya sūtra, one of the Prajñāpāramitā sutras.

Highest Continuum; see *Great Vehicle Highest Continuum Treatise*.

Highest Continuum Commentary; Asaṅga's commentary to the *Highest Continuum* treatise.

In Praise of Dharmadhātu; Skt. dharmadhātu stotra (some give as dharmadhātu stava) by Nāgārjuna.

"Instructions for Practising the View of Other Emptiness" A Text of Oral Instructions by Jamgon Kongtrul; by Tony Duff, published by PKTC, 2011, ISBN: 978-9937-572-03-3.

Kalama Sutra; Skt. kalama sūtra.

King Dharaṇeśhvara Sutra; see *Sutra Petitioned by King Dharaṇeśhvara*.

King of Samādhis; Skt. samādhi rājā sūtra.

Lion's Roar Proclaiming Other Emptiness; Tib. gzhan stong khas blangs sengge nga ro, by Ju Mipham. A sister text to *Lion's Roar Proclaiming the Sugata essence*. Published in English under the title *Lion's Roar Proclaiming Other Emptiness*, by Tony Duff, second edition, February 2011, ISBN Paper: 978-9937-824-46-0.

Lion's Roar That is a Great Thousand Doses of the Sugata Essence; Tib. bde gshegs snying po'i stong thun chen mo sengge nga ro, by Ju Mipham.

Nirvana Sutra; see *Great Nirvana Sutra*.

Noble One, Descent Into Laṅgka Sutra; Skt. laṅkāvatāra sutra; a Great Vehicle sutra of the final turning of the wheel regarded as one of the four main Mind Only sutras. Other Emptiness followers additionally classify it as one of the sutras representing the profound view and meditation system of Maitreya. Included in the *Translated Word*. A translation into English is available.

Ornament of Manifest Realizations; Skt. abhisamayālaṅkāra, one of the Five Dharmas of Maitreya. An electronic version of the whole text with reader software is available from Padma Karpo Translation Committee.

Other Emptiness, Entering Wisdom Beyond Emptiness of Self by Tony Duff, published by PKTC, 2014, ISBN: 978-9937-572-67-5.

Ratnagotravibhāṅga; "Distinguishing the Precious Species", an alternative name for the *Great Vehicle Highest Continuum Treatise*.

Rigpa Self-Shining Forth; Tib. rig pa rang shar, one of the seventeen root tantras of innermost extra secret Great Completion

Root Prajñā; Skt. mūlaprajñā, Tib. rtsa ba shes rab by Nāgārjuna. Included in the *Translated Treatises*. An electronic version of the whole text with reader software is available from Padma Karpo Translation Committee.

Samādhi of Wisdom Mudrā Sutra; Skt. jñānamudrā samādhi sūtra.

Sutra Gathering All the Threads; Skt. sarvavaidalyasaṃgrāha sūtra.

Showing the Dharmas Conducive to Enlightenment Sutra; Skt. bodhipakṣhanirdeśha sūtra.

Showing the Tathāgata's Great Sutra; Skt. tathāgata mahākaruṇā nirdeśha sūtra.

Sutra called "Samādhi due to Miracles that Fully Ascertain Utter Peace"; Skt. prasanta vinischaya piatiharya samādhi sūtra, Tib. rab tu rnam par nges pa'i cho phrul gyis ting nge 'dzin zhes pa'i mdo.

Sutra Petitioned by Braḥmā Viśheṣhachinti; Skt. brahmaviśeṣacinti paripṛiccha sūtra.

Sutra Petitioned by Brahmadatta; Skt. brahmadattaparipṛiccha sūtra.

Sutra Petitioned by Gaganagañja; Skt. gaganagañjaparipṛiccha sūtra.

Sutra Petitioned by King Dharaṇeśhvara; Skt. sharaṇeśhvara paripṛiccha sūtra one of the definitive meaning essence sutras of the final turning of the wheel.

Sword of Prajñā Ascertaining Superfact; Tib. shes rab ral dri, by Ju Mipham.

Ten Levels Sutra; Skt. daśhabhumika sūtra, A Great Vehicle sutra on the ten levels of the bodhisatvas.

Translated Treatises; Tib. bstan 'gyur.

Translated Word; Tib. bka' 'gyur.

Treasury of Abhidharma; Skt. abhidharmakoṣha by Vasubandu.

Unending Auspiciousness, The Sutra of the Recollection of the Noble Three Jewels; by Tony Duff, published by PKTC, 2010, ISBN: 978-9937-838-61-0.

Vajra Cutter Sutra; Skt. vajraceddikā sūtra, one of the Prajñāpāramitā sutras of the second turning of the wheel.

Verse Summary Prajñāpāramitā; Skt. prajñāpāramitā ratna guṇa sañcayagātha, one of the six prajñāpāramitā sutras.

GLOSSARY OF TERMS

Actuality, Tib. gnas lugs: The actuality of any given situation is how (lugs) the situation actuality sits or is present (gnas).

Adventitious, Tib. glo bur: This term has the connotations of popping up on the surface of something and of not being part of that thing. Therefore, even though it is often translated as "sudden", that only conveys half of the meaning. In Buddhist literature, something adventitious comes up as a surface event and disappears again precisely because it is not actually part of the thing on whose surface it appeared. It is frequently used in relation to the afflictions because they pop up on the surface of the mind of buddha-nature but are not part of the buddha-nature itself.

Affliction, Skt. kleśha, Tib. nyon mongs: This term is usually translated as emotion or disturbing emotion, etcetera, but the Buddha was very specific about the meaning of this word. When the Buddha referred to the emotions, meaning a movement of mind, he did not refer to them as such but called them "kleśha" in Sanskrit, meaning exactly "affliction". It is a basic part of the Buddhist teaching that emotions afflict beings, giving them problems at the time and causing more problems in the future.

Appearance and becoming, Tib. snang srid: This is a stock phrase usually meaning all of samsara and nirvana, though occasionally meaning all of samsara. Appearance refers to the worlds and becoming refers to the beings in those worlds whose existence is called "becoming".

Authoritative statement, Skt. āgama, Tib. lung: See the introductory section of the commentary for an explanation of this term.

Awareness, Skt. jñā, Tib. shes pa: "Awareness" is always used in our translations to mean the basic knower of mind or, as Buddhist teaching itself defines it, "a general term for any registering mind", whether dualistic or non-dualistic. Hence, it is used for both samsaric and nirvanic situations; for example, consciousness (Tib. rnam par shes pa) is a dualistic form of awareness, whereas rigpa, wisdom (Tib. ye shes), and so on are non-dualistic forms of awareness.

Becoming, Skt. bhāvanā, Tib. srid pa: This is another name for samsaric existence. Beings in samsara have a samsaric existence but, more than that, they are constantly in a state of becoming—becoming this type of being or that type of being in this abode or that, as they are driven along without choice by the karmic process that drives samsaric existence.

Bodhichitta, Tib. byang chub sems: See under enlightenment mind.

Bodhisatva, Tib. byang chub sems dpa': A bodhisatva is a person who has engendered the bodhichitta, enlightenment mind, and, with that as a basis, has undertaken the path to the enlightenment of a truly complete buddha specifically for the welfare of other beings. Note that, despite the common appearance of "bodhisattva" in Western books on Buddhism, the Tibetan tradition has steadfastly maintained since the time of the earliest translations that the correct spelling is bodhisatva; see under satva and sattva.

Clinging, Tib. zhen pa: In Buddhism, this term refers specifically to the twofold process of dualistic mind mis-taking things that are not true, not pure, as true, pure, etcetera and then, because of seeing them as highly desirable even though they are not, attaching itself to or clinging to those things. This type of clinging acts as a kind of glue that keeps a person joined to the unsatisfactory things of cyclic existence because of mistakenly seeing them as desirable.

Complete purity, rnam dag: This term refers to the quality of a buddha's mind, which is completely pure compared to a sentient being's mind. The mind of a being in samsara has its primordially pure nature covered over by the muck of dualistic mind. If the being practises correctly, the impurity can be removed and mind can be returned to its original state of complete purity.

Concept labels, Tib. mtshan ma: This is the technical name for the structures or concepts which function as the words of conceptual mind's language. They are the very basis of operation of the third skandha and hence of the way that dualistic mind communicates with its world. For example, a table seen in direct visual perception will have no concept labels involved with knowing it. However, when thought becomes involved and there is the thought "table" in an inferential or conceptual perception of the table, the name-tag "table" will be used to reference the table and that name tag is the concept label.

Although we usually reference phenomena via these concepts, the phenomena are not the dualistically referenced things we think of them as being. The actual fact of the phenomena is quite different from the concept labels used to discursively think about them and is known by wisdom rather than concept-based mind. Therefore, this term is often used in Buddhist literature to signify that dualistic samsaric mind is involved rather than non-dualistic wisdom.

Confusion, Tib. 'khrul pa: In Buddhism, this term mostly refers to the fundamental confusion of taking things the wrong way that happens because of fundamental ignorance, although it can also have the more general meaning of having lots of thoughts and being confused about it. In the first case, it is defined like this: "Confusion is the appearance to rational mind of something being present when it is not" and refers, for example, to seeing an object, such as a table, as being truly present, when in fact it is present only as mere, interdependent appearance.

Consciousness, Skt. vijñāna, Tib. rnam shes: The term literally means "awareness of superficies". A consciousness is a dualistic (jñā) awareness which simply registers a certain type of (vi) superfice, for example, an eye consciousness by definition registers only the superficies of visual form. A very important point is that the addition of the "vi" to the basic term (jñā) for awareness conveys the sense of a less than perfect way of being aware. This is not a wisdom awareness which knows every superfice in an utterly uncomplicated way but a limited type of awareness which is restricted to knowing one kind of superfice or another and which is part of the complicated—and highly unsatisfactory process—called (dualistic) mind. Note that this definition, which is a crucial part of understanding the role of consciousness in samsaric being, is fully conveyed by the Sanskrit and Tibetan terms but not at all by the English term.

Cyclic existence: See under samsara.

Dharmadhatu, Skt. dharmadhātu, Tib. chos kyi dbyings: A *dhātu* is a place or basis from or within which something can come into being. In the case of a dharma dhātu, it is the place or space which is a basis from and in which all dharmas or phenomena, can and do come into being. If a flower bed is the place where flowers grow and are found, the dharmadhātu is the dharma or phenomena bed in which all phenomena come into being and are found. The term is used in all levels of Buddhist teaching with that general meaning but the explanation of it becomes more profound as the teaching becomes more profound.

Dharmakaya, Skt. dharmakāya, Tib. chos sku: In the general teachings of Buddhism, this refers to the mind of a buddha, with "dharma" meaning reality and "kāya" meaning body. Dharmakāya refers to that aspect of enlightened being in which the being sees the truth for himself and, in doing so, fulfils his own needs for enlightenment. The dharmakāya is purely mind, without form.

Dharmin and dharmata, Tib. chos can, chos nyid: The explanations of definitive meaning sugata essence use this important pair of Sanskrit terms in their explanations. Each term starts with dharma, meaning a thing, a phenomenon. Each term has a suffix that gives it a precise meaning: the "in" on dharmin makes the whole term into "that possessing a thing" and the "tā" on dharmatā makes the whole term into "thing-ness" meaning the inherent property of something. For example, you have water, which is a thing or phenomenon. A samsaric consciousness knowing that water is called the water's dharmin mind. The most fundamental property or dharmatā of the dharmin mind is its emptiness, therefore terms like "emptiness of the dharmatā" or "dharmatā emptiness" are used.

When speaking of a dharmin or dharma-possessing mind, it is understood through the use of the term "mind" that the dharmin or dharma-possessing mind is a dualistic consciousness. However, when dharmin is used without "mind", while it most often refers to a dualistic consciousness, it can also refer to a non-dualistic wisdom.

Note that dharmatā does *not* mean "reality". It is a much more general term that that, meaning the property or properties of any given phenomenon. Thus there is the dharmatā of water which is not one dharmatā but several: the dharmatā of water is that it is wet, liquid, transparent, drinkable, and so on. The dharmatā of samsaric or dualistic mind also is manifold. However, in Buddhist texts it is frequently used to mean the most fundamental property of samsaric mind which is that it is empty luminosity. Because of that, many Western students have come to think that dharmatā means that reality but, as explained, dharmatā is much more general than that. In Mipham's text, dharmatā is mainly used to refer to the inherent property of samsaric mind, the sugata essence, an essence which, when correctly understood, is empty and luminous.

Dhatu, Skt. dhātu, Tib. khams, dbyings: See the introductory section of the commentary for an explanation of this term.

Discursive thought, Skt. vikalpa, Tib. rnam rtog: This means more than just the superficial thought that is heard as a voice in the head. It includes the entirety of conceptual process that arises due to mind contacting any object of any of the senses. The Sanskrit and Tibetan literally mean "(dualistic) thought (that arises from the mind wandering among the) various (superficies *q.v.* perceived in the doors of the senses)".

Elaboration, Tib. spro ba: This is a general name for what is given off by dualistic mind as it goes about its conceptual business. The term is pejorative in that it implies that a story has been made up, unnecessarily, about something which is actually nothing, which is empty. Elaborations, because of what they are, prevent a person from seeing emptiness directly.

Freedom from elaboration or being elaboration-free implies direct sight of emptiness. It is important to understand that these words are used in a theoretical or philosophical way in the second turning sutra teachings but are used in an experiential way in the final teachings of the final turning sutras. In the former, being free of elaborations is a definition of what could happen according to the tenets of the Middle Way, and so on; in the latter it is a description of a state of being, one which, because it is empty of all the elaborations of dualistic being, is the actual sphere of emptiness.

Eliminative differentiation Tib. dbye bsal: means that of two things one is decided on with the result that the other is necessarily eliminated. For example, which of the middle and final wheels is provisional and which definitive in meaning is usually decided using eliminative differentiation—one is decided on as definitive meaning which eliminates the possibility of the other being definitive meaning and similarly for provisional meaning.

Enlightenment mind, Skt. bodhichitta, Tib. byang chub sems: This is a key term of the Great Vehicle. It is the type of mind that is connected not with the lesser enlightenment of an arhat but the enlightenment of a truly complete buddha. As such, it is a mind which is connected with the aim of bringing all sentient beings to that same level of buddhahood. A person who has this mind has entered the Great Vehicle and is either a bodhisatva or a buddha.

It is important to understand that "enlightenment mind" is used to refer equally to the minds of all levels of bodhisatva on the path to buddhahood and to the mind of a buddha who has completed the path. Therefore, it is not "mind striving for enlightenment" as is so often translated, but "enlightenment mind", meaning that kind of mind which is connected with the full enlightenment of a truly complete buddha and which is present in all those who belong to the Great Vehicle. The term is used in the conventional Great Vehicle and also in the Vajra Vehicle. In the Vajra Vehicle, there are some special uses of the term where substances of the pure aspect of the subtle physical body are understood to be manifestations of enlightenment mind.

Element, Skt. dhātu, Tib. khams: See the introductory section of the commentary for an explanation of this term.

Entity, Tib. ngo bo: The entity of something is just exactly what that thing is. In English we would often simply say "thing" rather than entity. However, in Buddhism, "thing" has a very specific meaning rather than the general meaning that it has in English. It has become common to translate this term as "essence" *q.v.* However, in most cases "entity", meaning what a thing is rather than an essence of that thing, is the correct translation for this term. And entity and its nature are not the same; see the introductory section of the commentary for an explanation of this.

Essence, Skt. garbha, Tib. snying po: See the introductory section of the commentary for an explanation of this term.

Evil, evil deed, Skt. papaṃ, Tib. sdig pa: The original Sanskrit means something which someone has done which is truly bad, rotten. Anyone who has done such a thing is looked down upon.

Fact, Skt. artha, Tib. don: "Fact" is that knowledge of an object that occurs to the surface of mind or wisdom. It is not the object but what the mind or wisdom understands as the object. Thus there are two usages of "fact": fact known to dualistic and non-dualistic minds.

Fictional, Skt. saṃvṛtti, Tib. kun rdzob: This term is paired with the term "superfactual" *q.v.* In the past, these terms have been translated as "relative" and "absolute" respectively, but those translations are nothing like the original terms. These terms are extremely important in the Buddhist teaching so it is very important that they be corrected, but more than that, if the actual meaning of these terms is not presented, then the teaching connected with them cannot be understood.

The Sanskrit term saṃvṛtti means a deliberate invention, a fiction, a hoax. It refers to the mind of ignorance which, because of being obscured and so not seeing suchness, is not true but a fiction. The things that appear to that ignorance are therefore fictional. Nonetheless, the beings who live in this ignorance believe that the things that appear to them through the filter of ignorance are true, are real. Therefore, these beings live in fictional truth.

Fictional and superfactual, Skt. saṃvṛiti, paramārtha: Fictional and superfactual are our greatly improved translations for "relative" and "absolute" respectively. Briefly, the original Sanskrit word for fiction means a deliberately produced *fiction* and refers to the world projected by a mind controlled by ignorance. The original word for superfact means "that *superior fact* that appears on the surface of the mind of a noble one who has transcended samsara" and refers to reality seen as it actually is. Relative and absolute do not convey this meaning at all and, when they are used, the meaning being presented is simply lost.

Fictional truth, Skt. saṃvṛtisatya, Tib. kun rdzob bden pa: See under fictional.

Five paths, Tib. lam lnga: In the Prajñāpāramitā teachings of the Great Vehicle, the Buddha explained the entire Buddhist journey as a set of five paths called the paths of accumulation, connection, seeing, cultivation, and no more training. The first four paths are part of journeying to enlightenment; the fifth path is that one has actually arrived and has no more training to undergo. There are a set of five paths that describe the journey of the Lesser Vehicle and a set of five paths that describe the journey of the Greater Vehicle. The names are the same in each case but the details of what is accomplished at each stage are different.

Forders, Skt. tīrthika, Tib. mu stegs pa: A Forder literally speaking is someone who has deliberately gone to the brink of a body of water. The Buddha explained that he used this term to refer to people of other religious traditions of his time. He explained that they were people who had made an effort to go beyond the world but had entered religions or philosophies that were not true paths leading beyond the world. Therefore, unlike ordinary people, they were on the path to enlightenment and had to be respected for that, but were only on the brink of entering the true path, the one that the buddhas teach, that leads across the ocean of samsara to emancipation.

In other words, though this term is mostly translated as "non-buddhist", it does not mean that at all. It is a term of respect for those who have made the effort to liberate themselves, even if they are now only on the brink of doing so because of having entered a wrong path.

It is important to know that the term was used occasionally by the Buddha himself and by his followers to mean "all non-Buddhists" but was mostly used to refer to Hindu and other schools of the time who believed in a permanent self, such as the "atman" of various Hindu schools.

Foremost instruction, Skt. upadeśha, Tib. man ngag: There are several types of instruction mentioned in Buddhist literature: there is the general level of instruction which is the meaning contained in the words of the texts of the tradition; on a more personal and direct level there is oral instruction which has been passed down from teacher to student from the time of the buddha; and on the most profound level there are foremost instructions which are not only oral instructions provided by one's guru but are special, core instructions that come out of personal experience and which convey the teaching concisely and with the full weight of personal experience. Foremost instructions or upadeśha are crucial to the Vajra Vehicle because these are the special way of passing on the profound instructions needed for the student's realization.

Formative, Skt. saṃskāra, Tib. 'du byed. This term is usually translated as "formations", but a formation is the product of that which caused its formation, whereas this term refers to the agent which will cause a formation. The formatives, which are the contents of the fourth of the five aggregates, cause the production of a future set of aggregates for the mindstream involved. There are two types of formatives, ones which are a type of mind and ones which are not. The former includes all of the afflictions.

Fortune, fortunate person, Tib. skal ldan: To meet with any given dharma teaching, a person must have accumulated the karmic fortune needed for such a rare opportunity, and this kind of person is then called "a fortunate one" or "fortunate person".

Garbha, Skt. garbha, Tib. snying po: See the introductory section of the commentary for an explanation of this term.

Gotra, Skt. gotra, Tib. rigs: See the introductory section of the commentary for an explanation of this term.

Grasped-grasping, Tib. gzung 'dzin: When mind is turned outwardly as it is in the normal operation of dualistic mind, it has developed two faces that appear simultaneously. Special names are given to these two faces: mind appearing in the form of the external object being referenced is called "that which is grasped" and mind appearing in the form of the consciousness that is registering it is called the "grasper" or "grasping" of it. Thus, there is the pair of terms "grasped-grasper" or "grasped-grasping". When these two terms are used, it alerts one to the fact that a Mind Only style of presentation is being discussed. This pair of terms pervades Mind Only, Middle Way, and tantric writings and is exceptionally important in all of them.

Note that one could substitute the word "apprehended" for "grasped" and "apprehender" for "grasper" or "grasping" and that would reflect one connotation of the original Sanskrit terminology. The solidified duality of grasped and grasper is nothing but an invention of dualistic thought; it has that kind of character or characteristic.

Great Vehicle, Skt. mahāyāna, Tib. theg pa chen po: The Buddha's teachings as a whole can be summed up into three vehicles where a vehicle is defined as that which can carry a person to a certain destination. The first vehicle, called the Lesser Vehicle, contains the teachings designed to get an individual moving on the spiritual path through showing the unsatisfactory state of cyclic existence and an emancipation from that. However, that path is only concerned with personal emancipation and fails to take account of all of the beings that there are in existence. There used to be eighteen schools of Lesser Vehicle in India but the only one surviving nowadays is the Theravāda of south-east Asia. The Greater Vehicle is a step up from that. The Buddha explained that it was great in comparison to the Lesser Vehicle for seven reasons. The first of those is that it is concerned with attaining the truly complete enlightenment of a truly complete buddha for the sake of every sentient being where the Lesser Vehicle is concerned only with a personal liberation that is not truly complete enlightenment and which is achieved only for the sake of that practitioner. The Great Vehicle has two divisions: a conventional form in which the path is taught in a logical, conventional way, and an unconventional form in which the path is taught in a very direct way. This latter vehicle is called the Vajra Vehicle because it takes the innermost, indestructible (vajra) fact of reality of one's own mind as the vehicle to enlightenment.

Guardian, Skt. nātha, Tib. mgon po: This name is a respectful title reserved for the buddhas. It means that they both protect and nurture sentient beings who they oversee, like a child who, having no parents has been given or has found a guardian. It is often translated as "protector" but that correctly translates another Sanskrit term to start with and on top of that is insufficient because it does not include the aspect of nurturing. It is also given to other beings such as bodhisatvas who have a similar quality, for example, Guardian Nāgārjuna and Guardian Maitreya.

Kagyu, Tib. bka' brgyud: There are four main schools of Buddhism in Tibet—Nyingma, Kagyu, Sakya, and Gelug. Nyingma is the oldest school dating from about 800 C.E. Kagyu and Sakya both appeared in the 12th century C.E. Each of these three schools came directly from India. The Gelug school came later and did not come directly from India but came from the other three. The Nyingma school holds the tantric teachings called Great Completion (Dzogchen); the other three schools hold the tantric teachings called Mahāmudrā. Kagyu practitioners often join Nyingma practice with their Kagyu practice and Kagyu teachers often teach both, so it is common to hear about Kagyu and Nyingma together.

Kaya, Skt. kāya, Tib. sku: The Sanskrit term means a functional or coherent collection of parts, similar to the French "corps", and hence also comes to mean "a body". It is used in Tibetan Buddhist texts specifically to distinguish bodies belonging to the enlightened side from ones belonging to the samsaric side.

Enlightened being in Buddhism is said to be comprised of one or more kāyas. It is most commonly explained to consist of one, two, three, four, or five kāyas, though it is pointed out that there are infinite aspects to enlightened being and therefore it can also be said to consist of an infinite number of kāyas. In fact, these descriptions of enlightened being consisting of one or more kāyas are given for the sake of understanding what is beyond conceptual understanding so should not be taken as absolute statements.

Kayas and wisdoms, Tib. sku dang ye shes: Enlightened being might be empty of samsaric phenomena but it does have enlightened content. "Kāyas and wisdoms" or "bodies and wisdoms" is a stock phrase used to indicate either the content of enlightenment or to imply that it does have content. The phrase is used as a summation of all of the good qualities of enlightenment, with kāyas being the form aspect and wisdoms being the mind aspect.

Knower, Tib. ha go ba: "Knower" is a generic term for that which knows. There are many types of knower, with each having its own qualities and name, too. For example, *wisdom* is a non-dualistic knower, *mind* is the dualistic samsaric version of it, *consciousness* refers to the individual "registers" of samsaric mind, and so on. Sometimes a term is needed which simply says "that which knows" without further implication of what kind of knowing it might be; *knower* is one of a few terms of that sort.

Knowledgeability, Tib. spob pa: Knowledgeability is a quality of both mind and speech. It refers to having the ability to instantly recall the knowledge needed when something needs to be expressed verbally, for example when teaching, and therefore also a confidence of knowledge that comes with it. Knowledgeability can be developed by anyone but the knowledgeability in the case of a buddha is inconceivable: a buddha's wisdom knows all things throughout all times so he can recall an inconceivable array of knowledge and with that a buddha has an ultimate level of confidence that he can do so. This then means that a buddha's verbal presentation of his knowledge is inconceivable: his abilities of speech are miraculous and beyond the reach of ordinary being's spoken abilities. For example, with one instance of speech he can answer the questions of countless numbers of beings, with each answer appearing to each listener in a language that the listener understands, and in a way that the listener can comprehend.

Lesser Vehicle, Skt. hīnayāna, Tib. theg pa dman pa: See under Great Vehicle.

Luminosity or illumination, Skt. prabhāsvara, Tib. 'od gsal ba: The core of mind has two aspects: an emptiness factor and a knowing factor. The Buddha and many Indian religious teachers used "luminosity" as a metaphor for the knowing quality of the core of mind. If in English we would say "Mind has a knowing quality", the teachers of ancient India would say, "Mind has an illuminative quality; it is like a source of light which illuminates what it knows".

This term has been translated as "clear light" but that is a mistake that comes from not understanding the etymology of the word. It does not refer to a light that has the quality of clearness (something that makes no sense, actually!) but to the illuminative property which is the nature of the empty mind.

Note also that in both Sanskrit and Tibetan Buddhist literature, this term is frequently abbreviated just to Skt. "vara" and Tib. "gsal ba" with no change of meaning. Unfortunately, this has been thought to be another word and it has then been translated with "clarity", when in fact it is just this term in abbreviation.

Mara, Skt. māra, Tib. bdud: The Sanskrit term is closely related to the word "death". Buddha spoke of four classes of extremely negative influences that have the capacity to drag a sentient being deep into samsara. They are the "māras" or "kiss of death": of having a samsaric set of five skandhas; of having afflictions; of death itself; and of the son of gods, which means being seduced and taken in totally by sensuality.

Migrator, Tib. 'gro ba: Migrator is one of several terms that were commonly used by the Buddha to mean "sentient being". It shows sentient beings from the perspective of their constantly being forced to go here and there from one rebirth to another by the power of karma. They are like flies caught in a jar, constantly buzzing back and forth. The term is often translated using "beings" which is another general term for sentient beings but doing so loses the meaning entirely: Buddhist authors who know the tradition do not use the word loosely but use it specifically to give the sense of beings who are constantly and helplessly going from one birth to another, and that is how the term should be read. The term "six migrators" refers to the six types of migrators within samsaric existence—hell-beings, pretas, animals, humans, demi-gods, and gods.

Mind, Skt. chitta, Tib. sems: There are several terms for mind in the Buddhist tradition, each with its own, specific meaning. This term is the most general term for the samsaric type of mind. It refers to the type of mind that is produced because of fundamental ignorance of enlightened mind. Whereas the wisdom of enlightened mind lacks all complexity and knows in a non-dualistic way, this mind of un-enlightenment is a very complicated apparatus that only ever knows in a dualistic way.

Noble one, Skt. ārya, Tib. 'phags pa: In Buddhism, a noble one is a being who has become spiritually advanced to the point that he has passed beyond cyclic existence. According to the Buddha, the beings in cyclic existence were ordinary beings, spiritual commoners, and the beings who had passed beyond it were special, the nobility.

Output, Tib. gdangs: Output is a general term for that which is given off by something, for example, the sound that comes from a loudspeaker. Wisdom has an output that does not happen because of cause and effect but is self-occurring, which is then referred to as "self-output".

Outflow, Skt. āsrāva, Tib. zag pa: The Sanskrit term means a bad discharge, like pus coming out of a wound. Outflows occur when wisdom loses its footing and falls into the elaborations of dualistic mind. Therefore, anything with duality also has outflows. This is sometimes translated as "defiled" or "conditioned" but these fail to capture the meaning. The idea is that wisdom can remain self-contained in its own unique sphere but, when it loses its ability to stay within itself, it starts to have leakages into dualism that are defilements on the wisdom. See also under un-outflowed.

Own Appearance, Tib. rang snang: This is regarded as one of the more difficult terms to explain within Buddhist philosophy. It does not mean "self-appearance" in the sense of something coming into appearance of itself. Suffice it to say that it refers to a situation that is making its own appearances in accord with its own situation.

Prajna, Skt. prajñā, Tib. shes rab: The Sanskrit term, literally meaning "best type of mind" is defined as that which makes correct distinctions between this and that and hence which arrives at correct understanding. It has been translated as "wisdom" but that is not correct because it is, generally speaking, a mental event belonging to dualistic mind where "wisdom" is used to refer to the non-dualistic knower of a buddha. Moreover, the main feature of prajñā is its ability to distinguish correctly between one thing and another and hence to arrive at a correct understanding.

Provisional and definitive meaning, Skt. neyārtha and nītārtha, Tib. drangs don and nges don: This is a pair of terms used to distinguish which is an ultimate or final teaching and which is not. A teaching which guides a student along to a certain understanding where the understanding led to is not an ultimate understanding is called "provisional meaning". The teaching is not false even though it does not show the final meaning; it is a technique of skilful means used to lead a student in steps to the final meaning. A teaching which shows a student the final meaning directly is called "definitive meaning". The understanding presented cannot be refined or shown in a more precise way; it is the final and actual understanding to be understood. These terms are most often used in Buddhism when discussing the status of the three turnings of the wheel of dharma.

Rational mind, Tib. blo: Rational mind is one of several terms for mind in Buddhist terminology. It specifically refers to a mind that judges this against that. With rare exception it is used to refer to samsaric mind, given that samsaric mind only works in the dualistic mode of comparing this versus that. Because of this, the term is mostly used in a pejorative sense to point out samsaric mind as opposed to an enlightened type of mind.

Realization, Tib. rtogs pa: Realization has a very specific meaning: it refers to correct knowledge that has been gained in such a way that the knowledge does not abate. There are two important points here. Firstly, realization is not absolute. It refers to the removal of obscurations, one at a time. Each time that a practitioner removes an obscuration, he gains a realization because of it. Therefore, there are as many levels of realization as there are obscurations. Maitreya, in the *Ornament of Manifest Realizations*, shows how the removal of the various obscurations that go with each of the three realms of samsaric existence produces realization.

Secondly, realization is stable or, as the Tibetan wording says, "unchanging". As Guru Rinpoche pointed out, "Intellectual knowledge is like a patch, it drops away; experiences on the path are temporary, they evaporate like mist; realization is unchanging".

Reasoning of the Force of the Thing, Tib. dngos stobs kyi rigs pa: This is an inferential type of reasoning. It is used to validly establish that something is so by applying the test of whether the thing in question is actually the way that is has been proposed to be. Thus, through the *force of* what *the thing* itself is, we correctly know whether the proposal is true or not. For example, it is said that "fire is hot". One way to determine whether that is true or not is to look at the qualities of fire. If we find that one of those qualities is "hot" then the statement is proved to be true.

Reference and Referencing, Tib. dmigs pa: Referencing is the name for the process in which dualistic mind references an actual object by using a conceptual label instead of the actual object. Whatever is referenced is then called a reference. Note that these terms imply the presence of dualistic mind and their opposites, non-referencing and being without reference imply the presence of non-dualistic wisdom.

Samsara, Skt. saṃsāra, Tib. 'khor ba: This is the most general name for the type of existence in which sentient beings live. It refers to the fact that they continue on from one existence to another, always within the enclosure of births that are produced by ignorance and experienced as unsatisfactory. The original Sanskrit means to be constantly going about, here and there. The Tibetan term literally means "cycling", because of which it is frequently translated into English with "cyclic existence" though that is not quite the meaning of the term.

Satva and sattva: According to the Tibetan tradition established at the time of the great translation work done at Samye under the watch of Padmasambhava not to mention one hundred and sixty-three of the greatest Buddhist scholars of Sanskrit-speaking India, there is a difference of meaning between the Sanskrit terms "satva" and "sattva", with satva meaning "an heroic kind of being" and "sattva" meaning simply "a being". According to the Tibetan tradition established under the advice of the Indian scholars mentioned above, satva is correct for the words Vajrasatva and bodhisatva, whereas sattva is correct for the words samayasattva, samādhisattva, jñānasattva, and mahāsattva and is also used alone to refer to any or all of these three sattvas.

Self-arising wisdom, Tib. rang byung ye shes: The words "self-arising" are added to wisdom to indicate that it is not caused, that it is outside the samsaric process of cause and effect.

Shift and change, Tib. 'pho 'gyur: This phrase is used to refer to the shifts in time and the changes that come with them in the dualistic world. For example, in our dualistic world, we always speak in reference to time and change that occur with it; we have past, present, and future and the things of our world are always shifting and changing throughout those three times. Being without shift and change is usually referred to, as is being done here, to make the point that the dharmatā is simply outside the world of time and the changes that occur with it.

Shiftless or changeless and shiftless, Tib. 'pho 'gyur med pa: See under shift and change.

Species, Skt. gotra, Tib. rigs: See the introductory section of the commentary for an explanation of this term.

State, Tib. ngang: A state is a certain, ongoing situation.

Superfactual, Skt. paramārtha,Tib. don dam: This term is paired with the term "fictional" *q.v.* In the past, the terms have been translated as "relative" and "absolute" respectively, but those translations are nothing like the original terms. These terms are extremely important in the Buddhist teaching so it is very important that their translations be corrected but, more than that, if the actual meaning of these terms is not presented, the teaching connected with them cannot be understood.

The Sanskrit term literally means "the fact for that which is above all others, special, superior" and refers to the wisdom mind possessed by those who have developed themselves spiritually to the point of having transcended samsara. That wisdom is *superior* to an ordinary, un-developed person's consciousness and the *facts* that appear on its surface are superior compared to the facts that appear on the ordinary person's consciousness. Therefore, it is superfact or the holy fact, more literally. What this wisdom knows is true for the beings who have it, therefore what the wisdom sees is superfactual truth.

Superfactual truth, Skt. paramārthasatya, Tib. don dam bden pa: See under superfactual.

The authentic, Tib. yang dag: A name for reality, that which is real. For example "the view of the authentic" means "the view of reality".

The four reliances, Tib. rton pa bzhi: The four reliances were taught by the Buddha to the townspeople of Kalama in north India as the way to determine for oneself what of what other's say should and should not be accepted. The four are: rely on the dharma not the person speaking it; rely on the meaning, not the words spoken; rely on the definitive meaning, not the provisional meaning; and rely on wisdom, not consciousness.

The element, Skt. dhātu, Tib. khams. See the introductory section of the commentary for an explanation of this term.

Three types of analysis, Tib. dpyad pa gsum: See the introductory section of the commentary for an explanation of this term.

Total affliction and complete purification, Tib. kun nas nyon rmongs pa dang rnam par byang ba: The Buddha divided all types of existence into two: enlightened existence and un-enlightened existence. He taught his disciples that their unenlightened existence was total (through and through) affliction, but if they followed the path to enlightenment, they would arrive, through the practice of purification of that affliction, at the state of enlightened existence, which he then referred to as "complete purification". In this way, he made the character of these two types of existence clear and at the same time goaded his disciples to get on the path and reach the point of complete purification. Note that "complete purification" refers to the result of having followed the path and is only used in relation to "total affliction"; it is not the same as complete purity, which is also mentioned in this sutra.

Un-outflowed, Skt. anāśhrāva, Tib. zag pa med pa: Un-outflowed dharmas are ones that are connected with wisdom that has not lost its footing and leaked out into a defiled state; it is self-contained wisdom without any taint of dualistic mind and its apparatus. See also outflowed.

Vajra Vehicle, Skt. vajrayāna, Tib. rdo rje'i theg pa: See under Great Vehicle.

Valid cognizer, valid cognition, Skt. pramāṇa, Tib. tshad ma: The Sanskrit term "pramāṇa" literally means "best type of mentality" and comes to mean "a valid cognizer". Its value is that is can be used to validate anything that can be known. The Tibetans translated this term with "tshad ma" meaning an "evaluator"—something which can be used to evaluate the truth or not of whatever it is given to know. It is the term used in logic to indicate a mind which is knowing validly and which therefore can be used to validate the object it is knowing.

Valid cognizers are named according to the kind of test they are employed to do. A valid cognizer of the conventional or a valid cognizer of the fictional tests within conventions, within the realm of rational, dualistic mind. A valid cognizer of the ultimate or valid cognizer of superfact tests for the superfactual level, beyond dualistic mind.

Wisdom, Skt. jñāna, Tib. ye shes: This is a fruition term that refers to the kind of mind—the kind of knower—possessed by a buddha. Sentient beings do have this kind of knower but it is covered over by a very complex apparatus for knowing, that is, dualistic mind. If they practise the path to buddhahood, they will leave behind their obscuration and return to having this kind of knower.

The Sanskrit term has the sense of knowing in the most simple and immediate way. This sort of knowing is present at the core of every being's mind. Therefore, the Tibetans called it "the particular type of awareness which is there primordially". Because of the Tibetan wording it has often been called "primordial wisdom" in English translations, but that goes too far; it is just "wisdom" in the sense of the most fundamental knowing possible.

Wisdom does not operate in the same way as samsaric mind; it comes about in and of itself without depending on cause and effect. Therefore it is frequently referred to as "self-arising wisdom" *q.v.*

About the Author, Padma Karpo Translation Committee, And Their Supports for Study

I have been encouraged over the years by all of my teachers to pass on the knowledge I have accumulated in a lifetime dedicated to study and practice, primarily in the Tibetan tradition of Buddhism. On the one hand, they have encouraged me to teach. On the other, they are concerned that, while many general books on Buddhism have been and are being published, there are few books that present the actual texts of the tradition. Therefore they, together with a number of major figures in the Buddhist book publishing world, have also encouraged me to translate and publish high quality translations of individual texts of the tradition.

My teachers always remark with great appreciation on the extraordinary amount of teaching that I have heard in this life. It allows for highly informed, accurate translations of a sort not usually seen. Briefly, I spent the 1970's studying, practising, then teaching the Gelugpa system at Chenrezig Institute, Australia, where I was a founding member and also the first Australian to be ordained as a monk in the Tibetan Buddhist tradition. In 1980, I moved to the United States to study at the feet of the Vidyadhara Chogyam Trungpa Rinpoche. I stayed in his Vajradhātu community, now called Shambhala, where I studied and practised all the Karma Kagyu, Nyingma, and Shambhala teachings being presented there and was a senior member of the Nalanda Translation Committee. After the vidyadhara's nirvana, I moved in 1992 to Nepal, where I have been continuously involved with the study, practise, translation, and teaching of the Kagyu system and especially of the Nyingma system of Great Completion. In recent years, I have spent extended times in Tibet with the greatest living Tibetan masters of Great Completion, receiving very pure transmissions of the ultimate levels of this teaching directly in Tibetan and practising them there in retreat. In that way, I have studied and practised extensively not in one Tibetan tradition as is usually done, but in three of the four Tibetan traditions—Gelug, Kagyu, and Nyingma—and also in the Theravada tradition, too.

With that as a basis, I have taken a comprehensive and long term approach to the work of translation. For any language, one first must have the lettering needed to write the language. Therefore, as a member of the Nalanda Translation Committee, I spent some years in the 1980's making Tibetan word-processing software and high-quality Tibetan fonts. After that, reliable lexical works are needed. Therefore, during the 1990's I spent some years writing the Illuminator Tibetan-English Dictionary and a set of treatises on Tibetan grammar, preparing a variety of key Tibetan reference works needed for the study and translation of Tibetan Buddhist texts, and giving our Tibetan software the tools needed to translate and research Tibetan texts. During this time, I also translated full-time for various Tibetan gurus and ran the Drukpa Kagyu Heritage Project—at the time the largest project in Asia for the preservation of Tibetan Buddhist texts. With the dictionaries, grammar texts, and specialized software in place, and a wealth of knowledge, I turned my attention in the year 2000 to the translation and publication of important texts of Tibetan Buddhist literature.

Padma Karpo Translation Committee (PKTC) was set up to provide a home for the translation and publication work. The committee focusses on producing books containing the best of Tibetan literature, and, especially, books that meet the needs of practitioners. At the time of writing, PKTC has published a wide range of books that, collectively, make a complete program of study for those practising Tibetan Buddhism, and especially for those interested in the higher tantras. All in all, you will find many books both free and for sale on the PKTC website. Most are available both as paper editions and e-books.

It would take up too much space here to present an extensive guide to our books and how they can be used as the basis for a study program. However, a guide of that sort is available on the PKTC web-site, whose address is on the copyright page of this book and we recommend that you read it to see how this book fits into the overall scheme of PKTC publications. In short, given that this book is about sugata essence and also about Other Emptiness, other books of interest would be:

- *The Lion's Roar that Proclaims Other Emptiness*, a text by Ju Mipham which shows the view of Other Emptiness then goes through arguments raised by Tsongkhapa's followers against the Other Emptiness system;
- *Other Emtpiness, Entering Wisdom, Entering Wisdom Beyond Emptiness of Self*, a complete exposition on the entire subject of Other Emptiness that should be read in conjunction with this books;
- *The Noble One Called "Point of Passage Wisdom", A Great Vehicle Sutra*, the root sutra of the twenty sutras of Other Emptiness of the final turning of the wheel;
- *Instructions for Practising the View of Other Emptiness*, a text by the first Jamgon Kongtrul showing the practice of Other Emptiness according to the Jonang tradition;
- *Maitripa's Writings on the View*, a selection of important texts written by the Indian master Maitrīpa showing his understanding of the Other Emptiness approach;
- *A Juggernaut of the Non-Dual View, Ultimate Teachings of the Second Drukchen, Gyalwang Je*, a set of sixty-six teachings on the non-dual view of the tantras which shows clearly the Other Emptiness view of the Kagyus.

We make a point of including, where possible, the relevant Tibetan texts in Tibetan script in our books. We also make them available in electronic editions that can be downloaded free from our web-site, as discussed below. The Tibetan text for this book is included at the back of the book.

ELECTRONIC RESOURCES

PKTC has developed a complete range of electronic tools to facilitate the study and translation of Tibetan texts. For many years now, this software has been a prime resource for Tibetan Buddhist centres throughout the world, including in Tibet itself. It is available through the PKTC web-site. The wordprocessor TibetDoc has the only complete set of tools for creating, correcting, and formatting Tibetan text according to the norms of the Tibetan language. It can also be used to make texts with mixed Tibetan and English or other languages. Extremely high quality Tibetan fonts, based on the forms of Tibetan calligraphy learned from old masters from pre-Communist Chinese Tibet, are also available. Because of their excellence, these typefaces have achieved a legendary status amongst Tibetans.

TibetDoc is used to prepare electronic editions of Tibetan texts in the PKTC text input office in Asia. Tibetan texts are often corrupt so the input texts are carefully corrected prior to distribution. After that, they are made available through the PKTC web-site. These electronic texts are not careless productions like so many of the Tibetan texts found on the web, but are highly reliable editions useful to non-scholars and scholars alike. Some of the larger collections of these texts are for purchase, but most are available for free download.

The electronic texts can be read, searched, and even made into an electronic library using either TibetDoc or our other software, TibetD Reader. Like TibetDoc, TibetD Reader is advanced software with many capabilities made specifically to meet the needs of reading and researching Tibetan texts. PKTC software is for purchase but we make a free version of TibetD Reader available for free download on the PKTC web-site.

A key feature of TibetDoc and Tibet Reader is that Tibetan terms in texts can be looked up on the spot using PKTC's electronic dictionaries.

PKTC also has several electronic dictionaries—some Tibetan-Tibetan and some Tibetan-English—and a number of other reference works. The *Illuminator Tibetan-English Dictionary* is renowned for its completeness and accuracy.

This combination of software, texts, reference works, and dictionaries that work together seamlessly has become famous over the years. It has been the basis of many, large publishing projects within the Tibetan Buddhist community around the world for over thirty years and is popular amongst all those needing to work with Tibetan language or deepen their understanding of Buddhism through Tibetan texts.

TIBETAN TEXT

༄༅། །བདེ་གཤེགས་སྙིང་པོའི་སྟོང་ཐུན་ཆེན་མོ་སེང་གེའི་ང་རོ་
བཞུགས་སོ།།

༄༅། །ན་མོ་གུ་ར་བེ། གདོད་ནས་དྲི་མེད་སེམས་ཀྱི་ཆོས་ཉིད་ན། །ངེས་དོན་འཇམ་དཔལ་དཔའ་བོའི་བདག་ཉིད་དུ། ངེས་པའི་རིགས་ལམ་རལ་གྲིའི་རྣོ་རྒྱུན་གྱིས། །ཀུན་རྨོངས་སྲིད་པའི་དྲྭ་བ་རྣམ་པར་གཅོད། །དེ་ལ་འདིར་དུས་གསུམ་གཤེགས་པའི་རྒྱལ་བ་ཐམས་ཅད་ཀྱི་གསུང་གི་སྙིང་པོ་དགོངས་པའི་མཐིལ། མདོ་དང་སྔགས་ཀྱི་ཆོས་ཀུན་གྱི་གནད་གཅིག་པུ་ནི་ཀུན་ཁྱབ་བདེ་གཤེགས་སྙིང་པོ་འདི་ཁོ་ན་ཡིན་ཞིང་། ཚུལ་འདི་ཤིན་ཏུ་ཟབ་པས་ས་བཅུའི་དབང་ཕྱུག་ཆེན་པོ་རྣམས་ཀྱིས་ཀྱང་མཚན་མོའི་གཟུགས་ལྟར་ཇི་ལྟ་བ་བཞིན་དུ་རྟོགས་དཀའ་བར་གསུངས་ན་ཕལ་པས་ལྟ་ཅི་སྨོས། དེ་ཡང་སྟོན་པ་བདེ་བར་གཤེགས་པས་གསུང་གི་སྐབས་ལ་ལར་སྟོང་པ་ཉིད་བསྟན་པའི་སྒོ་ནས་བདེ་གཤེགས་སྙིང་པོའི་ངོ་བོ་གསལ་བར་མཛད། ལ་ལར་སྟོབས་སོགས་ཀྱི་ཡོན་ཏན་ཡེ་ལྡན་དུ་བསྟན་པའི་ཆ་ནས་བདེ་གཤེགས་སྙིང་པོའི་རང་བཞིན་གསལ་བར་མཛད་དེ། དེ་གཉིས་འགལ་མེད་ཟུང་དུ་འཇུག་པ་དགོས་ཀྱང་། བདེན་གཉིས་དབྱེར་མེད་པའི་གནད་ཟབ་པ་ལས་ཤིན་ཏུ་ཟབ་པ་ལ་ཡིད་ཆེས་མ་སྐྱེད་པའི་

དབང་གིས་ལ་ལས་ནི་བདེ་གཤེགས་སྙིང་པོ་ངོ་བོས་མི་སྟོང་པའི་རྟག་པར་བལྟ། ལ་ལས་ནི་སྟོང་རྐྱང་ཙམ་ལ་བཟུང་ནས་སྐུ་དང་ཡེ་ཤེས་ཀྱི་ཡོན་ཏན་འབྲལ་མེད་ཡེ་ལྡན་དུ་བཞག་ཏུ་མེད་པའི་ཆད་ལྟ་སྐུར་འདེབས་ཀྱི་ཕྱོགས་ལ་གནས་པར་གྱུར་ནས། སོ་སོའི་ཞེ་འདོད་གྲུབ་ཏུ་རེ་བའི་དགག་སྒྲུབ་ཀྱི་ཅ་ཅོ་སྣ་ཚོགས་རྒྱ་མཚོ་འཁྲུགས་པ་ལྟར་སྒྲོགས་ན་ཡང་། བླ་མའི་མན་ངག་གིས་ཟིན་པའི་སྐལ་བཟང་དག་ནི་བདུད་རྩིའི་བཅུད་བཟང་སྙིང་ལ་སིམས་པ་ལྟར་སྟོང་པའི་དབྱིངས་དང་འོད་གསལ་བའི་ཡེ་ཤེས་འགལ་མེད་ཟུང་འཇུག་གི་དོན་ལ་ཡིད་ཆེས་པའི་ངང་ནས་སྣང་སྟོང་གང་རུང་གི་མཐའ་ལ་ཕྱོགས་སུ་འཛིན་པ་རྣམ་པར་ཞིག་ནས་གནས་པ་རྣམས་འདི་སྐད་དུ་སྨྲའོ། །དེ་ལ་སྤྱིར་དེ་བཞིན་གཤེགས་པའི་བཀའ་ཚད་མ་ནི་མི་བསླུ་བའི་ལུང་ཡང་དག་ཡིན་མོད་ཀྱི། དེ་མི་བསླུ་བ་ངེས་པ་ལ་དཔྱད་པ་གསུམ་གྱིས་དག་པས་ལུང་རྣམ་དག་ཏུ་ངེས་པ་སྤྱིར་བཏང་། ཁྱད་པར་གཞུང་དེའི་སྒྲ་ཇི་བཞིན་པའི་བསྟན་དོན་ལ། རིག་པས་གནོད་པ་མེད་ཅིང་། སྒྲུབ་བྱེད་ཡང་དག་ཡོད་པའི་སྒོ་ནས་ངེས་པའི་དོན་དུ་བཟུང་དགོས་ཀྱི། ལུང་གི་དག་བྱེད་རིགས་པ་བོར་ནས། གང་གཤད་པ་ལ་དེ་བཞིན་དུ་ཡིད་ཆེས་པ་ཙམ་ཁོ་ནས་མི་ཆོག་སྟེ། སྤྱིར་ལུང་ལ་ཡག་དག་དང་ལྟར་སྣང་། ལུང་ཡང་དག་ལའང་དྲང་ངེས་ཀྱི་ཁྱད་པར་ཡོད་པ་བསྙོན་དུ་མེད་པའི་ཕྱིར་རོ། །དེས་ན་སོ་སྐྱེས་ཐོས་བསམ་གྱིས་སྒྲོ་འདོགས་བཅད་ནས་འཇུག་བྱའི་གནས་རྣམས་ཚད་མ་གསུམ་གྱིས་ངེས་ནུས་པ་རྣམས་ལ་ལོག་མེད་ཀྱི་ཡིད་ཆེས་འབྱུང་གི གཞན་དུ་རང་གི་ཚད་མས་མ་ངེས་ཤིང་གཞན་གྲོལ་བའི་ངོར་སྒྲུབ་པར་མ་ནུས་ན། ཤ་ཟ་བསྐལ་དོན་དུ་སོང་བའི་གང་ཟག་ཞིག་གིས་མདུན་གྱི་གཞི་འདིར་ཤ་ཟ་ཡོད་ཅེས་དམ་བཅའ་བ་དང་འདྲ་བས་ཚིག་དེ་འདྲས་རང་གཞན་ལ་ཡིད་ཆེས་སྐྱེད་མི་ནུས་སོ། །དེ་བས་ན་ཡང་དག་པའི་རིགས་ལམ་དང་མཐུན་པར་སྨྲ་བ་སྐྱེ་བོ་མཁས་པའི་ཚུལ་ཡིན་ལ། རིགས་པས་གྲུབ་ན་གྲོལ་བའི་ལྟེ་རང་བཞིན་གྱིས་ཐུང་ངུར་འགྱུར་ཞིང་རང་གི་ཕྱོགས་འཛིན་པ་དག་སྤྲོ་བ་ལོག་མེད་དུ་སྐྱེ་ལ། རིགས་པས་མི་འགྲུབ་པའི་ལམ་དེ་སྨྲ་བ་མང་པོས་ཇི་ལྟར་བརྒྱན་ཀྱང་ཀླན་ཀའི་ཚོགས་ལུ་མའི་ཆུ་ལྟར་འཕེལ་བར་འགྱུར་བའི་ཕྱིར། འདིར་རྒྱལ་བ་དང་རྒྱལ་སྲས་

ཆེན་པོ་བརྒྱུད་པར་བཅས་པའི་ལམ་སྲོལ་རྟོག་གེ་མ་དཀྲུགས་པ་ལ་ཞུགས་ནས། ཕྱོགས་སུ་ཞེན་པ་བོར་ཏེ་གཟུ་བོའི་བློས་བདེ་གཤེགས་སྙིང་པོའི་རྣམ་གཞག་བསྟན་པའི་ཚུལ་དེ་དག་གི་སྒྲུབ་བྱེད་རིགས་པ་རྣམ་དག་ལ་གཞལ་ལ་ན་བདེ་གཤེགས་སྙིང་པོ་ངོ་བོ་མི་སྟོང་པའི་བདེན་གྲུབ་རྟག་པ་དང་། ཡོན་ཏན་མེད་པའི་སྟོང་པ་ཕྱང་ཆད་དུ་འདོད་པ་གཉིས་ཀ་ལ་སྒྲུབ་བྱེད་མེད་ལ་གནོད་བྱེད་མཐོང་ཞིང་། ངོ་བོ་སྟོང་པ་དང་རང་བཞིན་ཡོན་ཏན་ཡེ་ལྡན་གྱི་སྙིང་པོ་འགྲོ་བའི་ཁམས་ན་ཡོད་པ་ལ། གནོད་བྱེད་མེད་ཅིང་སྒྲུབ་བྱེད་ཡང་དག་ཡོད་པར་མཐོང་ངོ་། །དེ་ལ་དང་པོ་ཁམས་བདེ་གཤེགས་སྙིང་པོ་འགྲོ་བའི་རྒྱུད་ལ་ཡོད་པའི་སྒྲུབ་བྱེད་གང་ཞེ་ན། ཐེག་པ་ཆེན་པོ་རྒྱུད་བླ་མ་ལས། རྫོགས་སངས་སྐུ་ནི་འཕྲོ་ཕྱིར་དང་། །དེ་བཞིན་ཉིད་དབྱེར་མེད་ཕྱིར་དང་། །རིགས་ཡོད་ཕྱིར་ན་ལུས་ཅན་ཀུན། །རྟག་ཏུ་སངས་རྒྱས་སྙིང་པོ་ཅན། །ཞེས་གསུངས་པའི་དོན་རིགས་པས་གཏན་ལ་དབབ་པ་ལ། གཞན་ལུགས་བརྗོད་པ་དང་། ཡང་དག་པའི་རང་ལུགས་རྣམ་པར་བཞག་པ་གཉིས། །དང་པོ་བོད་སྔ་རབས་པ་རྣམས་རྫོགས་སངས་སྐུ་འཕྲོ་བ་ཞེས་ཡེ་ཤེས་ཆོས་སྐུས་ཡུལ་ཀུན་ལ་ཁྱབ་པ་ཙམ་དང་། དེ་བཞིན་ཉིད་སྟོང་ཕྲུང་ཙམ་དུ་རིགས་འདྲ་བ་དང་། རིགས་ཡོད་ཅེས་སངས་རྒྱ་རུང་ཡིན་པ་ཙམ་ལ་བཤད་ནས་རྒྱུད་བླ་མའི་གཞུང་གི་སྙིང་པོ་འདིའི་ཐད་ནས་གནད་མ་བསླངས་བའི་ཚིག་ཙུང་ངུར་སྨྲོ། །དེ་ལ་ཆོས་སྐུས་ཡུལ་ཁྱབ་པ་ཙམ་གྱིས་རིགས་མཚན་ཉིད་པ་མི་འགྲུབ་སྟེ། གཞན་རྒྱུད་ཀྱིས་བསྡུས་པར་སྣང་བའི་སངས་རྒྱས་ཀྱི་མཁྱེན་པས་ཡུལ་ལ་ཁྱབ་པ་ཙམ་དངོས་པོ་ཀུན་ལ་ཡོད་ཀྱང་། དེ་ཡོད་པ་ཙམ་གྱིས་དེ་ཀུན་སངས་རྒྱ་བའི་རྒྱུ་མཚན་མེད་ལ། རང་རྒྱུད་ཀྱི་ཆོས་སྐུ་ནི་ད་ལྟ་མངོན་དུ་མ་གྱུར་པས་རྟགས་ལ་ཐེ་ཚོམ་ཟ་བ་དང་། སྟོང་པ་རྣམ་གྲངས་པ་ཙམ་ལ་རིགས་ཀྱི་དོན་གང་ཡང་མེད་དེ། ཁྱོད་ཀྱི་བསམ་ངོར་རིགས་འདི་ས་བོན་མྱུ་གུར་གོ་འཕོ་བ་བཞིན་དུ་ད་ལྟ་སངས་རྒྱས་ཀྱི་ཡོན་ཏན་ཅི་ཡང་མེད་ཀྱང་། ལམ་རྐྱེན་གྱིས་ཟིན་ན་གཟོད་འགྱུར་རུང་ཡིན་པར་འདོད་ན། བདེན་སྟོང་མེད་དགག་གི་ལྡོག་ཆ་དེ་འདུས་མ་བྱས་དོན་བྱེད་ནུས་པས་སྟོང་པ་དེ་འདྲའི་ཁྱད་པར་གང་ཡང་འཐད་པ་མེད་དེ། འདུས་བྱས་ས་བོན་

གྱི་ཆ་ནི་ཐ་སྙད་དུ་སྒྱུ་གུར་གནས་འགྱུར་རུང་གི་ས་བོན་གྱི་སྟེང་གི་བདེན་མེད་ཀྱི་ཆ་ནི་སྒྱུ་གུར་གནས་འགྱུར་བ་ནམ་ཡང་མི་སྲིད་པ་བཞིན་ནོ། །གཞན་ཡང་བདེན་སྟོང་ཡིན་པའི་གནད་ཀྱིས་སངས་རྒྱ་རུང་ཡིན་པར་སྒྲུབ་པའང་བབ་བཅོལ་ཏེ། སེམས་བདེན་གྲུབ་ཡིན་ན་སངས་རྒྱ་མི་རུང་བ་ཙམ་ཡིན་པ་བདེན་ཀྱང་། བདེན་གྲུབ་མེད་པ་ཡིན་ན་སངས་རྒྱ་བའི་ངེས་པ་མེད་དེ། ས་རྫི་ལ་སོགས་པ་ཆོས་ཐམས་ཅད་ཀྱང་བདེན་མེད་ཡིན་ཀྱང་། བདེན་མེད་ཡིན་ཚད་སངས་རྒྱ་རུང་བར་སུས་སྒྲུབ་པར་ནུས། བདེན་མེད་ལ་དམིགས་པས་སྒྲིབ་པ་སྤོང་ནུས་པ་ཁོ་ནས་རིགས་སུ་འཇོག་པའང་གྱི་ན་སྟེ། སྟོང་པ་ཉིད་ལ་དམིགས་པ་ཁོ་ནས་ཤེས་སྒྲིབ་སྤོང་བའི་རྒྱུ་མཚན་མེད་པར་སླར་ཚོགས་མཐའ་ཡས་པས་བརྒྱན་དགོས་པར་ཁྱོད་རང་འདོད་བཞིན་དུ། མེད་དགག་དེ་འདྲ་ལ་བདེ་གཤེགས་སྙིང་པོ་ཞེས་འདོད་པ་དོན་མེད་དེ། འདི་ཉན་རང་དང་ཐུན་མོང་བའི་རིགས་སུ་འགྱུར་གྱི། འདིས་སངས་རྒྱས་རུང་མི་འགྲུབ་སྟེ་འདི་ཙམ་ལ་ཤེས་སྒྲིབ་སྤངས་ནས་རྣམ་པ་ཐམས་ཅད་མཁྱེན་པའི་ཡེ་ཤེས་འབྱུང་བའི་འཐད་པ་གང་ཡང་སྒྲུབ་མ་ནུས་པ་དང་། མེད་དགག་རང་གི་ངོ་བོ་ལ་མཁྱེན་ཆ་མེད་པས་སངས་རྒྱས་དུས་ཀྱང་དེས་ཅི་ཡང་མཁྱེན་མི་སྲིད་པའི་ཕྱིར་རོ། །དེས་ན་གནས་གྱུར་འདུས་བྱས་ཀྱི་རིགས་ཀྱི་ཚུལ་འདི་ཡིད་ལ་མཛོད་ན། སེམས་ཅན་ཐམས་ཅད་ཀྱི་སེམས་ཀྱི་རྒྱུད་ན་ཐོག་མ་མེད་པ་ནས་ཡོད་པའི་མཁྱེན་བརྩེ་ནུས་གསུམ་གྱི་ས་བོན། གཅན་གཟན་དང་སྲིན་པོ་སོགས་ཀྱང་རང་གི་བུ་ལ་བརྩེ་བ་དང་། ཕན་གནོད་ངོ་ཤེས་པ་སོགས་ཡོད་པ་དེ། ལམ་གྱིས་ཟིན་ནས་གེགས་བྲལ་ཏེ་ཇེ་འཕེལ་དུ་སོང་བ་ན་ཚད་མེད་པའི་མཁྱེན་བརྩེ་ནུས་གསུམ་མངའ་བ་སངས་རྒྱས་སུ་འགྱུར་རུང་བ་ཙམ་ལ་འདོད་ན་མེད་དགག་ལ་རིགས་སུ་འདོད་པ་ལས་དེ་ལེགས་ཏེ། སྐྱེད་བྱེད་ཀྱི་རྒྱུ་འབྲས་ཡིན་དགོས་ཕན་ཆད། སྐད་ཅིག་ཅན་དངོས་པོར་གྱུར་པའི་རྒྱུ་སྐྱེད་བྱེད་ཡིན་པ་བོར་ནས། དངོས་མེད་འདུས་མ་བྱས་སྐྱེད་བྱེད་མིན་པ་ལ་རྒྱུར་འདོད་པ་ནི་ཡ་མཚན་པའི་གནས་སོ། །ཁ་ཅིག་འདི་སྙམ་དུ་བདེན་མེད་ཡིན་ཚད་རིགས་མ་ཡིན་ཀྱང་སེམས་ཀྱི་རང་བཞིན་བདེན་མེད་ཁོ་ན་རིགས་སུ་འཐད་དོ་སྙམ་ནས། སེམས་ཀྱི་བདེན་མེད་ཡིན་ཀྱང་རུང་དེས་ནི་སྐྱེད་པའི་

བྱ་བ་ཅི་ཡང་མི་ནུས་ལ། ཆོས་ཅན་སེམས་ཀྱི་སྐད་ཅིག་མ་རྣམས་ཕྱི་མའི་སྐྱེད་བྱེད་དུ་
འོས་པས་འདུས་མ་བྱས་པའི་རིགས་འདི་ཁྱེད་ལ་མི་མཁོ་འདྲ་བས་བོར་ཅིག །ཀལ་
ཏེ་བདེན་གཉིས་སོ་སོར་ཕྱེ་ནས་མི་འཛོག་སྟེ། ཆོས་ཅན་སེམས་ཀྱི་གསལ་བ་དང་
ཆོས་ཉིད་སྟོང་པ་ཉིད་དབྱེར་མེད་པའི་གནས་ལུགས་རིགས་སུ་འདོད་དོ་སྙམ་ན།
འདི་ཡང་རྣམ་ཤེས་དང་ཡེ་ཤེས་ཀྱི་རླབས་ཕྱེ་བའི་ཡེ་ཤེས་འགྱུར་མེད་འདུས་མ་བྱས་ལ་
འདོད་ན་ནི་དེ་ལྟར་ལུང་དང་རིགས་པས་གྲུབ་པའི་ཕྱིར་ཤིན་ཏུ་ཡིན་མོད་ཀྱི། སྟོང་པ་
དང་ཟུང་དུ་འཇུག་རྒྱུའི་ཆོས་ཅན་དེ་རྣམ་ཤེས་སྐད་ཅིག་མའི་ཆ་འདི་ཞེ་ལ་བཞག་ནས་འདི་
རིམ་གྱིས་སངས་རྒྱས་སུ་གོ་འཕོའོ་སྙམ་པ་ནི་ཀྱི་ན་སྟེ། རིགས་ལ་འདུས་བྱས་དང་
འདུས་མ་བྱས་ཀྱི་ཆ་གཉིས་ཡོད་པར་ཐལ་ཞིང་། དེ་ལྟ་ན་དགོས་ནུས་མེད་པའི་འདུས་
མ་བྱས་ནི་རིགས་བཏགས་པ་བ་དང་། འདུས་བྱས་ནི་འབྲས་བུ་སྐྱེད་ནུས་ཀྱི་རིགས་
མཚན་ཉིད་པར་འགྲོ་བས་རང་བཞིན་གནས་རིགས་འདུས་མ་བྱས་ཆོས་ཀྱི་དབྱིངས་ལ་
བཞེད་པའི་ཐེག་ཆེན་གྱི་མདོ་སྡེ་ཀུན་གྱི་དགོངས་པ་སྟོང་པར་ཟད་དོ། །དེས་ན་བསྐྱེད་
བྱ་སྐྱེད་བྱེད་ཀྱི་རྒྱུ་འབྲས་སུ་གྱུར་པའི་སྒོ་ནས་བཞག་པའི་རིགས་ཞིག་སེམས་ཀྱིས་འདོར་
མི་ནུས་པར་ཆོས་དབྱིངས་རྣམ་དག་ལ་རང་བཞིན་གནས་རིགས་སུ་སྨྲས་ཀྱང་ཞེ་འདོད་
དང་རང་ཚིག་འགལ་བའི་རྟགས་ངེས་པ་ཙམ་ལས་མ་མཆིས་པས་ཆོས་དབྱིངས་
འགྱུར་མེད་ལ་སངས་རྒྱས་ཀྱི་རིགས་སུ་འདོད་ཕན་ཆད། ཐོག་མར་ཆོས་ཀྱི་དབྱིངས་
ཞེས་པ་གང་ལ་གདགས་པའི་གཞི་རྣམ་གྲངས་མིན་པའི་དོན་དམ་བདེན་གཉིས་ཟུང་
འཇུག་ཆེན་པོ་རབ་ཏུ་མི་གནས་པ་དབུ་མའི་དོན་དེ་ཉིད་ངོས་ཟིན་པར་བྱ་སྟེ། དེ་ངོས་
མ་ཟིན་པར་རྣམ་གྲངས་པའི་དོན་དམ་ཙམ་ལ་འདོད་ན་ནགས་སུ་སྤྲེའུའི་ཚོགས་མཐོང་བ་
ལ་སུམ་ཅུ་རྩ་གསུམ་པའི་ལྟར་འཕྲུལ་པ་ལྟར་ཆོས་དབྱིངས་མ་ཡིན་པ་ལ་ཆོས་དབྱིངས་
སུ་བཟུང་ནས་དེ་ལ་སངས་རྒྱས་ཀྱི་རིགས་སུ་འདོད་པ་དང་། དེ་ཉིད་དམིགས་པས་
ཤེས་རབ་ཀྱི་ཕ་རོལ་ཏུ་ཕྱིན་པ་སྒོམ་པ་དང་། དེ་ངོ་བོ་ཉིད་སྐུའི་རྒྱུར་འདོད་པ་སོགས་
རྣམ་གཞག་ཀུན་ཐེག་པ་ཆེན་པོ་ལྟར་བཅོས་པའི་ལམ་ཡིན་པར་གྲུབ་ཅིང་ཤེར་མདོ་
སོགས་ལས་ཀྱང་དེ་ལྟར་གསུངས་སོ། །དེ་བས་ན་བདེན་གཉིས་ཟུང་འཇུག་གི་

དབྱིངས་སྤྲོས་པའི་དྲྭ་བ་ཀུན་གྱིས་དབེན་པའི་དོན་སོ་སོ་རང་གིས་རིག་པར་བྱ་བ་ལ་རང་བཞིན་རྣམ་པར་དག་པ་ཆོས་ཀྱི་དབྱིངས་དང་སྟོང་པ་ཉིད་ཅེས་བྱ་སྟེ་དེ་ནི་སངས་རྒྱས་ཀྱི་རིགས་མཚན་ཉིད་པ་དང་དག་པ་གཉིས་ལྡན་གྱི་ངོ་བོ་ཉིད་སྐུར་འགྱུར་བ་ཡིན་པར་ཐེག་ཆེན་གྱི་མདོ་དང་དགོངས་འགྲེལ་ཐམས་ཅད་ལས་གསུངས་པས་ན། རང་བཞིན་གནས་རིགས་འདི་འདུས་མ་བྱས་སུ་འདོད་པ་ལས་འོས་མ་མཆིས་ལ། འདུས་མ་བྱས་ཡིན་ཕན་ཆོད་འདི་རང་གི་ངོ་བོ་ཉིད་ཀྱིས་འབྲས་བུ་གཞན་བསྐྱེད་ནས་རང་ཉིད་འགག་པའི་བྱ་བ་བྱེད་པ་མི་འཐད་པའི་ཆོས་སྐུའི་ཡོན་ཏན་རྣམས་ཀྱང་བྲལ་འབྲས་སུ་ཁས་ལེན་པ་ལས་འོས་མེད་ལ། དེ་ལྟར་ཡིན་པར་རྒྱལ་ཚབ་ས་བཅུའི་སེམས་དཔའ་ཆེན་པོས་རྒྱུད་བླ་མ་ལས་གསུངས་པ་དང་། དཔལ་མགོན་འཕགས་པ་ཀླུ་སྒྲུབ་ཀྱིས་ཆོས་དབྱིངས་བསྟོད་པ་ལས་ཀྱང་གསལ་པོར་གསུངས་པའི་ཕྱིར་གཞུང་དེ་དག་གི་རྗེས་སུ་འབྲངས་ནས་རང་ལུགས་ཆོས་དབྱིངས་འདུས་མ་བྱས་པ་རིགས་སུ་འདོད་ཅིང་། དབྱིངས་དེ་ཉིད་ཆོས་ཐམས་ཅད་ཀྱི་གནས་ལུགས་ཡིན་ལ་དེའི་ངོ་བོ་སྐྱེ་འགག་མེད་པ་དང་། སྣང་སྟོང་དབྱེར་མེད་པའི་བདག་ཉིད་དུ་གནས་ཀྱི་ཕྱོགས་སུ་ལྷུང་བ་མེད་པ་ཡིན་ནོ། །འདི་ལྟར་སྐྱེ་ཞིང་འགག་བར་སྣང་བའི་འདུས་བྱས་རྣམས་ནི་སྣང་བ་ལྟར་མ་གྲུབ་པའི་ཕྱིར་དབྱིངས་ཀྱི་གཤིས་ལ་དེས་གོས་པ་ཡོད་མ་མྱོང་བས། འཁོར་བ་རྒྱུ་འབྲས་ཡེ་ནས་དག་ཅིང་རང་བཞིན་ལྷུན་གྱིས་གྲུབ་པའི་འོད་གསལ་ཟག་མེད་ཀྱི་སྣང་བ་རྣམས་དང་འདུ་འབྲལ་མེད་པའི་གནད་འདིས་བདེ་བར་གཤེགས་པའི་སྙིང་པོའི་ཚུལ་ཕྱིན་ཅི་མ་ལོག་པ་ངེས་ཟིན་པར་བྱ་དགོས་སོ། །དེ་བས་ན་གཉིས་པ་རང་ལུགས་བརྗོད་པ་ལ། གོང་གི་རྐང་པ་དང་པོའི་དོན་ནི། ཡང་དག་པར་རྫོགས་པའི་སངས་རྒྱས་ཀྱི་སྐུ་མཐར་ཐུག་པ་ཆོས་ཀྱི་སྐུ་ཡོན་ཏན་ནམ་མཁའ་དང་མཉམ་པ་དེ་ལྟ་བུ། སྟོན་ཐ་མལ་པ་འཆིང་བ་ཀུན་ལྡན་དུ་གྱུར་པའི་གང་ཟག་གི་རྒྱུད་དེ་ལས་ཕྱིས་གསལ་བའམ། འཁྲོ་བའམ། མངོན་དུ་གྱུར་པ་ཡོད་པས་ན་ད་ལྟ་ནས་སེམས་ཅན་གྱི་རྒྱུད་ན་བདེ་གཤེགས་སྙིང་པོ་ཡོད་ཅེས་བསྒྲུབ་པ་ཡིན་ནོ། །འདིས་ཇི་ལྟར་འགྲུབ་པའི་འཐད་པ་ནི། ཐུན་མོང་དང་ཐུན་མོང་མ་ཡིན་པ་གཉིས་སུ་ཡོད་དེ། དང་པོ་ཡེ་ཤེས་ཆོས་སྐུ་མངོན་

དུ་མཛད་པའི་སེམས་ཅན་ཡོད་ན་སེམས་ལ་སངས་རྒྱ་རུང་གི་རིགས་ཡོད་པས་ཁྱབ་ཅིང་། རིགས་གཏན་མེད་པ་ལ་དེ་ལྟར་མི་འཐད་པའི་ཕྱིར་ཏེ། ཆོས་དབྱིངས་བསྟོད་པ་ལས། ཁམས་ཡོད་ན་ནི་ལས་བྱས་པས། །ས་ལེ་སྦྲམ་དག་མཐོང་བར་འགྱུར། །ཁམས་མེད་པ་ན་ལས་བྱས་ཀྱང་། ཉོན་མོངས་འབའ་ཞིག་སྐྱེ་བར་ཟད། །ཅེས་གསུངས་པ་བཞིན་ནོ། །གཉིས་པ་དེ་ལྟར་འཐད་པ་བསྟན་པ་དཔེ་ཞིང་ས་ལ་ལོ་ཏོག་སྐྱེ་རུང་ལྟར་སེམས་འདི་སངས་རྒྱ་རུང་གི་རྒྱུ་ཙམ་དུ་གྲུབ་ཀྱང་། སངས་རྒྱས་ཀྱི་ཡོན་ཏན་ཡེ་ལྡན་གྱི་རིགས་ཁྱད་པར་པ་ཇི་ལྟར་འགྲུབ་སྙམ་ན། དེ་ཡང་འགྲུབ་སྟེ་སངས་རྒྱས་བཅོམ་ལྡན་འདས་རྣམས་ནི་འདུས་མ་བྱས་ཀྱིས་རབ་ཏུ་ཕྱེ་བའི་བདག་ཉིད་ཡེ་ཤེས་ཀྱི་སྐུ་ཅན་ཏེ། འདུས་བྱས་མི་རྟག་པའི་རང་བཞིན་ཅན་མིན་པར་ལུང་དང་རིགས་པས་གྲུབ་པའི་ཕྱིར་རོ། །དེ་ཡང་ལུང་ནི་མྱ་ངན་ལས་འདས་པའི་མདོ་ལས། དགེ་སློང་ཚུལ་ཁྲིམས་ཕུན་སུམ་ཚོགས་པ་དེ་བཞིན་གཤེགས་པ་འདུས་མ་བྱས་པ་ལ། དེ་བཞིན་གཤེགས་པ་འདུས་བྱས་ཡིན་ནོ་ཞེས་ཟེར་བས་ནི་མུ་སྟེགས་པར་འགྱུར་ཏེ་ཤི་ཡང་སླའོ། །ཞེས་དང་། རིགས་ཀྱི་བུ། ད་ནི་དེ་བཞིན་གཤེགས་པ་རྟག་པའི་སྐུ་དང་། མི་ཤིགས་པའི་སྐུ་དང་། རྡོ་རྗེའི་སྐུ་དང་། ཤའི་སྐུ་མ་ཡིན་པ་དང་། ཆོས་ཀྱི་སྐུར་ལྟོས་ཤིག །ཅེས་དང་། ཡང་། དེ་བཞིན་གཤེགས་པའི་པ་མི་རྟག་གོ་ཞེས་བྱ་བའི་ཚིག་སྨྲ་བས་ནི་ཤིང་གི་ཕུང་པོ་འབར་བ་འདི་ལ་ལྕེས་ཀུན་ནས་རེག་པར་བྱས་ཏེ་ཤི་ཡང་སླའི། ཚིག་དེ་ནི་མཉན་པར་མི་བྱའོ། །ཞེས་དང་། མེད་དགག་གི་ཆ་ཙམ་མྱང་འདས་སུ་མི་རུང་བ་ཡང་ལུང་དེ་ལས། སྟོང་པ་ཉིད་སྟོང་པ་ཉིད་ཅེས་བྱ་བ་ནི་གང་གི་ཚེ་བཙལ་ཀྱང་ཅི་ཡང་མ་རྙེད་པ་སྟེ། ཅི་ཡང་མེད་པ་ཞེས་བྱ་བ་ནི་གཅེར་བུ་པ་རྣམས་ལའང་ཡོད་མོད་ཀྱི། ཐར་པ་ནི་དེ་ལྟ་མ་ཡིན་ནོ། །ཞེས་དང་། ཐར་པ་གང་ཡིན་པ་དེ་ནི་བཅོས་མ་མ་ཡིན་པའི་ཁམས་ཡིན་ཏེ། དེ་ནི་དེ་བཞིན་གཤེགས་པའོ། །ཞེས་དང་། རྡོ་རྗེ་གཅོད་པ་ལས་ཀྱང་། གང་དག་ང་ལ་གཟུགས་སུ་མཐོང་། །གང་དག་ང་ལ་སྒྲར་ཤེས་པ། །ལོག་པའི་ལམ་དུ་ཞུགས་པ་སྟེ། །སྐྱེ་བོ་དེ་དག་ང་མི་མཐོང་། །སངས་

རྒྱས་རྣམས་ནི་ཆོས་ཉིད་ལྟ། །འདྲེན་པ་རྣམས་ནི་ཆོས་ཀྱི་སྐུ། །ཆོས་ཉིད་ཤེས་པར་བྱ་མིན་པས། །དེ་ནི་རྣམ་པར་ཤེས་མི་ནུས། །ཞེས་གསུངས་པ་ལ་སོགས་པས་མཚོན་ཏེ་ངེས་དོན་གྱི་མདོ་སྡེ་ཀུན་ལས་རྒྱ་ཆེར་བསྟན་པ་དང་། རིགས་པ་ཡང་། གདོད་མའི་ཆོས་དབྱིངས་དང་གཉིས་སུ་མེད་པར་རོ་མཉམ་པའི་འབྲས་བུ་མཐར་ཐུག་པ་རྣམ་མཁྱེན་གྱི་ཡེ་ཤེས་ཉིད་རྒྱུ་རྐྱེན་གྱིས་གསར་དུ་འདུས་བྱས་པའི་མི་རྟག་པ་ཡིན་ན། རང་བྱུང་གི་ཡེ་ཤེས་མ་ཡིན་པ་དང་། འགྱུར་བའི་ཟུག་རྡུ་མ་སྤངས་པ་དང་། ཡང་འགགས་ཡང་སྐྱེ་བའི་ཆ་དང་བཅས་པ་དང་། རང་གི་ངོ་བོས་འཇིག་པས་བསླུ་བ་ཅན་དང་། གཏན་གྱི་སྐྱབས་སུ་མ་གྱུར་པ་རང་ཉིད་སྐྱེས་མ་ཐག་ཏུ་འགགས་པའི་ཕྱིར་དང་། རྒྱུའི་ཚོགས་པ་ཚང་བ་གང་དུ་ཉི་ཚེ་བར་གནས་པའི་ཕྱིར་དང་། ཆོས་ཀུན་ལ་རོ་མཉམ་དུ་མ་སོང་བ་དང་། མཐའ་ཀུན་ལས་མ་འདས་པ་དང་། ཡིད་ཀྱི་རང་བཞིན་གྱི་སྐྱེ་བ་སོགས་མ་འགགས་པ་དང་། རང་དབང་མེད་པར་འདུ་བྱེད་པའི་གཞན་དབང་ཅན་དུ་ཐལ་བ་སོགས་ཀྱི་སྐྱོན་དང་བཅས་པས་དེ་ལྟར་ཁས་ལེན་པ་ལ་རྡོ་རྗེའི་སྐུ་ལ་མི་རྟག་པར་བལྟ་བའི་ཉེས་པ་ཤིན་ཏུ་རྒྱ་ཆེར་འབྱུང་བས་ན། ལམ་ངན་པ་འདི་དོར་ནས་གཉིས་སུ་མེད་པའི་ཡེ་ཤེས་ཀྱི་སྐུ་འདུས་མ་བྱས་དང་རྟག་པ་དམ་པ་བལྟ་བར་བྱ་སྟེ། ཐུན་མོང་ཚུ་རོལ་མཐོང་བ་ལ་བརྟེན་པའི་རིགས་པ་ཙམ་གྱིས་གཞལ་ནས་ཡེ་ཤེས་འདུས་མ་བྱས་པ་མི་སྲིད་དེ། ཤེས་པ་དང་རྟག་པའི་གཞི་མཐུན་མི་སྲིད་པས་སོ་སྙམ་པ་ནི་གྱི་ན་སྟེ། ཡུལ་ཤེས་པའི་ཤེས་པ་ཉི་ཚེ་བ་ལ་མི་རྟག་པས་ཁྱབ་ཀྱང་། ཤེས་དང་ཤེས་བྱ་རོ་གཅིག་པའི་ཡེ་ཤེས་མཁའ་ཁྱབ་མཁའ་ཡི་རྡོ་རྗེ་ཅན་ནི་དེ་དང་མི་འདྲ་སྟེ། འདུས་མ་བྱས་པའི་རང་གདངས་འོད་གསལ་མི་འགྱུར་བའི་ངང་དེར་འཁོར་འདས་ཀྱི་ཆོས་ཀུན་འུབ་ཆུབ་པས་ན་དེའི་ངོ་བོ་ལ་སྐྱེ་འགགས་ཡེ་ནས་མེད་པར་མཐར་ཐུག་དཔྱོད་པའི་རིག་ཤེས་ཀྱིས་གྲུབ་པའི་ཕྱིར་རོ། །དེས་ན་དེ་འདྲ་བའི་ཡེ་ཤེས་དེ་ནི་འདུས་བྱས་དང་འདུས་མ་བྱས་ཀྱི་མཐའ་གང་ལའང་མི་གནས་པའི་འདུས་མ་བྱས་ཆེན་པོ་སྟེ། དངོས་མེད་རྐྱང་པ་དང་གཏན་མི་འདྲ་ལ། དངོས་དངོས་མེད་གཉིས་ཀ་ཆོས་ཅན་ཡིན་ཞིང་། དེ་དག་བརྟེན་ནས་སྐྱེས་པའམ་བརྟེན་ནས་བཏགས་པའི་ཕྱིར་ན

ཡང་དག་པར་དཔྱད་ན་འདུས་བྱས་དང་གསོག་གསོབ་རྫུན་པ་བསླུ་བ་ཡིན་ལ། བདེ་
གཤེགས་སྙིང་པོ་ནི་དངོས་དངོས་མེད་ཀྱི་ཆོས་ཀུན་གྱི་ཆོས་ཉིད་འདུས་མ་བྱས་ཆེན་པོ་
ཡང་དག་པར་མི་བསླུ་བ་ཡིན་ཏེ། རྩ་བ་ཤེས་རབ་ལས། རང་བཞིན་དག་ནི་
བཅོས་མིན་དང་། །གཞན་ལ་ལྟོས་པ་མེད་པ་ཡིན། །ཞེས་དང་། དངོས་དང་
དངོས་མེད་འདུས་བྱས་ཡིན། །མྱ་ངན་འདས་པ་འདུས་མ་བྱས། །ཞེས་གསུངས་
པ་བཞིན་ནོ། །དེ་ལྟར་མཐར་ཐུག་ཆོས་སྐུའི་ཡེ་ཤེས་དེ་ནི་སྲིད་ཞི་ཀུན་ཁྱབ་དང་
མཉམ་པ་ཉིད་དང་འདུས་མ་བྱས་པ་དང་། འགྱུར་མེད་དོན་དམ་པའི་རང་བཞིན་དུ་
ངེས་པ་དོན་གྱི་མདོ་སྡེའི་ལུང་དང་མཐར་ཐུག་དཔྱོད་པའི་རིགས་པས་གྲུབ་པ་ན། དེ་
ནམ་ཞིག་མངོན་དུ་འགྱུར་རུང་གི་རྒྱུད་ན་ད་ལྟ་ནས་ཡེ་ཤེས་ཆོས་སྐུའི་རང་བཞིན་ཆོས་
ཉིད་ཀྱི་ཚུལ་བྲི་གང་དང་བྲལ་བར་བཞུགས་པ་དེ་ཉིད་ལ། གློ་བུར་གྱི་དྲི་མ་བྲལ་མ་
བྲལ་གྱི་སྣང་ཚུལ་ལ་མངོན་དུ་གྱུར་མ་གྱུར་ཡོད་ཀྱང་། གནས་ཚུལ་ལ་སྔ་ཕྱིར་བཟང་
ངན་གྱི་ཁྱད་པར་ཏིལ་ཙམ་མེད་དེ། འགྱུར་མེད་འདུས་མ་བྱས་ཀྱི་རང་བཞིན་ཡིན་
པའི་ཕྱིར་ཏེ། རྒྱུད་བླ་མ་ལས། ཇི་ལྟར་སྔར་བཞིན་ཕྱིས་དེ་བཞིན། །འགྱུར་བ་
མེད་པའི་ཆོས་ཉིད་དོ། །ཞེས་དང་། སེམས་ཀྱི་རང་བཞིན་འོད་གསལ་གང་ཡིན་
པ། དེ་ནི་ནམ་མཁའ་བཞིན་དུ་འགྱུར་མེད་དེ། །ཡང་དག་མིན་རྟོག་ལས་བྱུང་
འདོད་ཆགས་སོགས། །གློ་བུར་དྲི་མས་དེ་ཉོན་མོངས་མི་འགྱུར། །ཞེས་སོགས་
འཁོར་བའི་ཆོས་ཐམས་ཅད་འགྱུར་ཞིང་མི་བརྟན་པ་ཡིན་ལ་དེ་ཀུན་ཆོས་ཉིད་དེའི་ངང་དུ་
འཕོ་འགྱུར་བྱེད་པ་ལྟར་སྣང་ཡང་། སེམས་ཀྱི་དག་པ་བདེ་གཤེགས་སྙིང་པོ་ནི་ནམ་
མཁའ་ལྟར་འཕོ་འགྱུར་མེད་པར་ཡང་ནས་ཡང་དུ་གསུངས་པ་ལྟར་ཤེས་པར་བྱ་ལ།
དེ་ལྟར་འདུས་མ་བྱས་འོད་གསལ་བའི་དབྱིངས་ལ་འཁྲུལ་པས་གོས་པ་མེད་པར་རང་
བཞིན་གྱིས་རྣམ་པར་དག་ཅིང་། མ་འཁྲུལ་པ་གཤིས་ཀྱི་རང་གདངས་ལ་ལྷུན་གྱིས་
གྲུབ་པའི་སྟོབས་སོགས་འབྲས་ཆོས་ཀྱི་ཡོན་ཏན་འབྲལ་མེད་དུ་གནས་ཏེ་ཉི་མ་དང་འོད་
ཟེར་བཞིན་ནོ། །དེ་ལྟར་ཡང་རྒྱུད་བླ་མ་ལས། རྣམ་དབྱེར་བཅས་པའི་མཚན་ཉིད་
ཅན། གློ་བུར་དག་གིས་ཁམས་སྟོང་གི རྣམ་དབྱེར་མེད་པའི་མཚན་ཉིད་

ཅན། །བླ་མེད་ཆོས་ཀྱིས་སྟོང་མ་ཡིན། །ཞེས་འཁོར་བའི་ཉེས་པ་ཐམས་ཅད་ནི་ངདང་ཆོས་ཀྱི་བདག་ཏུ་འཛིན་པ་འཁྲུལ་པའི་སེམས་ལས་བྱུང་ལ། འཁྲུལ་སེམས་དེ་ཡང་གདོད་མའི་གཤིས་འོད་གསལ་ལ་ཡེ་ནས་མ་གོས་མ་འདྲེས་པར་མཁའ་ལ་སྤྲིན་ལྟར་གློ་བུར་བ་ཡིན་པས་སྐྱོན་དེ་དག་གི་ཁམས་དང་སོ་སོར་འབྱེད་ཅིང་འབྲལ་རུང་བ་ཡིན་པས་ཁམས་ཀྱི་ངོ་བོ་ལ་སྐྱོན་དེས་སྟོང་པ་སྟེ་མ་གོས་པ་ཡིན་ལ། འཁྲུལ་པས་བསླད་པ་ལ་མི་ལྟོས་པར་རང་གི་ངང་གིས་འོད་གསལ་ཞིང་ཆོས་ཀུན་གྱི་དེ་ཁོ་ན་ཉིད་དུ་ཞུགས་པའི་རང་བྱུང་གི་ཡེ་ཤེས་ལས་རྣམ་དབྱེར་བྱར་མེད་པའི་མཐར་ཐུག་གི་ཡོན་ཏན་རྣམས་ཀྱི་ཁམས་དེ་མི་སྟོང་སྟེ། རང་གི་ངོ་བོ་ལ་འབྲལ་མེད་ཀྱི་གཤིས་ཡིན་པས་ཉི་མ་དང་ཟེར་བཞིན་ནོ། །དེ་ལྟར་རང་བཞིན་གནས་རིགས་དེ་འདུས་མ་བྱས་པ་ཡོན་ཏན་ཡེ་ལྡན་ཆོས་སྐུའི་ངོ་བོར་གྲུབ་པ་ན་སངས་རྒྱ་རུང་བས་སེམས་ཅན་ཐམས་ཅད་ཀྱི་རྒྱུད་ན་ཡེ་ཤེས་ཆོས་སྐུ་བྲི་གང་དང་བྲལ་བར་བཞུགས་དགོས་ཏེ། ལམ་བསྒོམས་ན་སངས་རྒྱ་རུང་བར་དངོས་སྟོབས་ཀྱིས་གྲུབ་ལ། སངས་རྒྱས་དུས་ཀྱི་ཆོས་སྐུ་དེ་འདུས་མ་བྱས་ཡིན་པས་གསར་དུ་རྒྱུ་རྐྱེན་གྱིས་འདུས་བྱས་པ་མི་སྲིད་པའི་ཕྱིར་ད་ལྟ་ནས་སངས་རྒྱས་ཀྱི་ངོ་བོར་བཞུགས་ཞེས་གྲུབ་བོ། །དེ་ལ་ཁ་ཅིག་འདི་སྙམ་དུ་ད་ལྟ་ནས་སངས་རྒྱས་པའི་ངོ་བོར་བཞུགས་ན་རྣམ་པ་ཐམས་ཅད་མཁྱེན་པའི་ཡེ་ཤེས་དེས་སེམས་ཅན་དེ་དག་གི་སྒྲིབ་པ་ཅི་ལ་མི་སེལ་སྙམ་པ་དང་། ཡང་ཐེག་པ་ཐུན་མོང་པའི་གོ་ཡུལ་ལ་ཞེན་ནས་སངས་རྒྱས་ནི་འབྲས་བུ་དང་སེམས་ཅན་རྒྱུ་ཡིན་པས་རྒྱུ་ལ་འབྲས་བུ་ཡོད་ན་ཟན་ཟ་མི་གཙང་ཟ་བའི་རིགས་པ་སོགས་ཀྱིས་གནོད་དོ་སྙམ་ན། ཤིན་ཏུ་ཟབ་པའི་ངེས་དོན་གྱི་མདོ་སྡེའི་དོན་ལ་བློ་མ་སྦྱངས་པ་ཁྱོད་ལ་ཐུན་མོང་པའི་གཞུང་གི་གོ་བ་ཙམ་གྱིས་ཁྲིད་ནས་དོགས་པ་དེ་ལྟར་སྐྱེ་བ་ལ་ཁགས་མེད་ཀྱང་། དེ་མ་ཡིན་ཏེ་ཆོས་ཉིད་འོད་གསལ་བའི་ཡེ་ཤེས་ཀུན་ལ་ཁྱད་མེད་པར་ཡོད་ཀྱང་། རང་སེམས་འཁྲུལ་པ་གློ་བུར་བ་འདི་སྐྱེས་པའི་ཚེ་འཁྲུལ་སེམས་ཡུལ་དང་བཅས་པ་འདི་ཙམ་འཁོར་བའི་གདགས་གཞི་ཡིན་ལ་འཁྲུལ་པ་དེས་རང་ལ་ཡོད་པའི་ཆོས་ཉིད་ཇི་ལྟ་བ་བཞིན་ཏུ་མི་ཤེས་ཏེ། དཔེར་ན་གཉིད་ཀྱི་དུས་ན་ཡིད་ཀྱི་ཤེས་པ་གཅིག་པུའི་དབང་གིས་ལུས་དང་ཡུལ་

དང་མིག་ཤེས་ལ་སོགས་པའི་སྣང་བ་སླུ་མེད་པ་བྱུང་བ་ལ། དེ་དུས་ཡུལ་ཡུལ་ཅན་སོ་སོར་འཛིན་ཅིང་དམིགས་ཀྱི། ཡིད་ཤེས་ཁོ་རང་གིས་རང་གི་ཡིན་ལུགས་གཟུང་འཛིན་ཐ་དད་དུ་མ་གྲུབ་པ་ཤེས་མི་ནུས་ལ། མ་ཤེས་ཀྱང་ཡིན་ལུགས་དེ་ལས་གཞན་དུ་གྱུར་པ་མེད་པ་དང་། ཆོས་ཐམས་ཅད་སྟོང་པ་ཉིད་དུ་གནས་ཀྱང་དེ་ལྟར་ཡིན་པ་ཙམ་གྱིས་ཀུན་གྱིས་རྟོགས་དགོས་པ་མ་ཡིན་པ་བཞིན་ཏེ། གནས་སྣང་མི་མཐུན་པའི་འཁྲུལ་པ་སྲིད་པའི་ཕྱིར་རོ། །དེས་ན་སེམས་དང་སྙིང་པོའི་ཡེ་ཤེས་གཉིས་ཆོས་ཅན་དང་ཆོས་ཉིད་ཡིན་ལ་སངས་རྒྱས་དང་སེམས་ཅན་ཀྱང་གནས་ཚུལ་དང་སྣང་ཚུལ་གྱི་དབང་དུ་བྱས་ནས་སྟོན་པའི་ཕྱིར་རྒྱུ་ལ་འབྲས་གནས་ཀྱི་རིགས་པའི་གནོད་པ་སྟོན་པ་ནི་ཕྱོགས་མ་གོ་བར་ཟད་དོ། །དེ་ལྟར་རིགས་པ་འདི་ནི་འབྲས་དུས་ཀྱི་ཆོས་སྐུ་མངོན་དུ་གསལ་བའི་རྟགས་ཀྱིས་རྒྱུ་དུས་ཀྱི་རིགས་ཡོན་ཏན་ཡེ་ལྡན་ཅན་ཡོད་པར་སྒྲུབ་པ་སྟེ། གནས་ཚུལ་ལ་སྔ་ཕྱི་རྒྱུ་འབྲས་སུ་མེད་ཀྱང་སྣང་ཚུལ་ལ་ལྟོས་ནས་རྒྱུ་འབྲས་སུ་བཞག་དགོས་པའི་ཕྱིར་འབྲས་བུ་ལས་རྒྱུ་བསྒྲུབ་པ་ལྟོས་པའི་རིགས་པ་ཞེས་བྱ་བ་ཡིན་ནོ། ། །

རྐང་པ་གཉིས་པ། དེ་བཞིན་ཉིད་དབྱེར་མེད་ཕྱིར་དང་། ཞེས་པའི་དོན་ནི། འཁོར་འདས་ཀྱི་ཆོས་ཐམས་ཅད་གནས་ལུགས་སྟོང་པ་ཉིད་གདོད་མའི་འོད་གསལ་ཆེན་པོར་དབྱེར་མེད་རོ་གཅིག་པས་ན། སངས་རྒྱས་དང་སེམས་ཅན་ཀྱང་དོན་དམ་པར་དབྱེ་བ་མེད་དེ་སྲིད་ཞི་མཉམ་པ་ཉིད་དོ། །དེའི་ཕྱིར་འཁྲུལ་པ་གློ་བུར་བས་སྦྲུལ་པའི་སེམས་ཅན་ལྟར་སྣང་བ་རྣམས་ཀྱང་གནས་ལུགས་དོན་དམ་པའི་ཆོས་ཉིད་ལས་ཅུང་ཟད་ཀྱང་མ་གཡོས་པར་ཆོས་ཉིད་ཀྱི་རིགས་པས་གྲུབ་པས་ན་སངས་རྒྱས་ཀྱི་སྙིང་པོ་ཅན་དུ་ངེས་ཏེ། མདོ་ལས་ཀྱང་ཆོས་ཐམས་ཅད་གདོད་མ་ནས་འོད་གསལ་བ་དང་། མྱ་ངན་ལས་འདས་པ་དང་མངོན་པར་སངས་རྒྱས་པའི་རང་བཞིན་དུ་གསུངས་པ་ཡིན་ནོ། །འོ་ན་ཁྱོད་ཀྱིས་སྔར་གཞན་ལ་བརྗོད་པ་ལྟར་དེ་བཞིན་ཉིད་དུ་དབྱེར་མེད་པ་ཙམ་གྱིས་རིགས་ཡོད་པར་འགྱུར་ན། ས་རྡོ་སོགས་ལའང་རིགས་ཡོད་པར་ཐལ་ལོ་སྙམ་ན། རིགས་ཞེས་བྱ་བ་ནི་འཁྲུལ་པའི་སེམས་ཀྱི་དབང་གིས་འབྱུང་བའི་སྒྲིབ་གཉིས་ཟད་པར་སྦྱངས་ནས་ཤེས་བྱའི་རང་བཞིན་ལ་མ་འཁྲུལ་པའི་བློ་རྒྱས་པའི་སངས་རྒྱས་ཀྱི་

རྒྱུ་སྐྱོན་མེད་ལ་འཇོག་དགོས་ན། དེ་སེམས་མ་ཡིན་པ་ས་རྡོ་སོགས་བེམ་པོ་ལ་ལམ་སྒྲུབ་པ་མེད་པ་ཐ་སྙད་དུ་དེ་བཞིན་ཉིད་དུ་དབྱེར་མེད་ནའང་དེ་ལ་རིགས་ཡོད་པར་འཇོག་མི་དགོས་ཏེ། སེམས་ཀྱི་དབང་གིས་ས་རྡོ་སོགས་སྣང་གི །ས་རྡོ་སོགས་ཕྱི་རོལ་གྱི་དབང་གིས་སེམས་བྱུང་བ་མ་ཡིན་པ། རྨི་ལམ་གྱི་སྣང་བ་དང་དེ་དུས་ཀྱི་ཤེས་པའི་དཔེས་མཚོན་ཏེ་ཤེས་པར་བྱ་ལ། ཁམས་གསུམ་གྱི་བྱེད་པ་པོ་སེམས་འདི་ལ་ཆོས་ཉིད་བདེ་གཤེགས་སྙིང་པོ་དོན་དམ་པའི་དགེ་བ་ཟག་མེད་ཀྱི་རང་བཞིན་ཅན་ཉིད། རྒྱུ་ལ་ཧླན་ལྟར་བཞུགས་པར་ཤེས་པས་འཁོར་འདས་ཀྱི་སྣང་བ་རྣམས་ནི་རྣམ་ཤེས་དང་ཡེ་ཤེས་དེ་དག་གི་རོལ་པ་ཙམ་ཡིན་པས་ཐ་དད་དུ་མི་དགོས་ལ། ཡང་དག་པའི་དོན་དུ་ཆོས་ཉིད་ཡེ་སངས་རྒྱས་པའི་ངང་ལས་མ་གཡོས་པའི་སྣང་བ་ཐམས་ཅད་ཀྱང་དེ་བཞིན་གཤེགས་པའི་ངང་ཚུལ་ལས་མི་འདའ་བར་ཤིན་ཏུ་ཡང་ཁས་ལེན་ཏེ། སྡུད་པ་ལས། གཟུགས་ཀྱི་དག་པ་འབྲས་བུ་དག་པར་རིག་པར་བྱ། །འབྲས་བུ་གཟུགས་དག་ཐམས་ཅད་མཁྱེན་ཉིད་དག་པར་འགྱུར། །ཐམས་ཅད་མཁྱེན་ཉིད་འབྲས་བུ་དག་དང་གཟུགས་དག་པ། །ནམ་མཁའི་ཁམས་དང་མཚུངས་ཏེ་དབྱེར་མེད་བཅད་དུ་མེད། །ཅེས་གསུངས་པ་ལྟར། ཡུལ་ཅན་སྒྲིབ་པ་ལས་གྲོལ་བའི་དག་པ་གང་ཡིན་པ། ཡུལ་གཟུགས་ལ་སོགས་པའི་དག་པའམ་རང་བཞིན་ཡིན་ཏེ། རང་སྣང་གི་སྒྲིབ་པ་རིམ་བྲལ་གྱི་མཐོང་ཚུལ་ཙམ་ལས་དོན་གྱི་ངོ་བོ་ཡེ་ནས་སྒྲིབ་བྲལ་དུ་གནས་པའི་ཕྱིར་རོ། །དེས་ན་ཡུལ་ཅན་རིག་པའི་ཁམས་ཀྱི་དྲི་མ་ཟད་དེ་སངས་རྒྱས་པ་ན། ཡུལ་གྱི་དངོས་པོས་དག་པར་ལྷག་མར་མི་ལུས་ཏེ། མིག་སྐྱོན་དག་ན་རབ་རིབ་རང་སངས་པ་བཞིན་ནོ། །འོ་ན་གཅིག་སངས་རྒྱས་དུས་སྣང་བ་མ་དག་པ་ཀུན་འགག་གོ་སྙམ་ན་མ་ཡིན་ཏེ། གང་ཟག་སོ་སོའི་རང་སྣང་གི་སྒྲིབ་པས་རང་བསྒྲིབས་ནས་གནས་སྣང་འགལ་བར་མཐོང་བ་ཡོད་པའི་ཕྱིར་རོ། །འོ་ན་གནས་སྣང་རྣམ་པ་ཀུན་ཏུ་མཐུན་པ་སངས་རྒྱས་ཀྱི་ས་ན་མ་དག་པའི་སྣང་བ་འདི་ཀུན་མངའ་འམ་མི་མངའ། མངའ་ན་ཆོས་ཐམས་ཅད་མངོན་པར་རྫོགས་པར་སངས་མ་རྒྱས་ལ། མི་མངའ་ན་ཀུན་ཏུ་འགྲོ་བའི་ལམ་ལ་སོགས་པ་མཁྱེན་པར་མི་སྲིད་དོ་སྙམ་ན། རྣམ་པ་ཐམས་

ཅན་མཁྱེན་པའི་ཡེ་ཤེས་ཀྱིས་འཁོར་འདས་ཀྱི་ཆོས་སྲིད་དོ་ཅོག་ཀུན་རང་དང་རོ་མཉམ་པའི་ངང་ནས་འབད་མེད་ལྷུན་གྲུབ་ཏུ་མཁྱེན་ཅིང་། དེ་ལ་རང་ངོར་ཐམས་ཅད་དག་པ་ཆེན་པོར་གཟིགས་པ་ལས་མ་འདས་བཞིན་དུ་འགྲོ་བ་རིགས་དྲུག་གི་སྣང་བ་རྣམས་ཀྱང་སོ་སོའི་སྣང་ཚུལ་ལྟར་གཟིགས་པ་འདི་ནི། ཡུལ་དང་ཡུལ་ཅན་གྱི་གཉིས་སྣང་གི་སྒྲིབ་པ་མཐའ་དག་ཟད་པའི་སྟོབས་ཀྱིས་ཆོས་ཅན་ཇི་སྙེད་པ་མ་འདྲེས་ཡོངས་རྫོགས་ཀྱི་ཚུལ་དུ་ཆོས་ཉིད་ཀྱི་ཀློང་དུ་ཆུད་པའི་གནད་ཀྱིས་རོ་མཉམ་པའི་ཡེ་ཤེས་སྐྱེ་འགག་དང་བྲལ་བས་ཅིག་ཆར་གཟིགས་པ་སྟེ། ཚུར་མཐོང་གིས་ལྟ་ཅི། ས་ལ་གནས་པས་ཀྱང་བསམ་པར་དཀའ་བའོ། །དེའི་ཚུལ་ཀྱང་ཇི་སྐད་དུ་བྱང་ཆུབ་སེམས་དཔའི་སྡེ་སྣོད་ལས། ཆོས་ཀུན་མཉམ་པ་ཉིད་མཉམ་པར། །རང་བྱུང་པས་ནི་རྗེས་སུ་རྟོགས། །དེ་ཕྱིར་ཡང་དག་མངོན་སངས་རྒྱས། །དེ་བཞིན་གཤེགས་པ་གཟིགས་པ་མཉམ། །ཞེས་དང་། སེམས་རང་བཞིན་གྱི་འོད་གསལ་བ་དེ་བཞིན་དུ་ཤེས་པས་དེ་དེའི་ཕྱིར་སེམས་ཀྱི་སྐད་ཅིག་གཅིག་དང་ལྡན་པའི་ཤེས་རབ་ཀྱིས་བླ་ན་མེད་པ་ཡང་དག་པར་རྫོགས་པའི་བྱང་ཆུབ་མངོན་པར་རྫོགས་པར་སངས་རྒྱས་པ་ཞེས་བྱའོ། །ཞེས་གསུངས་པ་ལྟར་སློབ་དཔོན་ཟླ་བ་གྲགས་པའི་ཞལ་ནས། ཇི་ལྟར་སྣོད་ཀྱི་དབྱེ་བས་མཁའ་ལ་དབྱེ་བ་མེད་དེ་ལྟར། །དངོས་བྱས་དབྱེ་བ་འགའ་ཡང་དེ་ཉིད་ལ་མེད་དེ་ཡི་ཕྱིར། །རོ་མཉམ་ཉིད་དུ་ཡང་དག་ཐུགས་སུ་ཆུད་པར་མཛད་གྱུར་ན། །མཁྱེན་བཟང་ཁྱོད་ཀྱིས་སྐད་ཅིག་གིས་ནི་ཤེས་བྱ་ཐུགས་སུ་ཆུད། །ཅེས་གསུངས་པ་ལྟར་དབྱིངས་དང་གཉིས་སུ་མེད་པའི་ཡེ་ཤེས་ཆེན་པོས། ཆོས་ཐམས་ཅད་ཁྱབ་ཅིང་འབད་མེད་གཟིགས་པ་རྒྱ་མཚོ་ལ་ཟླ་སྐར་ཤར་བའི་ཚུལ་དུ་ཁྱབ་ཅིང་རྟོག་པ་ཉེ་བར་ཞི་བའི་ངང་ནས་གཟིགས་པ་འདི་རང་བྱུང་འོད་གསལ་བའི་ཡེ་ཤེས་གཞི་ལ་བཞུགས་པའི་ཆོས་ཉིད་དེ་སྒྲིབ་པ་མཐའ་དག་ཟད་ནས་ཇི་བཞིན་མངོན་དུ་གྱུར་པའི་སྟོབས་ཀྱིས་ཡིན་པས་མཐར་ཐུག་དཔྱོད་པའི་ཆོས་ཉིད་ཀྱི་རིགས་པ་ཡང་དག་ལ་བརྟེན་ན་མི་ལྡོག་པའི་ཡིད་ཆེས་སྐྱེད་པར་འགྱུར་གྱི། གཞན་དུ་ཉི་ཚེ་བའི་བློས་གཞལ་ནས་སངས་རྒྱས་ཀྱི་ས་ན་ཡེ་ཤེས་མེད་པའམ། ཡོད་ཀྱང་འགྱུར་བཅས་ཀྱི་བློ་ཐ་མལ་པ་

དང་མཚུངས་པར་སྒྲུབ་པ་དང་། སེམས་ཅན་གྱི་ཁམས་མི་གཟིགས་པའམ་ཡང་ན་མ་དག་པའི་སྣང་བ་ཡོད་པར་འདོད་པ་དང་། ཇི་ལྟ་ཇི་སྙེད་ངོ་བོ་རོ་མཉམ་དུ་སྒྲུབ་མ་ནུས་པ་སོགས་འགལ་འདུ་དང་ཀུན་རྟོག་གི་ཚོགས་མ་མང་དུ་སྤྱོང་བ་མཐོང་ངོ་། །རྐྱང་པ་གསུམ་པ་རིགས་ཡོད་ཕྱིར་ན། ཞེས་པའི་དོན་ནི། སེམས་ཅན་ཐམས་ཅད་ལ་སངས་རྒྱ་རུང་གི་རིགས་ཡོད་དེ། དྲི་མ་གློ་བུར་བ་སྤང་རུང་དུ་གྲུབ་ཅིང་། ཡོན་ཏན་ཡེ་ལྡན་གྱི་ཆོས་སྐུ་ཀུན་ལ་ཁྱད་མེད་པར་ཡོད་པར་གྲུབ་པས་སོ། །དེ་ལྟར་སངས་རྒྱ་རུང་གི་རིགས་ཡོད་ན་ལུས་ཅན་དེ་དག་སངས་རྒྱས་ཀྱི་སྙིང་པོ་ཅན་དུ་ངེས་ཏེ། །དེ་དག་སངས་རྒྱས་པའི་གནས་སྐབས་ཡོད་ལ། སངས་རྒྱས་ཆོས་སྐུ་དེ་ཡང་ངོ་བོ་འདུས་མ་བྱས་སུ་གྲུབ་པས་སྔ་ཕྱི་ལ་བཟང་ངན་གྱི་ཁྱད་པར་ངོ་བོའི་ཆ་ནས་མེད་པའི་ཕྱིར་རོ། །རིགས་པ་གསུམ་པ་འདིས་རྒྱུ་ལས་འབྲས་བུ་སྐྱེད་པར་ཤེས་པ་བྱ་བ་བྱེད་པའི་རིགས་པ་ཡིན་ནོ། །འདིར་རྒྱུ་ཡོད་ཙམ་གྱིས་འབྲས་བུ་འབྱིན་པར་དཔོག་པ་ཙམ་མིན་ཏེ། ཆོས་ཉིད་དེ་བཞིན་ཉིད་ཀྱི་རིགས་ལ་འགྱུར་བ་མེད་པ་དང་། དེ་འབྲས་དུས་ངོ་བོ་ལ་བཟང་ངན་མེད་པ་དང་། གློ་བུར་བའི་དྲི་མ་རྣམས་ཡུན་ཇི་ལྟར་རིང་ཡང་འབྲལ་རུང་ཡིན་པས་རིགས་དེ་སངས་རྒྱ་བ་ལ་ནམ་ཡང་ཆུད་ཟ་བ་མི་སྲིད་པའི་གནད་ཀྱིས་སོ། །དེ་ལྟར་རྒྱུ་རིགས་ཡོད་པ་དེ་འབྲས་དུས་ཀྱི་ཆོས་སྐུ་དང་ངོ་བོ་ཁྱད་མེད་དང་། འབྲས་དུས་ཀྱི་ཆོས་སྐུ་ཡོད་ན་དེ་སེམས་ཅན་གྱི་དུས་ནའང་འཕེལ་འགྲི་མེད་པར་ཡོད་དགོས་པ་དང་། རྒྱུ་འབྲས་དང་སྔ་ཕྱིར་བཏགས་ཀྱང་དོན་ལ་ཆོས་དབྱིངས་འགྱུར་མེད་ཀྱི་ངོ་བོར་རོ་གཅིག་པའི་རིགས་པ་དེ་གསུམ་གྱིས་སེམས་ཅན་ཐམས་ཅད་དེ་བཞིན་གཤེགས་པའི་སྙིང་པོ་ཅན་དུ་འགྲུབ་སྟེ་དངོས་པོའི་སྟོབས་ཀྱིས་ཞུགས་པའི་རིགས་པ་ཡང་དག་གི་ལམ་ནས་སོ། །དེ་ལྟར་དེ་བཞིན་གཤེགས་པའི་སྙིང་པོ་སེམས་ཅན་ཐམས་ཅད་ལ་ཡོད་པར་སྒྲུབ་པའི་རིགས་པ་འདིས་མཐར་ཐུག་གི་ཐར་པ་དང་། དེ་བཞིན་གཤེགས་པ་དང་ཆོས་ཐམས་ཅད་ཀྱི་གནས་ལུགས་དོན་དམ་པ་རྣམས་ཐ་དད་དུ་མེད་ལ། དེ་ཡང་དེ་བཞིན་གཤེགས་པའི་སྙིང་པོ་ཉིད་ཀྱི་སྟོབས་ལས་བྱུང་བར་ཤེས་ན་མཐར་ཐུག་ཐེག་གཅིག་ཏུ་འགྲུབ་ཀྱི། གཞན་དུ་བདེ་གཤེགས་སྙིང་པོ་ཞེས་པ་སེམས

ཅན་གྱི་ཁམས་ན་མེད་པ་དང་། སངས་རྒྱས་ཀྱི་དུས་ན་མེད་པ་དང་། རྒྱུ་དུས་ཡོན་ཏན་མེད་པ་ལ་འབྲས་དུས་གསར་དུ་ཡོན་ཏན་ཅན་དུ་སྨྲ་བ་སོགས་ཐེག་པ་ཆེན་པོའི་དོན་ལ་རྒྱབ་ཀྱིས་ཕྱོགས་པ་དག་གི་ལུགས་ལ་མཐར་ཐུག་ཐེག་གཅིག་སྒྲུབ་པའི་རིགས་པ་པྲ་ཡས་པར་འགྱུར་རོ། །དེའི་ཕྱིར་ཐེག་པ་མཆོག་གི་གནས་ལ་མོས་པ་རྣམས་ཀྱིས་གནས་འདི་ལ་ཤིན་ཏུ་བློ་གྲོས་འབྱོར་པར་བྱ་དགོས་སོ། །དེ་ལྟར་སེམས་ཅན་གྱི་དུས་ན་ཡོན་ཏན་ཡེ་ལྡན་གྱི་ཁམས་ཡོད་པར་བཞག་པ་དེ་ནི་བསམ་གྱིས་མི་ཁྱབ་པའི་གནས་ཟབ་མོ་ཡིན་པས་སངས་རྒྱས་ཀྱིས་ཀྱང་འཁོར་རྣམས་ལ་ངའི་གསུང་གིས་ཡིད་ཆེས་པར་གྱིས་དང་མི་བསླུ་བར་འགྱུར་གྱི་རང་སྟོབས་ཀྱིས་ཤེས་པར་དཀའ་བའི་ཚུལ་གྱིས་བཀའ་སྩལ་པས་ཟབ་མོའི་མཐར་ཐུག་ཏུ་བསྟན་པ་ཡིན་པས། འདི་ལ་བློ་ཆུང་རྟོག་གེ་རྣམས་ཧྲོལ་བ་བརྒྱུད་མར་བྱེད་དེ། སངས་རྒྱས་དང་སེམས་ཅན་གྱི་གཞི་མཐུན་གྱི་སེམས་ཡོད་པར་ཐལ་བ་སོགས་ཐ་སྙད་ལ་བརྟེན་པའི་ཀླན་ཀ་ཇི་སྙེད་པ་ནི་གྱི་ནར་སྨྲ་བ་སྟེ། ཇི་སྐད་དུ་དགོངས་པ་ངེས་པར་འགྲེལ་བའི་མདོ་ལས། འདུ་བྱེད་ཁམས་དང་དོན་དམ་མཚན་ཉིད་ན། །གཅིག་དང་ཐ་དང་བྲལ་བའི་མཚན་ཉིད་དེ། །གཅིག་དང་ཐ་དད་དུ་ཡང་གང་རྟོགས་པ། །དེ་དག་ཚུལ་བཞིན་མ་ཡིན་ཞུགས་པ་ཡིན། །ཞེས་གསུངས་པ་ལྟར། སེམས་ཀྱི་ཆོས་ཉིད་སྙིང་པོའི་ཁམས་དང་། ཆོས་ཅན་གྱི་སེམས་གཉིས་གཅིག་ཐ་དད་གང་དུའང་ཁས་བླང་མི་དགོས་ལ། གནས་ཚུལ་ཆོས་ཉིད་ཀྱི་དོན་ལས་མ་འདས་ཀྱང་། སྣང་ཚུལ་འཁྲུལ་པ་སྲིད་པ་ལ་འགལ་པ་མེད་པར་མ་ཟད། དེ་ལས་གཞན་དུ་ཐར་པ་མེད་པའམ། སུ་ཡང་འཁྲུལ་མི་སྲིད་པ་སོགས་ཀྱི་སྐྱོན་དུ་འགྱུར་ལ། གནས་སྣང་མི་མཐུན་པ་ཡོད་པའི་ཕྱིར་འཁྲུལ་བའི་སེམས་ཅན་སྲིད་ཅིང་། དེ་ལམ་ལ་ཞུགས་པས་འཁྲུལ་བ་སྤངས་ནས་སངས་རྒྱས་པའང་ཡོད་པར་འགྲུབ་པ་ཡིན་ནོ། །དོན་དམ་དཔྱོད་པའི་རིགས་པས་ཆོས་ཐམས་ཅད་སྟོང་པ་ཉིད་དུ་གྲུབ་ཀྱང་དེས་སྙིང་པོའི་ཡོན་ཏན་འགོག་པར་མི་འགྱུར་ཏེ་ཡོན་ཏན་བླ་ན་མེད་པ་ཡོད་ཀྱང་ངོ་བོ་སྟོང་པར་འདི་པས་ཀྱང་ཞལ་གྱིས་བཞེས་པའི་ཕྱིར་རོ། །དེས་ན་འཁོར་ལོ་བར་པས་བསྟན་དོན་ཀུན་བྱང་གི་ཆོས་ཐམས་ཅད་སྟོང་པར་བསྟན་པ་ནི་དེ་དེ་བཞིན་དུ་

གྲུབ་སྟེ་བདེ་གཤེགས་སྙིང་པོའང་སྟོང་པ་ཉིད་ཀྱི་རང་བཞིན་ཡིན་པའི་ཕྱིར་རོ། །འོན་ཀྱང་སྟོང་པའི་རང་བཞིན་ཅན་གྱི་སྐུ་དང་ཡེ་ཤེས་ཀྱི་སྣང་བ་དང་འདུ་འབྲལ་མེད་པས་ཁྱད་པར་དུ་བྱས་པའི་སྙིང་པོ་བསྟན་པ་འདི་འཁོར་ལོ་ཐ་མའི་ངེས་དོན་གྱི་མདོ་སྡེ་རྣམས་ཀྱི་དགོངས་པ་ཡིན་པས། ཚུལ་དེ་ཙམ་གྱི་ཆ་ནས་འཁོར་ལོ་བར་པ་ལས་ལྷག་པའི་ཕྱིར། མདོ་སྡེ་དགོངས་འགྲེལ་ལས་འཁོར་ལོ་ཐ་མའི་དོན་ལ་མཆོག་ཏུ་བསྔགས་པའང་འཁོར་ལོ་ཐ་མར་གཏོགས་ཚད་མ་ཡིན་གྱི་སྙིང་པོ་བསྟན་པའི་ངེས་དོན་གྱི་ཕྱོགས་ནས་དེ་ལྟར་གསུངས་པ་སྟེ། རིག་ཁམས་ནོར་བུ་སྦྱོང་བའི་དཔེ་བསྟན་པ་སོགས་མདོ་གཞན་གྱིས་དེ་ལྟར་གསལ་བར་ངེས་ནུས་སོ། །དེས་ན་འཁོར་ལོ་བར་པར་བསྟན་པའི་སྟོང་པ་ཉིད་དང་། ཐ་མར་བསྟན་པའི་སྐུ་དང་ཡེ་ཤེས་དག་སྣང་སྟོང་ཟུང་དུ་ཆུད་པར་བྱ་དགོས་པས། འཁོར་ལོ་བར་པ་དང་ཐ་མའི་ངེས་དོན་གྱི་སྐོར་རྣམས་དབྱེ་བསལ་མེད་པར་གཉིས་ཀ་ངེས་དོན་དུ་ཀུན་མཁྱེན་ཀློང་ཆེན་རབ་འབྱམས་ཀྱིས་བཞེད་པ་འདི་ཁོ་ན་ལྟར་གཟུང་བར་བྱ་སྟེ། དེ་གཉིས་གཅིག་ངེས་དོན་བྱས་ན་གཅིག་དྲང་དོན་བྱ་དགོས་པའི་འགལ་བ་མེད་པར་མ་ཟད། ཟུང་དུ་ཚོགས་པར་བྱས་ནས་བདེ་གཤེགས་སྙིང་པོ་དེ་ལྟ་བུ་ལ་རྒྱུ་རྒྱུད་ཀྱི་དོན་དུ་བྱས་ནས་རྡོ་རྗེ་ཐེག་པའི་མན་ངག་གི་གནད་འབྱུང་བས་སངས་རྒྱས་ཀྱི་བསྟན་པ་དེ་དག་གནད་གཅིག་ཏུ་འབབ་པར་ཤེས་དགོས་ཤིང་། མཐར་ཐུག་གི་དོན་འདི་ལ་ཀླུ་ཐོགས་རྣམ་གཉིས་སོགས་འཕགས་པ་རྣམས་དགོངས་པ་གཅིག་སྟེ་ཆོས་དབྱིངས་བསྟོད་པ་དང་སེམས་འགྲེལ་ལ་སོགས་པ་དང་། རྒྱུད་བླ་མའི་འགྲེལ་པ་སོགས་ཀྱིས་གསལ་བར་རྟོགས་པའི་ཕྱིར་རོ། །དེ་ལྟར་ཡང་སློབ་དཔོན་ཀླུ་སྒྲུབ་ཀྱིས། སྟོང་པ་ཉིད་ནི་སྟོན་པའི་མདོ། །རྒྱལ་བས་ཇི་སྙེད་གསུངས་པ་སྟེ། །དེ་དག་ཀུན་གྱིས་ཉོན་མོངས་ལྡོག །ཁམས་དེ་ཉམས་པར་བྱེད་མ་ཡིན། །ཞེས་གསུངས་པ་ལྟར་དོན་དམ་དཔྱོད་པས་དཔྱད་ནས་གྲུབ་འབྲས་མཐར་ཐུག་བདེན་པ་དབྱེར་མེད་རྡོ་རྗེ་ལྟ་བུའི་དོན། རྟོག་གེའི་ཤེས་པས་མི་ཕྱེད་པའི་དབྱིངས་ཡིན་པས་དོན་དམ་པ་ལ་བརྟེན་པའི་ཀླན་ཀ་འཛུག་པའི་གཞི་མེད་དོ། །ད་ནི་ཁམས་དེ་དག་སེམས་ཅན་གྱི་རྒྱུད་ན་ཇི་ལྟར་བཞུགས་པའི་ཚུལ་བཤད་ན། གནས་

ལུགས་རང་གི་ངོ་བོའི་དབང་དུ་བྱས་ན་ཆོས་ཐམས་ཅད་ཆོས་ཉིད་དེ་ཡི་ཀློང་དུ་ཆུད་ཅིང་ཆོས་ཉིད་རང་གི་ངོ་བོ་ལ་སྐྱེ་འགག་མེད་པར་མཉམ་པ་ཉིད་དུ་གནས་ལ་འཁོར་འདས་ལ་སོགས་པའི་བཟང་ངན་དང་། ཕ་རོལ་ཚུ་རོལ་བདག་དང་གཞན་ཆེ་དང་ཆུང་བ་སོགས་ཀྱི་ཆ་དང་། སྔ་ཕྱིའི་དུས་ཀྱི་ཁྱད་པར་སོགས་མེད་དེ་ཆོས་དབྱིངས་ཐིག་ལེ་ཉག་གཅིག་འཕོ་འགྱུར་མེད་པའོ། །གནས་ལུགས་ལ་དེ་ལྟར་ཡིན་ཀྱང་འཁྲུལ་པ་གློ་བུར་བའི་སྣང་ངོ་དང་བསྟུན་ན་འདི་ལྟར་ཁམས་གསུམ་འཁོར་བའི་ལུས་སེམས་ཡུལ་གྱི་སྣང་བར་ཤར་ནས་ཆོས་ཉིད་ཀྱི་རང་བཞིན་མི་མཐོང་བའི་ཚེ་ནའང་། ཆོས་ཉིད་ནི་མེད་པ་མ་ཡིན་ཏེ་རང་གི་རང་བཞིན་ལས་གཡོ་བ་ཙུང་ཟད་ཀྱང་མེད་པར་ཡོད་པས་ན། སེམས་ཀྱི་ཆོས་ཉིད་དེ་ལྟ་བུ་གློ་བུར་གྱི་དྲི་མས་སྒྲུབས་སུ་བྱས་ནས་མི་མངོན་ཡང་བཙུད་དམ་དབྱུས་ན་སྙིང་པོའི་ཚུལ་གྱིས་གནས་པ་ལ་རིགས་སམ་སྙིང་པོ་ཞེས་བརྗོད་དེ། དཔེར་ན་ས་འོག་གི་གཏེར་ལ་སོགས་པའི་དཔེ་དགུས་མཚོན་ནས་ཤེས་པར་བྱ་བར་གསུངས་སོ། །དེ་གློ་བུར་གྱི་དྲི་མ་ལ་ལྟོས་ནས་མ་དག་པར་དང་། དག་མ་དག་ཅི་རིགས་པ་དང་། ཤིན་ཏུ་རྣམ་དག་གི་གནས་སྐབས་གསུམ་དུ་བཞག་ཀྱང་ཁམས་རང་གི་ངོ་བོ་ལ་ཁྱད་པར་མེད་དེ། རྒྱུད་བླ་མ་ལས། སངས་རྒྱས་ཡེ་ཤེས་སེམས་ཅན་ཚོགས་ཞུགས་ཕྱིར། རང་བཞིན་དྲི་མེད་དེ་ནི་གཉིས་མེད་དེ། །སངས་རྒྱས་རིགས་ལ་དེ་འབྲས་ཉེར་བཏགས་པས། །འགྲོ་ཀུན་སངས་རྒྱས་སྙིང་པོ་ཅན་དུ་གསུངས། །ཞེས་དང་། །འདི་ཡང་རང་བཞིན་ཆོས་སྐུ་དང་། །དེ་བཞིན་ཉིད་དང་རིགས་ཀྱང་སྟེ། །ཞེས་དང་། མ་དག་མ་དག་དག་པ་དང་། །ཤིན་ཏུ་རྣམ་དག་གོ་རིམ་བཞིན། །སེམས་ཅན་བྱང་ཆུབ་སེམས་དཔའ་དང་། །དེ་བཞིན་གཤེགས་ཞེས་མཚན་གསོལ་ཏོ། །ཞེས་གསུངས་པ་བཞིན་ནོ། །དེ་ལྟར་མ་ཤེས་པར་བདེ་གཤེགས་སྙིང་པོ་ཞེས་པ་མཁར་གཞོང་ལ་རྒྱ་ཤུག་བརྟེན་པ་ལྟར་ཕུང་ལྔའི་གཟེབ་ག་ཤེད་ན་འཁྲུལ་དང་མ་འཁྲུལ་བའི་བློ་གཉིས་སྣང་མུན་བཞིན་དུ་འགྲོགས་པ་ཞིག་གི་རྣམ་པ་ཡིད་ལ་བཟུང་ནས་དགག་སྒྲུབ་ཀྱང་དེ་དང་འཚམས་པར་བྱེད་པ་ནི་ཐེག་ཆེན་གྱི་དགོངས་དོན་ལ་རང་ཉིད་ཕྱོགས་སུ་མ་ཕྱིན་པའི་འོ་དོད་ཙམ་དུ་ཟད་དེ། དེ་

བས་ན་ཐེག་ཆེན་ལ་བློ་མ་སྦྱངས་པའི་རྟོག་གེ་ངན་པའི་ཁྲོད་དུ་སྙིང་པོའི་གཏམ་འདི་
བསྒྲགས་ཀྱང་དོན་མེད་ལ། ཟབ་མོའི་གཏམ་འདི་ལྟ་བུ་ཐོས་པ་དང་། མུ་སྟེགས་
ཅན་ལ་བསྟན་བྱ་མ་ཡིན་ཏེ། དེ་དག་ཆོས་ཟབ་མོ་འདི་མཉན་པའི་སྣོད་དུ་མི་རུང་བས་
ན་དེ་ལ་བདག་མེད་པ་དང་། མི་རྟག་པ་སོགས་ལས་བརྩམས་ཏེ་ཆོས་བསྟན་ཅིང་དེ་
རིགས་པས་སྒྲུབ་དགོས་ཀྱི། སྙིང་པོ་བསྟན་པ་དོན་མེད་དེ་དེ་ཚུར་མཐོང་ཁོ་ནས་སྒྲུབ་
མི་ནུས་པས་སྒྲོ་སྐུར་གྱི་གནས་སུ་འགྱུར་བའི་ཕྱིར་རོ། །ནང་པའི་གྲུབ་མཐའ་འོག་མ་
ནས་བློ་སྦྱངས་ཏེ་སྟོང་པ་ཆེན་པོ་རྣམ་གྲངས་མིན་པའི་དོན་ལ་ངེས་པ་ཁྱད་པར་ཅན་སྐྱེས་
པ་དག་ལ་རིམ་བཞིན་བདེ་གཤེགས་སྙིང་པོའི་གཏམ་བསྟན་ན་གདོད་ཡིད་ཆེས་པར་
འགྱུར་རོ། །དེས་ན་ལམ་རྣམ་དག་ཡིན་ཀྱང་རིགས་པས་སྒྲུབ་མི་ནུས་ཏེ་མྱོང་བས་
རྟོགས་དགོས་སོ་ཞེས་པ་དང་། ཚུར་མཐོང་གི་ལམ་དུ་མ་གྱུར་ན་ལམ་ཡང་དག་མིན་
ནོ་སྙམ་པའི་རྨོངས་མཚང་བརྗོལ་ནས་ལམ་སྒྲུབ་ཚུལ་གྱི་གནད་ལ་མཁས་པར་བྱ་དགོས་
སོ། །ད་ནི་ཁམས་ཀྱི་རང་བཞིན་ལ་ལོག་པར་རྟོག་པའི་ཕྱོགས་འགའ་ཞིག་བཟློག་པ་
ལ། མི་སྟོང་པར་བདེན་གྲུབ་ཏུ་ལྟ་བ་བཟློག་པ། སྟོང་པ་ཕྱང་ཆད་དུ་ལྟ་བ་བཟློག་
པ། མི་རྟག་པར་འདུས་བྱས་སུ་འཛིན་པ་བཟློག་པའོ། །དང་པོ་ནི་ཇི་སྐད་དུ།
འཕགས་པ་ལང་ཀར་གཤེགས་པ་ལས། བྱང་སེམས་བློ་གྲོས་ཆེན་པོས་བཅོམ་ལྡན་
འདས་ལ་གསོལ་བ། སངས་རྒྱས་ཀྱིས་མདོ་སྡེ་ལས་དེ་བཞིན་གཤེགས་པའི་སྙིང་པོ་
དྲི་མའི་སྦུབས་སུ་གནས་པ་རྟག་བརྟན་ཐེར་ཟུག་ཏུ་གསུངས་པ་དེ་མུ་སྟེགས་བྱེད་ཀྱི་
བདག་ཏུ་སྨྲ་བ་དང་ཇི་ལྟར་མི་འདྲ་ལགས། མུ་སྟེགས་བྱེད་རྣམས་ཀྱང་ཡོན་ཏན་མེད་
པ་སོགས་ཀྱིས་བདག་ཏུ་སྨྲ་བ་ཡིན་ཅེས་དྲིས་པའི་ལན་དུ། བཅོམ་ལྡན་འདས་ཀྱི་
བཀའ་སྩལ་བ། དེ་ནི་མི་མཚུངས་ཏེ། སངས་རྒྱས་རྣམས་ཀྱིས་རྣམ་ཐར་སྒོ་
གསུམ་དང་མྱ་ངན་ལས་འདས་པ་དང་མ་སྐྱེས་པའི་ཚིག་གི་དོན་རྣམས་ལ་དེ་བཞིན་
གཤེགས་པའི་སྙིང་པོར་བསྟན་པར་བྱས་ནས། བྱིས་པ་རྣམས་བདག་མེད་པས་
འཇིགས་པར་གྱུར་པའི་གནས་རྣམ་པར་སྤང་བའི་དོན་དུ་དེ་བཞིན་གཤེགས་པའི་སྙིང་
པོའི་སྒོ་བསྟན་པའི་རྣམ་པར་མི་རྟོག་པའི་གནས་སྣང་བ་མེད་པའི་སྤྱོད་ཡུལ་སྟོན་ཏེ་འདི་

ལ་བློ་གྲོས་ཆེན་པོ། །མ་འོངས་པ་དང་ད་ལྟར་བྱུང་བའི་བྱང་ཆུབ་སེམས་དཔའ་སེམས་དཔའ་ཆེན་པོ་རྣམས་ཀྱིས་བདག་ཏུ་མངོན་པར་ཞེན་པར་མི་བྱའོ། །ཞེས་གསུངས་པ་དང་། གཞན་ཡང་དངོས་པོའི་འདུ་ཤེས་ཅན་ལ་ཐར་པ་མེད་པར་གསུངས་པ་དང་། རང་གི་ངོ་བོ་མ་སྟོང་ན་ཆོས་གཞན་གྱིས་སྟོང་པ་ཡོད་ཀྱང་སྟོང་གོ་མི་ཆོད་དེ། སྟོང་པ་བདུན་གྱི་ནང་ནས་ཐ་ཤལ་པ་གཅིག་གཅིག་གིས་སྟོང་པ་སྟེ། དེ་སྤང་བར་བྱ་ཞེས་སོགས་མཐའ་ཡས་པ་དང་། གཞན་ཡང་བློ་གྲོས་ཆེན་པོ་དེ་བཞིན་གཤེགས་པ་རྟག་པ་མ་ཡིན་མི་རྟག་པ་ཡང་མ་ཡིན་ནོ། །དེ་ཅིའི་ཕྱིར་ཞེ་ན་འདི་ལྟ་སྟེ་གཉིས་ཀར་ཡང་ཉེས་པར་འགྱུར་བའི་ཕྱིར་རོ། །ཞེས་དང་། སྤྲོས་པ་བདུད་ཀྱིས་བཟུང་བ་ཡིན། །ཡོད་དང་མེད་ལས་འདའ་བར་བྱ། །ཞེས་དང་། ཆོས་མཆོག་མྱ་ངན་འདས་པ་ལས་ལྷག་པའི་ཆོས་ཞིག་ཡོད་ན་དེ་ཡང་སྒྱུ་མ་དང་རྨི་ལམ་ལྟ་བུའོ། །ཞེས་པ་ལ་སོགས་པའི་ལུང་གི་དོན་དེ་བཞིན་དུ། རིགས་པས་དཔྱད་ན་ཡང་བདེ་གཤེགས་སྙིང་པོ་ངོ་བོ་སྟོང་པ་ཡིན་པའི་གནད་ཀྱིས་སེམས་ཀྱིས་སེམས་ཀྱི་ཆོས་ཉིད་དུ་རུང་བ། ཡུལ་ཐམས་ཅད་ཁྱབ་པ། དུས་ཇི་སྲིད་དུ་རྟག་པ། བསམ་གྱིས་མི་ཁྱབ་པ། ཡོན་ཏན་རྣམ་པ་ཐམས་ཅད་པར་རིས་མེད་དུ་འཆར་བ་ཡིན་གྱི། རང་གི་ངོ་བོ་མི་སྟོང་པར་བདེན་པར་གྲུབ་པ་ལ་ཆོས་གཞན་གྱི་ཆོས་ཉིད་དུ་རུང་བ་སོགས་རྣམ་པ་ཀུན་ཏུ་མི་སྲིད་ཅིང་དོན་དམ་དཔྱོད་པའི་ཚད་མས་གཏན་ལ་ཕབ་པའི་གྲུབ་འབྲས་སུ་ཡང་མི་བཏུབ་སྟེ་ཆོས་ཐམས་ཅད་བདེན་མེད་དུ་དཔྱོད་པའི་ལག་རྗེས་ལ་བདེན་གྲུབ་གཅིག་འགྲུབ་པ་ནི་སྣང་བ་ལས་མུན་པ་ལྟར་གནས་མ་ཡིན་པའི་ཕྱིར་རོ། །ཐ་སྙད་དཔྱོད་པའི་ཚད་མས་ཀྱང་བདེན་གྲུབ་མི་འགྲུབ་སྟེ། དེའི་ངོར་བདེན་པར་གྲུབ་ཀྱང་དེ་ཙམ་གྱིས་ཆོས་དེ་མི་སྟོང་པར་རྣམ་པ་ཀུན་ཏུ་འགྲུབ་མི་ནུས་པའི་ཕྱིར་རོ། །ཚད་མ་གཉིས་ཀྱིས་སྒྲུབ་མ་ནུས་པར་གྱུར་པ་ལ་སྒྲུབ་བྱེད་ནམ་མཁའི་མེ་ཏོག་གི་རྗེས་སུ་འགྲོ་བས་དེ་སྒྲུབ་པ་དོན་མེད་ཀྱི་ངལ་བར་ཟད་དོ། །གཉིས་པ་ནི། སྣང་སྟོང་ཟུང་འཇུག་གི་དབྱིངས་ཕྱོགས་མ་གོ་བ་དག་རྣམ་གྲངས་པའི་དོན་དམ་མེད་དགག་ཙམ་ལ་རིགས་དང་ཆོས་དབྱིངས་དང་སྟོང་ཉིད་དུ་བཟུང་ནས་ཡོན་ཏན་ཡེ་ལྡན་དུ་སྨྲ་བའི་

གཞུང་ལ་འགལ་བ་སྒྲུབ་པ་ནི་ཤིན་ཏུ་མི་རུང་སྟེ། ཡེ་ཤེས་ཕྱག་རྒྱའི་ཏིང་ངེ་འཛིན་གྱི་མདོ་ལས། ཆོས་འདོད་མ་ཡིན་རྙེད་པ་དོན་གཉེར་བ། །བསྡམས་པ་མིན་དག་བྱང་ཆུབ་སློབ་བོ་ཞེས། །སྨྲ་འགྱུར་ཁ་ཅིག་ཕྱི་མའི་དུས་འབྱུང་སྟེ། སྨྲ་ལ་དགའ་ཞིང་ཐམས་ཅད་སྟོང་ཞེས་སྨྲ། །ཞེས་དང་། སྟོང་ཉིད་མ་སྐྱེས་སུས་ཀྱང་བྱས་མ་ཡིན། །མ་མཐོང་འོང་བ་མ་ཡིན་འཕོ་མིན་ན། །དམིགས་གནས་བདག་ཅག་སྟོང་ཉིད་ལེགས་བསླབས་ཞེས། །འཛེར་པ་དེ་དག་ཆོས་ཀྱི་རྐུན་པོ་ཡིན། །ཞེས་དང་། མེད་པའི་ཆོས་ལ་ཡོངས་སུ་རྟོག་པ་ན། །བྱིས་པ་གང་ཡིན་གཡོ་བ་དེ་ཡིས་བཅིངས། །ཞེས་དང་། སྡུད་པ་ལས། ཕུང་འདི་སྟོང་ཞེས་རྟོགས་ནའང་བྱང་ཆུབ་སེམས་དཔའ་ན། །མཚན་མ་ལ་སྤྱོད་སྐྱེ་མེད་གནས་ལ་དད་མ་ཡིན། །ཞེས་དང་། ཏིང་འཛིན་རྒྱལ་པོ་ལས། ཡོད་དང་མེད་ཅེས་བྱ་བ་གཉིས་ཀ་མཐའ། །གཙང་དང་མི་གཙང་འདི་ཡང་མཐའ་ཡིན་ཏེ། །དེ་ཕྱིར་གཉིས་ཀའི་མཐའ་ནི་རབ་སྤངས་ནས། །མཁས་པ་དབུས་ལའང་གནས་པ་ཡོང་མི་བྱེད། །ཅེས་དང་། སེར་ཕྲེང་ལ་ཕན་པའི་མདོ་ལས། ཀྱེ་མ་འཇིག་རྟེན་ན་དམ་པའི་ཆོས་འཇིག་པའི་སྐྱེས་བུ་གཉིས་ཡོད་དེ། །གང་ཤིན་ཏུ་སྟོང་པ་ཉིད་དུ་ལྟ་བ་དང་། གང་འཇིག་རྟེན་ན་བདག་ཏུ་སྨྲ་བ་འདི་གཉིས་ནི་དམ་པའི་ཆོས་འཇིག་པ་དང་། དམ་པའི་ཆོས་ཁས་འབུབས་པའོ་ཞེས་དང་། ལྟ་བ་ཀུན་འབྱིན་བྱེད་ཀྱི་གཉེན་པོ་སྟོང་ཉིད་ལ་དངོས་དངོས་མེད་དུ་ཞེན་ན་གསོར་མི་རུང་བའི་ལྟ་བར་གསུངས་པ་དང་། སྟོང་མི་སྟོང་གང་ཡང་དམིགས་པ་ལས་མ་འདས་ལ་དེ་ཀུན་སྤང་དགོས་པར་མདོ་བསྟན་བཅོས་རྣམས་ལས་ཡང་ཡང་གསུངས་སོ། །རིགས་པས་བརྟགས་ན་ཡང་བདེན་གྲུབ་བཅད་ཙམ་གྱི་མེད་དགག་གི་ལྡོག་ཆ་དེ་དགག་བྱ་བཅད་པ་འཛིན་པའི་རྟོག་བཅས་ཀྱིས་བཏགས་པ་ཙམ་ལས་གནས་ལུགས་སྤྲོ་འདོགས་བྲལ་བའི་ཕྱོགས་སུ་མ་ཕྱིན་པར་གཏིང་རྙེད་སླ་བའི་ཕྱིར་འདིར་མང་དུ་བརྗོད་མི་དགོས་སོ། །བདེན་སྟོང་མེད་དགག་གི་ཆ་ཙམ་ཆོས་དབྱིངས་དང་གནས་ལུགས་མཚན་ཉིད་པ་མིན་ཀྱང་། ལས་དང་པོ་པས་དེ་ལ་འཇུག་པའི་སྒོ་ཙམ་དུ་ཡིད་ལ་བྱ་བར་འོས་པ་ཡིན་ཅིང་། མདོ་ལས། འཇམ་དཔལ་བྱང་ཆུབ

སེམས་དཔའ་གང་ལ་ལས་ལྷའི་ལོ་སྟོང་དུ་དཀོན་མཆོག་གསུམ་ལ་ཅི་དགོས་པ་བྱིན་པ
བས། བྱང་ཆུབ་སེམས་དཔའ་གཞན་ཞིག་ཐ་ན་སེ་གོལ་གཏོགས་པ་སྲིད་དུ་འདུ་བྱེད
ཐམས་ཅད་ནི་མི་རྟག་པའོ། །འདུ་བྱེད་ཐམས་ཅད་ནི་སྡུག་བསྔལ་བའོ། །འདུ་བྱེད
ཐམས་ཅད་ནི་སྟོང་པའོ། །འདུ་བྱེད་ཐམས་ཅད་ནི་བདག་མེད་པའོ་སྙམ་དུ་དཔྱོད་ན་དེ
དེ་བས་བསོད་ནམས་ཆེས་གྲངས་མེད་པ་སྐྱེད་པར་བྱེད་དོ། །ཞེས་གསུངས་པ་བཞིན
ནོ། །གསུམ་པ་ནི། གཞི་བདེ་བར་གཤེགས་པའི་སྙིང་པོ་ཉི་མ་སྤྲིན་དང་བྲལ་བ
ལྟར་ཇི་བཞིན་པ་མངོན་དུ་གྱུར་པའི་རྣམ་པ་ཐམས་ཅད་མཁྱེན་པའི་ཡེ་ཤེས་དེ་རྟག་མི་རྟག
གང་ཡིན་སྙམ་ན་མདོ་རྣམས་ལས་རྣམ་མཁྱེན་ཉིད་རེས་རྟག་པར་ཡང་གསུངས།
རེས་མི་རྟག་པར་ཡང་གསུངས་མོད་ཀྱི་དེའི་དོན་ནི་འདི་ལྟ་སྟེ། གནས་ཡོངས་སུ་མ
གྱུར་པའི་གདུལ་བྱ་གཞན་གྱི་བསམ་ངོ་དང་བསྟུན་ཏེ་རྣམ་མཁྱེན་མི་རྟག་ཅེས་ལུང་ལས
གསུངས་ཤིང་། རིགས་པ་ཡང་རྣམ་འགྲེལ་ལས། ཚད་མ་རྟག་པ་ཉིད་ཡོད
མིན། །དངོས་ཡོད་རྟོགས་པ་ཚད་ཕྱིར་དང་། །ཤེས་བྱ་མི་རྟག་པ་ཉིད་ཀྱི། །དེ
མི་རྟག་པ་ཉིད་ཕྱིར་རོ། །ཞེས་གསུངས་ཏེ། སེམས་བསྐྱེད་པ་དང་སྟོང་ཉིད
གོམས་པ་ལ་སོགས་ལམ་གྱི་རྒྱུ་ལས་རྣམ་མཁྱེན་འབྱུང་གི་རྒྱུ་མེད་དུ་འབྱུང་བ་མི་རིགས
པ་དང་། དེ་ཆོས་ཐམས་ཅད་ལ་མངོན་སུམ་པའི་ཚད་མ་ཡིན་པའི་ཕྱིར། ཚད་མ
སྟེ་མི་བསླུ་བའི་བློ་ཡིན་ན་རྟག་པ་ཞིག་མེད་དེ་དངོས་པོ་ཡོད་པ་ལ་དེ་དེ་བཞིན་འཇལ་བ
ཚད་མ་ཡིན་ལ། དེའི་ཡུལ་ཤེས་བྱ་ནི་མི་རྟག་པ་ཉིད་ཀྱི་ཕྱིར་འཇལ་བྱེད་ཚད་མ་དེ
ཡང་མི་རྟག་སྟེ་རིམ་ཅན་དུ་འབྱུང་གི རྟག་པ་ཡིན་ན་དོན་བྱེད་པའི་ནུས་པས་སྟོང
པར་ཚད་མས་གྲུབ་པའི་ཕྱིར་ཡུལ་འཇལ་བ་ལ་སོགས་པའི་བྱེད་པ་མཐའ་དག་གིས་སྟོང
པར་ངེས་པས་ན་རྣམ་མཁྱེན་ནི་རྟག་པར་ཤིན་ཏུ་མི་རིགས་ཏེ་མི་རྟག་པར་འགྲུབ་ལ།
དེ་བཞིན་དངོས་པོ་ཐམས་ཅད་མི་རྟག་པ་དང་། དངོས་མེད་ལ་རྟག་པར་བཏགས་ཀྱང
རྟག་རྒྱུའི་གཞི་མེད་པས་རྟག་པ་མཚན་ཉིད་པའི་ཆོས་གང་ཡང་མི་རྙེད་པར་འགྱུར
རོ། །ཚུལ་འདི་ནི་ཕྱི་རོལ་མུ་སྟེགས་ཅན་དང་། བསམ་གྱིས་མི་ཁྱབ་པའི་ཆོས
ཉིད་ཀྱི་ངོ་བོར་གནས་གྱུར་པའི་ཚུལ་ལ་བློ་མ་སྦྱངས་པའི་ཐེག་པ་ཐུན་མོང་པའི་ངོར་དེ

ལྟར་སྒྲུབ་དགོས་ཏེ། རྣམ་ཤེས་ཀྱི་ངོར་སྣང་ཚུལ་ལ་དེ་ལས་གཞན་དུ་འཆར་བའི་ཐབས་ཅི་ཡང་མེད་དོ། །འོན་ཀྱང་གནས་ཡོངས་སུ་གྱུར་པའི་ཡེ་ཤེས་ཀྱི་གཟིགས་པའི་དབང་དུ་བྱས་ན་རྣམ་མཁྱེན་རྟག་པར་འགྲུབ་སྟེ། དེ་མི་རྟག་པའི་སྒྲུབ་བྱེད་དུ་བཀོད་པའི་ཤེས་བྱ་སྐད་ཅིག་མར་སྐྱེ་འགག་བྱེད་པ་དང་། ཡུལ་ཅན་ཡེ་ཤེས་ཀྱང་སྐད་ཅིག་རིམ་ཅན་དུ་འབྱུང་བ་སོགས་ནི་གནས་ཡོངས་སུ་མ་གྱུར་པ་རྣམས་ཀྱི་སྣང་ངོར་དེ་ལྟར་སྣང་བར་ཟད་ཀྱི། གནས་ཚུལ་དོན་ལ་དེ་ཁོ་ན་ལྟར་གྲུབ་པ་ནི་མ་ཡིན་ཏེ། ཆོས་གང་ཡང་སྐད་ཅིག་གཅིག་ཏུ་སྐྱེ་བའང་མེད་ན། དེས་བརྩམས་པའི་དུས་ཀྱི་གོ་རིམ་སོགས་མ་གྲུབ་པ་ལྟ་ཅི་སྨོས་ཏེ། དཔེར་ན་རྨི་ལམ་རང་ངོའི་སྣང་བ་ལ་སྔ་ཕྱིའི་དུས་ཀྱི་མཐའ་དང་ཕྱོགས་ཀྱི་ཆ་མུ་མེད་པར་སྣ་ཚོགས་སུ་སྣང་ཡང་དེ་ལྟར་མ་གྲུབ་པ་བཞིན་ནོ། །དེས་ན་ཆོས་ཉིད་སྐྱེ་འགག་མེད་པའི་དོན་དེ་བཞིན་དུ་གནས་ཡོངས་སུ་གྱུར་པའི་ཡེ་ཤེས་མཐར་ཐུག་པ་ན། ཤེས་དང་ཤེས་བྱ་དབྱེར་མེད་པའི་ཡེ་ཤེས་ཀྱི་སྐུ་ཡིན་ཅིང་། གནས་མ་གྱུར་པའི་སྐབས་ན་ཡང་སེམས་ཀྱི་གཤིས་སམ་ཆོས་ཉིད་ཟུང་འཇུག་རང་བཞིན་གྱིས་འོད་གསལ་བ་ནི་འགྱུར་བ་མེད་པའི་ཕྱིར། སྔ་ཕྱིའི་ཁྱད་མེད་པར་རང་བཞིན་དུ་གནས་པའི་རིགས་ཞེས་བྱ་ལ། འགྱུར་བཅས་གློ་བུར་འབྲལ་རུང་གི་དྲི་མ་གང་དག་སྐད་ཅིག་མའི་སྐྱེ་འགག་རིམ་གྱིས་འབྱུང་བ་དང་། འཁོར་འདས་དང་བཟང་ངན་ལ་སོགས་པའི་མི་མཉམ་པ་འདི་ནི་གནས་མ་གྱུར་པའི་གཉིས་སྣང་ཅན་ལ་དེ་ལྟར་བསླུ་མེད་བསློན་མེད་དུ་སྣང་ཡང་། གཤིས་ལ་སྐྱེ་འགག་དང་གཉིས་ཆོས་མ་གྲུབ་པར་མཉམ་པ་ཆེན་པོར་གནས་པ། དེའི་ངང་དུ་ཕྱོགས་ཀྱི་ཆ་དང་དུས་ཀྱི་འགྱུར་བ་ཐམས་ཅད་ཁྱབ་ཆུབ་ཅིང་། དེ་ནི་འཕགས་པ་རྣམས་ཀྱི་སོ་སོ་རང་རིག་པའི་ཡེ་ཤེས་ཀྱི་ཡུལ་དུ་ཡོད་པ་ཡིན་ཅིང་། དུས་གསུམ་གྱི་འགྱུར་བས་བསླད་དུ་མེད་པས་ན་དེ་ལ་རྟག་པ་ཆེན་པོའི་ཐ་སྙད་ཅིས་མི་གདགས་ཏེ། ཡོད་པ་གང་ཞིག་སྐད་ཅིག་གི་སྐྱེ་འགག་ཅན་མིན་པའི་ཕྱིར་རོ། །འདི་ལྟར་འགྱུར་བ་ཅན་དངོས་པོ་ཐམས་ཅད་དང་དངོས་མེད་ནམ་མཁའ་ལ་སོགས་པ་ཕྱོགས་དུས་ཀྱི་ཤེས་བྱ་ཐམས་ཅད་རོ་མཉམ་པར་ཆོས་ཉིད་དེའི་ཁོངས་སུ་ཆུད་ཀྱང་། ཆོས་ཉིད་དེ་འགྱུར་བ་ཅན་ལ་སོགས་པའི་ཆོས་

ཅན་གང་གིས་ཀྱང་བསྒྱུས་པ་མ་ཡིན་ཏེ། དཔེར་ན་ནམ་མཁའི་ཁོངས་སུ་སྤྲིན་འདུས་ཀྱང་། སྤྲིན་གྱི་ཁོངས་སུ་ནམ་མཁའ་མི་འདུས་པ་བཞིན་ནོ། །དེས་ན་ཆོས་ཉིད་མཉམ་པ་ཆེན་པོ་དབྱིངས་འོད་གསལ་བའི་གཤིས་དེ་ནི་རང་བྱུང་གི་ཡེ་ཤེས་ཉག་གཅིག་གིས་རང་བཞིན་གྱིས་དངོས་པོ་ཀུན་ལ་ཁྱབ་པར་ལྷུན་སྐྱེས་སུ་གནས་ཀྱང་། །གློ་བུར་གྱི་དྲི་མ་ཅན་ལ་རང་གི་རང་བཞིན་མངོན་དུ་མ་གྱུར་པ་ན། དྲི་མ་དེ་སེལ་བྱེད་ལམ་ལྷུས་བསྒྱུས་པའི་སྦྱང་རྟོགས་ཀྱི་མཐུ་ལས་ཤེས་དང་ཤེས་བྱ་དབྱེར་མེད་པའི་ཡེ་ཤེས་ཆེན་པོ་དེ་ཐོབ་པ་ན། རང་བྱུང་གི་ཡེ་ཤེས་འགྱུར་བ་མེད་པའི་ཤེས་པ་ཐམས་ཅད་ཆོས་ཉིད་ཀྱི་གཤིས་སུ་རོ་མཉམ་པར་མི་རྟོག་བཞིན་འབད་མེད་ལྷུན་གྲུབ་ཏུ་མཁྱེན་པའི་རྣམ་པ་ཐམས་ཅད་མཁྱེན་པའི་ཡེ་ཤེས་འཐོབ་བོ། །འོན་ཀྱང་ཚུལ་དེས་རང་བྱུང་གི་ཡེ་ཤེས་རྒྱུ་ལས་སྐྱེས་པར་མི་འགྱུར་ཏེ། ཡང་དག་པར་གློ་བུར་དྲི་བྲལ་གྱི་ཆོས་སྐུ་དེ་བྲལ་བའི་འབྲས་བུར་སོང་བ་ཡིན་ལ། རྒྱུ་ལས་གསར་དུ་སྐྱེ་བ་ལྟར་སྣང་བ་ཡང་གནས་མ་གྱུར་པའི་སྣང་ཚུལ་ལ་དེ་ལྟར་སྣང་བར་ཟད་ཀྱི། ཡང་དག་པའི་དོན་དུ་ཆོས་ཉིད་ཀྱི་རང་བཞིན་ཆོས་ཀྱི་སྐུའི་ངོ་བོ་ལ་སྐྱེ་འཇིག་མེད་པར་ཆོས་ཐམས་ཅད་གདོད་ནས་མཉམ་པ་ཉིད་དུ་མངོན་པར་སངས་རྒྱས་པའམ། གཟོད་མ་ནས་ཞི་བ་མྱ་ངན་ལས་འདས་པ། རང་བཞིན་གྱིས་འོད་གསལ་བ་སོགས་ཟབ་མོའི་མདོ་སྡེ་རྣམས་ཀྱི་དགོངས་པ་མཐར་ཐུག་འདི་དག་པའི་སེམས་དཔའ་རྣམས་ཀྱིས་ཀྱང་བསམ་པར་དཀའ་བའི་གནས་ཡིན་ན་ཕལ་པས་ལྟ་ཅི་སྨོས། འོན་ཀྱང་ཚུལ་བཞིན་ཡིད་ཆེས་སྐྱེས་ན་ཕྱིར་མི་ལྡོག་པར་ལུང་བསྟན་ཐོབ་པ་དང་མཚུངས་པར་བསྔགས་པའི་ཕྱིར་ཚུལ་འདི་ལ་མོས་པར་བྱའོ། །ཚུལ་དེ་ལྟར་དེ་བཞིན་གཤེགས་པའི་ཡེ་ཤེས་ཀྱི་སྐུ་རྟག་པར་བལྟས་ན་བསོད་ནམས་འབྱུང་སྟེ། རབ་ཏུ་ཞི་བ་རྣམ་པར་ངེས་པའི་ཆོ་འཕྲུལ་གྱིས་ཏིང་ངེ་འཛིན་ཞེས་པའི་མདོ་ལས་འཇམ་དཔལ་རིགས་ཀྱི་བུའམ་རིགས་ཀྱི་བུ་མོ་གང་ལ་ལས་ལྷའི་བསྐལ་པ་བྱེ་བར་ཕྱོགས་བཅུའི་འཇིག་རྟེན་གྱི་ཁམས་རེ་རེར་འཁོར་བཞི་ལ་ཅི་འདོད་པའི་སྦྱིན་པ་བྱིན་པས། རིགས་ཀྱི་བུའམ་རིགས་ཀྱི་བུ་མོ་གང་གཞན་གྱིས་མཐུན་པར་བྱ་བའི་དོན་དུ་གཡོས། དེ་བཞིན་གཤེགས་པ་ནི་རྟག་པའོ། །དེ་བཞིན་གཤེགས་པ་ནི་གཡུང་དྲུང་

ངོ། །ཞེས་ཚིག་ཏུ་སྨྲ་ན་ཡང་དེ་དེ་བས་ཆེས་བསོད་ནམས་གྲངས་མེད་པ་སྐྱེད་པར་བྱེད་དོ། །ཞེས་དང་། མྱ་ངན་ལས་འདས་པ་ཆེན་པོའི་མདོ་ལས། འོད་སྲུང་རིགས་ཀྱི་བུའམ་རིགས་ཀྱི་བུ་མོ་དག་གི་རྟག་ཏུ་རྩེ་གཅིག་པའི་སེམས་ཀྱིས་སངས་རྒྱས་རྟག་པ་དང་གནས་པའོ་ཞེས་བྱ་བའི་ཚིག་འདི་གཉིས་ལ་ནན་ཏན་བྱའོ། །ཞེས་དང་། གང་གིས་བསམ་གྱིས་མི་ཁྱབ་པ་དེ་ལ་རྟག་པའི་འདུ་ཤེས་ཀྱིས་ནན་ཏན་བྱེད་ན་དེ་ནི་སྐྱབས་སུ་འགྲོ་བའི་གནས་ཡིན་ནོ། །ཞེས་སོགས་དང་། དེ་བཞིན་གཤེགས་པའི་སྐུ་ལ་མི་རྟག་པར་བལྟ་བ་ལ་སྐྱབས་འགྲོ་ཙམ་ཡང་མེད་པ་དང་། རྡོ་རྗེའི་སྐུ་ལ་མི་རྟག་པར་བལྟས་ན་ཉེས་དམིགས་ཚད་མེད་པ་འབྱུང་བར་མདོ་ལས་གསུངས་པ་ལྟར་ཤེས་པར་བྱས་ནས་ཡང་དག་པའི་དོན་ལ་གུས་པར་བྱ་དགོས་སོ། །དེ་ལྟར་བདེ་བར་གཤེགས་པའི་སྙིང་པོ་རང་གི་ངོ་བོ་ནི་ཡོད་མེད་རྟག་ཆད་ལ་སོགས་པའི་སྤྲོས་པ་ཐམས་ཅད་བྲལ་བ་བདེན་པ་དབྱེར་མེད་ཐིག་ལེ་ཉག་གཅིག་མཉམ་པ་ཉིད་དེ། གནས་ལུགས་དེའི་ངང་དུ་སྣང་སྲིད་ཀྱི་ཆོས་ཐམས་ཅད་རོ་གཅིག་པ་དེ་ཁོ་ན་ཉིད་དུ་གྱུར་པ་དེ་དེ་བཞིན་དུ་མཐོང་བ་ནི་ཡང་དག་པ་བསལ་བཞག་མེད་པའི་དོན་མཐོང་བས་འཛིན་པ་མཐའ་དག་དང་བྲལ་བ་ནི་དོན་དམ་རྟོགས་པའི་ལྟ་བ་བཟང་པོ་སྟེ། བྱང་ཆུབ་ཀྱི་ཕྱོགས་བསྟན་པ་ཞེས་པའི་མདོ་ལས་འཇམ་དཔལ་སུས་ཆོས་ཐམས་ཅད་མི་མཉམ་པ་མེད་ལ་གཉིས་སུ་མེད་ཅིང་གཉིས་སུ་མེད་པར་མཐོང་བ་འདི་ནི་ཡང་དག་པའི་ལྟ་བའོ། །ཞེས་དང་། ནམ་མཁའ་མཛོད་ཀྱིས་ཞུས་པའི་མདོ་ལས། དངོས་དང་དངོས་མེད་རྣམ་ཤེས་ཤིང་། །ཡང་དག་མཐའ་ལ་གང་གནས་པ། །དངོས་པོ་དང་ནི་དངོས་མེད་པ། །ལྟ་བ་མཁས་པས་མི་འཛིན་ཏོ། །ཞེས་དང་། བྱང་ཆུབ་སེམས་དཔའི་སྡེ་སྣོད་ལས། དོན་དམ་པར་འཕགས་པའི་ཤེས་རབ་དང་ཡེ་ཤེས་ཀྱི་མདུན་ན་ཆོས་གང་ཡང་ཡོངས་སུ་ཤེས་པའམ། སྤང་པའམ་བསྒོམ་པའམ་མངོན་དུ་བྱ་བར་འགྱུར་བ་ནི་ཆོས་གང་ཡང་མི་འདུག་གོ། །ཞེས་གསུངས་པ་བཞིན་ནོ། །འོན་ཀྱང་ཐ་སྙད་དཔྱོད་པའི་ཚད་མས་ཤན་ལེགས་པར་འབྱེད་པའི་སྐབས་སུ་བདེན་པ་ལ་བདེན་པར་ཤེས་པ་འཕགས་པའི་ལམ་མི་བསླུ་བར་ཤེས་པ་ལྟ་བུ་དང་། མི་བདེན་པ་ལ་མི་བདེན་པར་

ཤེས་པ་བདག་བསྒོམས་པས་གྲོལ་བར་སྨྲ་བ་ལ་ལོག་པར་ཤེས་པ་ལྟ་བུ་དང་། མི་རྟག་པ་ལ་མི་རྟག་པར་ཤེས་པ་འདུས་བྱས་ཀྱི་དངོས་པོ་ཐམས་ཅད་སྐད་ཅིག་མར་ཤེས་པ་དང་། རྟག་པ་ལ་རྟག་པར་ཤེས་པ་བདེ་གཤེགས་སྙིང་པོ་རང་བྱུང་གི་ཡེ་ཤེས་རྣམ་པ་ཐམས་ཅད་པ་མི་འགྱུར་བར་ཤེས་པ་དང་། མེད་པ་ལ་མེད་པར་ཤེས་པ་བདག་དང་གཟུང་འཛིན་དུ་སྣང་བ་རང་བཞིན་མ་གྲུབ་པར་ཤེས་པ་ལྟ་བུ་དང་། ཡོད་པ་ལ་ཡོད་པར་འཛིན་པ་རྒྱུ་འབྲས་བསླུ་མེད་རྟེན་འབྲེལ་གྱི་སྣང་ཚུལ་དང་། སེམས་ཅན་ཐམས་ཅད་ལ་ཆོས་ཉིད་བདེ་གཤེགས་སྙིང་པོ་ལྷུན་གྱིས་གྲུབ་པའི་ཡོན་ཏན་རང་བཞིན་གྱིས་གནས་པར་ཤེས་པ་ལྟ་བུ་ལ་སོགས་པ་ནི་ཐ་སྙད་དུ་དངོས་པོའི་ཡིན་ལུགས་ལ་ཕྱིན་ཅི་མ་ལོག་པའི་ཤེས་རབ་ཀྱི་འཛིན་སྟངས་ཡིན་པས་དེ་ལྟར་ཤེས་ཤིང་བཞུགས་པ་ལས་ཡོན་ཏན་རྒྱ་ཆེན་པོ་ཐོབ་སྟེ་གཏི་མུག་མེད་པའི་དགེ་བའི་རྩ་བ་ཡིན་པའི་ཕྱིར་རོ། །དེ་ལྟར་མདོ་སྡེ་རྣམས་ལས་ཀྱང་སྤྱིར་བཏང་དང་དམིགས་ཀྱིས་བསལ་བའི་སྒོ་ནས་ཆོས་དུ་མ་བསྟན་ཅིང་། ཁྱད་པར་དུ་གང་ཟག་གི་བདག་མེད་ཀྱང་། བདག་དང་བདག་མེད་ཀྱི་སྤྲོས་པ་གཉིས་ལས་འདས་པའི་བདེ་གཤེགས་སྙིང་པོ་ནི་བདག་ཆེན་པོར་གསུངས་པ་སོགས་གཙང་བདེ་རྟག་བདག་གི་ཕ་རོལ་ཏུ་ཕྱིན་པའི་ཡོན་ཏན་མཆོག་ཏུ་བསྟན་པ་ནི་མི་གནས་པའི་མྱང་འདས་ཆེན་པོ་ཞི་བ་བསིལ་བ་གྲུ་ནོམ་པ་མཐར་ཐུག་པའི་ཡོན་ཏན་འགྱུར་བ་མེད་པ་ཡོད་པ་ལ་ཡོད་པར་ཤེས་པའི་སྐད་དུ་སྟེ། མྱ་ངན་ལས་འདས་པའི་མདོ་ལས། བདག་ཅེས་བྱ་བ་ནི་ཆོས་གང་བདེན་པ་ཡང་དག་པར་རྟག་པ། བདག་པོར་གྱུར་པ་མི་འགྱུར་མི་འཕོ་བ་དེ་ནི་བདག་ཅེས་བྱ་སྟེ། ཞེས་སོགས་གསུངས་པ་བཞིན་ནོ། །དེ་ལྟར་ཟབ་མོ་བདེ་གཤེགས་སྙིང་པོའི་ཚུལ་འདི་བཤད་པ་ཐོས་ནས་མོས་པ་ཙམ་ལའང་ཕན་ཡོན་ཚད་མེད་པ་འབྱུང་སྟེ་རྒྱུད་བླ་མ་ལས། བློ་ལྡན་རྒྱལ་བའི་ཡུལ་དེ་ལ་མོས་པ། །སངས་རྒྱས་ཡོན་ཏན་ཚོགས་ཀྱི་སྣོད་འགྱུར་ཏེ། །བསམ་མེད་ཡོན་ཏན་ཚོགས་ལ་མངོན་དགའ་བས། །སེམས་ཅན་ཀུན་གྱི་བསོད་ནམས་ཟིལ་གྱིས་གནོན། །གང་ཞིག་བྱང་ཆུབ་དོན་དུ་གཉེར་བས་གསེར་ཞིང་ནོར་བུས་སྤྲས་པ་ན། །སངས་རྒྱས་ཞིང་རྡུལ་མཉམ་པ་ཉིན་རེ་ཆོས་རྒྱལ་རྣམས་ལ་རྟག་འབུལ་ན། །

གཞན་གང་འདི་ལས་ཚིག་ཙམ་ཐོས་ཤིང་ཐོས་ནས་ཀྱང་ནི་མོས་ན་འདད། །སྦྱིན་པ་ལས་བྱུང་དགེ་བ་དེ་ལས་བསོད་ནམས་ཆེས་མང་ཐོབ་པར་འགྱུར། །བློ་ལྡན་གང་ཞིག་བླ་མེད་བྱང་ཆུབ་འདོད་པས་བསྐལ་པ་དུ་མར་ཡང་། །ལུས་ངག་ཡིད་ཀྱི་འབད་པ་མེད་པར་ཚུལ་ཁྲིམས་དྲི་མེད་སྲུང་བྱེད་པ། །གཞན་གང་འདི་ལས་ཚིག་ཙམ་ཐོས་ནས་ཀྱང་ནི་མོས་ན་འདད། །ཚུལ་ཁྲིམས་ལས་བྱུང་དགེ་བ་དེ་ལས་བསོད་ནམས་ཆེས་མང་ཐོབ་པར་འགྱུར། །གང་ཞིག་འདི་ན་སྲིད་པ་གསུམ་གྱི་ཉོན་མོངས་མེ་འཇིལ་བསམ་གཏན་ན། །ལྷ་དང་ཚངས་གནས་མཐར་སོན་རྫོགས་པའི་བྱང་ཆུབ་འཕོ་མེད་ཐབས་བསྒོམས་ལ། །གཞན་གང་འདི་ལས་ཚིག་ཙམ་ཐོས་ཤིང་ཐོས་ནས་ཀྱང་ནི་མོས་ན་འདད། །བསམ་གཏན་ལས་བྱུང་དགེ་བ་དེ་ལས་བསོད་ནམས་ཆེས་མང་ཐོབ་པར་འགྱུར། །ཞེས་གསུངས་པ་བཞིན་ནོ། །དེ་ལྟར་ཟབ་ཅིང་གཏིང་དཔག་དཀའ་ལ། ཤེས་ཤིང་མོས་ན་དོན་ཆེ་ཞིང་ཐེག་པ་མཆོག་གི་སྙིང་པོ་ཕྱིར་མི་ལྡོག་པའི་སེང་གེའི་སྒྲ་བདེ་བར་གཤེགས་པའི་སྙིང་པོའི་གཏམ་བསྟན་པ་འདི་ནི་ཆོས་ཟབ་མོ་ཡུལ་དུ་བྱུང་བའི་ཕྱིར། ཐོན་སྦྱངས་ཆུང་ཞིང་བློ་དམན་པ་དག་མོས་པར་དཀའ་སྟེ། དེ་བཞིན་གཤེགས་པ་འགྲོ་བའི་མདོ་ལས། ང་ཡི་ཡེ་ཤེས་འདི་ལ་ནི། །བྱིས་པའི་བློ་ཅན་ཐེ་ཚོམ་ཟ། །གནས་མི་འགྱུར་ཏེ་ནམ་མཁའ་ལ། །ཇི་ལྟར་མདའ་འཕངས་ལྟུང་བ་བཞིན། །ཞེས་དང་། རྣམ་པར་འཐག་པ་བསྡུས་པའི་མདོ་ལས། དེ་ལྟར་མི་བླུན་པོ་དེ་དག་ངན་སོང་དུ་འགྲོ་བར་བདུད་ཀྱིས་བྱིན་གྱིས་བརླབ་པའི་ཕྱིར། དེ་ལའང་སྐྱོན་འདོགས་པར་སེམས་སོ། །དེ་བཞིན་གཤེགས་པས་གསུང་བའི་ཆོས་སྨྲ་བ་དེ་དག་ལ་ཡང་སྐྱོན་འདོགས་པར་སེམས་སོ། །ཞེས་དང་། ཚངས་པ་བྱིན་གྱིས་ཞུས་པ་ལས། ལེགས་པར་གསུངས་པའི་ཆོས་ནི་སྟོན་པ་ན། །སྡིག་པའི་སྤྱོད་ཡུལ་ཅན་ཏེ་མི་འཐད་འཛིན། །དད་མེད་ཆོས་ལ་སོམ་ཉི་བསྐྱེད་ན་ན། །བསྐལ་བ་བྱེ་བ་མང་པོར་སྨྱོན་པར་འགྱུར། །མ་དད་པ་ཡི་བསམ་པས་སྡིག་ཅན་འགྱུར། །བློ་སྡང་གང་གི་ཡིད་ཀྱང་སྲུང་མི་བྱེད། །སྙིང་པོ་ཅན་ཀུན་རྣམ་པར་སྤངས་ནས་ན། ། དད་པ་མེད་པས་སྙིགས་མ་འཛིན་པར་བྱེད། །འཁྲིང་བར་བྱེད་ཅིང་རྟག་ཏུ་ཁེངས་པ་

སྟེ། །མ་དད་དེ་ནི་གཞན་ལ་འདུད་མི་བྱེད། །ཅེས་དང་། དེ་དག་ཆོས་མིན་ཚིག་གིས་འགལ་བར་བྱེད། །རྒྱལ་བ་རྣམས་ཀྱི་བསྟན་ལ་དྲི་མ་དེས། །སྨུ་སྟེགས་ཅན་ལྟར་ཐེ་ཚོམ་སོམ་ཉི་བཅས། །དེས་ནི་ཆོས་ལ་ཀླགས་གཏོང་འགལ་བྱས་ནས། །དད་མེད་དེ་ནི་ཆོས་ཀྱང་སྤོང་བར་བྱེད། །ཅེས་དང་། ཚུལ་འཆལ་ཚར་གཅོད་པའི་མདོ་ལས། ཤཱ་རིའི་བུ། འཚོ་བའི་ལམ་དུ་བྱིང་བ། སྟོད་པ་ལ་ཞེན་པ། བདག་དང་གཞན་ལ་གནོད་པ་བྱེད་པ་སྐྱེས་བུ་དམ་པ་མ་ཡིན་པ་དེ་ལྟ་བུ་དག་གིས་འཛམ་བུའི་གླིང་འདི་རབ་ཏུ་གང་བར་འགྱུར་རོ། །ཞེས་སོགས་གསུངས་པའི་ཚུལ་ལ་བསམས་ཏེ་དུས་ཀྱི་སྙིགས་མ་བདོ་ཞིང་བསྟན་ཞབས་སུ་སྐྱེས་པ་རྣམས་ཧོན་པ་བཞི་གོ་ལོག་པའི་ཚུལ་གྱིས་ཐེག་པ་མཆོག་གི་རིང་ལུགས་ཀྱི་གནད་ཕར་ཆེར་ཉམས་ཤིང་ཆོས་ལྟར་བཅོས་པ་བྱུང་བ་ན། ཐེག་ཆེན་ལམ་གྱི་སྲོག་ལྟ་བུ་འདི་ལ་ཕངས་པའི་སེམས་སུ་བྱེད་པའང་དཀོན་མོད་ཀྱི། སྔ་འགྱུར་རིག་འཛིན་བརྒྱུད་པའི་བསྟན་ཞབས་སུ་སྐྱེས་པའི་སྟོབས་ཀྱིས། བརྒྱུད་པའི་ཞལ་ལུང་རིན་པོ་ཆེ་དུ་མ་མཐོང་ཞིང་ཐོས་པ་དང་། རྒྱལ་དབང་པདྨའི་རྒྱལ་ཚབ་འཇམ་དཔལ་གཞོན་ནུ་མི་ཡི་རྣམ་པར་རོལ་པ་ཀུན་མཁྱེན་རྡོ་རྗེ་གཟི་བརྗིད་སོགས་ཡང་དག་པ་དགེ་བའི་བཤེས་གཉེན་དུ་མའི་ཞབས་པད་སྤྱི་བོས་ལེན་པའི་སྐལ་བ་བཟང་པོར་གྱུར་པའི་མཐུ་ལས་ན་ཚོད་དང་བློ་གྲོས་མ་སྨིན་པ་བདག་ཀྱང་ཟབ་མོའི་གནས་འདི་ལ་ཅུང་ཟད་སྤོབས་པ་སྐྱེས་པ་ཡིན་ནོ། །འདི་ལྟར་མཐའ་ཀུན་བྲལ་བའི་ཟུང་འཇུག་རབ་ཏུ་མི་གནས་པའི་ཚུལ་ཆོས་ཀྱི་དབྱིངས་རང་བཞིན་དུ་གནས་པ་རིགས་ཀྱི་དོན་ལེགས་པར་སྨྲ་བ་འདི་ནི་སེང་གེའི་སྒྲ་ཡིན་ཏེ། ཚངས་པ་ཁྱད་པར་སེམས་ཀྱིས་ཞུས་པའི་མདོ་ལས། ལྷའི་བུ་ཆོས་གང་ལ་ཡང་མངོན་པར་མ་ཆགས་པར་བརྗོད་པ་དེ་དག་སེང་གེའི་སྒྲ་ཡིན་ནོ། །གང་དེ་ལྟ་བུ་ལ་མངོན་པར་ཆགས་པར་བརྗོད་པ་དེ་དག་ནི་སེང་གེའི་སྒྲ་མ་ཡིན་ཏེ་ཝའི་སྒྲའོ། །གང་ལྟ་བ་ཀུན་ཏུ་སློང་བ་སྟོན་པ་དེ་དག་ལ་སེང་གེའི་སྒྲ་མེད་དོ། །ཞེས་དང་། མདོ་མྱང་འདས་ཆེན་པོ་ལས། སེང་གེའི་སྒྲ་སྒྲོགས་པ་ནི་སེམས་ཅན་ཐམས་ཅད་ལ་སངས་རྒྱས་ཀྱི་རང་བཞིན་ཡོད་པ་དང་། དེ་བཞིན་གཤེགས་པ་རྟག་ཏུ་གནས་ཤིང་མི་འགྱུར་བར་ངེས་པར་

བཤད་པའོ། །ཞེས་དང་། རིགས་ཀྱི་བུ་གནས་སྟོང་པར་མང་དུ་བཤད་ཀྱང་སེང་
གེའི་སྒྲ་བསྒྲགས་པ་ཞེས་མི་བྱ་སྟེ། མཁས་པ་ཤེས་རབ་ཅན་གྱི་འཁོར་མང་པོའི་ནང་
དུ་བསྒྲགས་པ་ནི་སེང་གེའི་སྒྲ་ཆེན་པོ་སྒྲོགས་པ་ཞེས་བྱའོ། །དེ་ལ་སེང་གེའི་སྒྲ་
སྒྲོགས་པ་ནི་ཆོས་ཐམས་ཅད་མི་རྟག་པ་སྡུག་བསྔལ་བ་བདག་མེད་པ་ཡོངས་སུ་མ་དག
པ་ཞེས་མི་འཆད་དེ། དེ་བཞིན་གཤེགས་པ་རྟག་པ་བདེ་བ་བདག་དང་ཡོངས་སུ་དག
པ་འབའ་ཞིག་འཆད་དོ། །ཞེས་སོགས་སེང་གེའི་སྒྲ་བསྒྲགས་པའི་དཔེ་དོན་རྒྱ་ཆེར་
གསུངས་པས་མཚོན་ཏེ་ཤེས་པར་བྱའོ། །གལ་ཏེ་དེ་ལྟར་བདེ་བར་གཤེགས་པའི་རང་
ལམ་དྲང་པོར་སྨྲས་པ་ཁ་ཅིག་དང་མ་མཐུན་ཡང་། ཡང་དག་པའི་ལམ་རྣམ་པར་
བཞག་པ་ཡིན་པས་གཞན་ཁོང་འཁྲུགས་པར་མི་བྱ་སྟེ། དབུ་མ་ལ་འཇུག་པ་ལས།
བསྟན་བཅོས་ལས་དཔྱད་རྩོད་ལ་ཆགས་པའི་ཕྱིར། །མ་མཛད་རྣམ་གྲོལ་ཕྱིར་ནི་དེ་
ཉིད་བསྟན། །གལ་ཏེ་དེ་ཉིད་རྣམ་པར་བཤད་པ་ན། །གཞན་གཞུང་འཇིག་པར་
འགྱུར་ན་ཉེས་པ་མེད། །ཅེས་པ་ལྟར་རོ། །དེ་ལྟ་བུའི་ཚུལ་འདི་ཆོས་སྲུང་བའང་
ཡིན་ཏེ། ཏིང་འཛིན་རྒྱལ་པོ་ལས། དེ་ལ་ཆོས་སྲུང་བ་གང་ཞེ་ན། འདི་ལྟ་སྟེ་
སངས་རྒྱས་ཀྱི་ཆོས་ལ་སྨོད་པ་རྣམས་ཆོས་དང་མཐུན་པར་ཚར་གཅོད་པའོ། །ཞེས་
དང་། ཆོས་འཛིན་པ་ཡང་ཡིན་པར་ནམ་མཁའ་མཛོད་ཀྱིས་ཞུས་པ་ལས། རྒྱལ་
བའི་བྱང་ཆུབ་མཚན་ཉིད་གང་བསྙེས་པ། །ཆོས་ཀྱི་མཚན་ཉིད་དེ་ནི་ཡོངས་འཛིན་
ཅིང་། །གང་གིས་རྟུལ་མེད་མཐའ་འདི་རབ་ཤེས་པ། དེ་ནི་སངས་རྒྱས་ཀུན་གྱི་
ཆོས་འཛིན་ཡིན། །ཞེས་དང་། དེ་ལྟར་ཆོས་བཟུང་བ་དེ་ནི་སངས་རྒྱས་ལ་བྱས་པ
གཟོ་བ་དང་། བསོད་ནམས་ཚད་མེད་པའང་འཐོབ་སྟེ། དེ་བཞིན་གཤེགས་པའི་
སྙིང་རྗེ་ཆེན་པོ་ངེས་པར་བསྟན་པའི་མདོ་ལས། འདི་ལྟར་རྒྱལ་བའི་ཆོས་ཀྱིས་ཉེར་
གནས་ཤིང་། །ཆོས་ཀྱིས་ངེས་པར་འབྱུང་གི་ཟང་ཟིང་མིན། དེ་བས་གང་ཞིག
བདེ་གཤེགས་ཆོས་འཛིན་པ། །དེ་ནི་སངས་རྒྱས་ཀུན་ལ་བྱས་པ་གཟོ། །ཞེས་
དང་། ནམ་མཁའ་མཛོད་ཀྱི་ཞུས་པའི་མདོ་ལས། ཇི་ལྟར་བསྐལ་པ་བྱེ་བ་སྟོང་
བརྗོད་ཀྱང་། །སངས་རྒྱས་ཡེ་ཤེས་མཐའ་ཡོད་མ་ཡིན་ལྟར། །དེ་བཞིན་གཤེགས

ཀྱི་དམ་ཆོས་འཛིན་པ་ཡ། །བསོད་ནམས་དེ་ཡང་ཚད་ཡོད་མ་ཡིན་ནོ། །ཞེས་གསུངས་པའི་ཕྱིར་རོ། །འདི་ན་ཐེག་པ་མཆོག་གི་གཞུང་ལུགས་ལ། །ཅུང་ཟད་སྦྱ་བའི་སྤོབས་པ་རྒྱས་གྱུར་ཀྱང་། །ན་ཚོད་གཞོན་ཞིང་སྦྱང་བ་མ་སྨིན་པ། །བན་སྨྲོན་བདག་གི་ངག་ལ་སུས་ཡིད་རྟོན། །དེང་དུས་སྐྱེ་བོ་གྲགས་པའི་རྗེས་སུ་འབྲངས། །ཚུལ་དང་ཚུལ་མིན་དཔྱོད་པའི་བློ་གྲོས་བྲལ། །ཕལ་ཆེར་ཕྲག་དོག་གདོན་གྱིས་རྣམ་པར་དཀྲུགས། །ལེགས་བཤད་སྨྲ་བའི་དུས་མིན་བདག་གིས་འཚལ། །འོན་ཀྱང་བླ་མ་མཆོག་དང་ལྷག་པའི་ལྷ། །སྙིང་གི་པདྨོར་རྟག་ཏུ་གུས་མཆོད་པས། །གཞུང་བཟང་རྣམས་ཀྱི་ཚིག་དང་དོན་གྱི་ཆ། །གསལ་བ་གསལ་བར་རིག་པའི་དབྱིངས་སུ་ཤར། །དེ་ཚེ་ལེགས་བཤད་གོམས་པ་ལྷུར་ལེན་ལ། །དགའ་བ་ཡུན་རིང་སྐྱེས་ནས་ཕྱི་མའི་མུར། །ཞིང་གཞན་དུ་ཡང་རྒྱལ་བའི་ཆོས་ཚུལ་ལ། །སྤྲོ་བ་དམ་པ་ཡར་ངོའི་ཟླ་བ་བཞིན། །ཟབ་མོའི་མཐར་ཐུག་པ་ཡི་གཏམ་འདི་ལས། །བློ་ལྡན་དགའ་བ་སྐྱེ་འགྱུར་དེ་ལྟ་བུ། །སྲིད་ཞིའི་མཐར་ལྷུང་བདེ་བ་གང་གིས་མིན། །དེ་ཕྱིར་སྐལ་བཟང་ཚོགས་ཀྱི་དགའ་སྟོན་ལགས། །མཛོན་པར་ཞེན་པ་མཐའ་དག་སྤངས་པ་ཡ། །སྣང་སྟོང་ཟུང་འཇུག་ཐེག་མཆོག་སེང་གེའི་སྒྲས། །ལྷ་ངན་རི་དྭགས་ཚོགས་རྣམས་ཟིལ་གནོན་ཞིང་། །རྒྱལ་བསྟན་སྙིང་པོར་ཕྱོགས་བཅུར་རྒྱས་གྱུར་ཅིག །ཅེས་པ་འདི་ཡང་བསླབ་གསུམ་ནོར་བུའི་མཛོད་འཆང་ཆོས་ཀྱི་མཆེད་པོ་གུ་རུའི་མིང་ཅན་གྱིས། རྫོགས་སངས་སྐུ་ནི་འཕྲོ་ཕྱིར་སོགས་ཀྱི་རྣམ་བཤད་ཡིད་ངོར་གང་ཐོན་ཞིག་བྲིས་ཞེས་ཆེད་བསྐུལ་ངོར་བརྩེ་བློ་གྲོས་དྲི་མེད་ཀྱིས་ཤར་མར་བྲིས་པ་དགེ་ལེགས་འཕེལ། །འདིའི་རྩོམ་དཔེ་རྗེ་བླ་མའི་ཕྱག་དཔེའི་ཁྲིད་དུ་འཚེབས་ནས་ལོ་སྐོར་ཚར་གཉིས་སོན་པའི་རྗེས་སུ་སླར་ཡང་དཔེ་རྙེད་པ་དང་དུས་མཚུངས་པར་བླ་མ་དམ་པ་ལུང་རྟོགས་ནས་སྤྱར་བཀྲ་རྒྱ་མཛད་ཐོག །སྤྱར་གྱི་སྐུལ་བ་པོ་ཡང་དེར་འཛོམས་པ་དང་མཁྱེན་ལྡན་ལེགས་པའི་བློ་གྲོས་བཅས་ཀྱིས་ད་དུང་བསྐྱར་བསྡུན་སོགས་དགོས་ན་ཅིས་ཀྱང་གྱིས་ཞེས་བསྐུལ་བ་ལ་བརྟེན་ནས་སྤྱར་གྱི་རྩོམ་དཔེའི་ཚིག་སྔ་འགའ་ཞིག་བསྡུས། གནད་རེ་ཟུང་གསར་བསྣན་བཅས་རབ་ཆོས་

ལྕགས་ཡོས་ས་ག་ཟླ་བའི་དམར་ཕྱོགས་ཀྱི་གྲལ་ཚེས་དགེ་བར་སྒྲུབ་ཁང་བདུད་ལས་
རྣམ་རྒྱལ་གླིང་དུ་བློ་གྲོས་དྲི་མེད་འཇམ་དཔལ་དགྱེས་པའི་རྡོ་རྗེས་ཞག་གཉིས་ལ་ངོས་
བཤུས་གྲུབ་པར་བགྱིས་པ་མངྒ་ལཾ།།

INDEX

abandonments and realizations 33, 152
ability to perform a function .. 6, 31, 83, 84, 149
actuality .. 8, 9, 17-19, 21, 24, 30, 35, 66, 80, 95, 99, 104, 114, 118, 119, 121, 122, 124, 127, 129, 130, 136, 147, 156, 173
adventitious ... 14-17, 20, 21, 24, 25, 32, 33, 94, 104-107, 113, 114, 119, 127, 128, 136, 137, 142, 151, 152, 173
adventitious appearances . 24, 136
adventitious confusion .. 16, 17, 114, 119
adventitious stains ... 14, 20, 21, 25, 32, 33, 94, 104, 105, 107, 127, 128, 136, 137, 142, 151, 152
affirming negation 7, 11, 28, 30, 80, 83-90, 99, 109, 110, 144, 145, 147
affliction 14, 23, 61, 94, 105, 173, 190
all-knowing wisdom .. 7, 12, 15, 19, 30, 31, 33, 88, 100, 101, 112, 123, 124, 148-152
analysis by reasoning 28, 147
appearance and becoming ... 35, 156, 173
appearance-emptiness . 9, 23, 28, 42, 96, 134, 144, 167
Asaṅga ... 23, 24, 55, 73, 77, 78, 111, 117, 132, 135, 142, 169, 170
assessed emptiness 6, 82, 84, 115, 145
assessed superfact 9
assessed superfactual truth .. 28, 93, 102, 144
authoritative statement ... 4, 55, 68, 70, 78, 174
authoritative statements . 39, 60, 66, 68, 153, 163
bare emptiness 3, 6, 66
basic meaning of guru 58
because suchness is without differentiation 5, 56, 77
because the complete buddha's kāya radiates 5, 56, 77
because the species exists . 5, 56, 77, 78
becoming and peace . 14, 17, 42, 119

birth and cessation 9, 24, 32, 136, 150
bodhisatva sutras ... 19, 35, 124, 157
buddha essence .. 20, 23, 26, 54, 55, 95, 100, 116, 125, 132, 138
buddha nature .. i, vi-viii, 47-54, 121
buddha qualities .. 15, 37, 66, 84, 85, 90, 96, 107-109, 116, 135, 160
buddha species .. 8, 9, 52, 92, 94, 119
causal tantra 23, 134
cause and effect ... 8, 17, 36, 54, 55, 84, 85, 89, 92, 96, 101, 102, 111, 115-117, 158, 186, 189, 191
cause and result 112
causes and conditions ... viii, 12, 15, 83, 84, 91, 92, 100, 102, 104-106, 108, 109
cause-and-result samsara 10
central issue 3, 47, 54, 62, 63
certainty ... 4, 26, 48, 68, 71, 72, 78, 139
clinging .. 15, 42, 107, 146, 167, 174
close-minded sophists ... 26, 138
colophon 167, 168
common vehicles 15, 159
complete buddha's kāya 5, 6, 56, 77, 78, 80, 97, 110
complete purification ... 23, 190
complete purity ... 8, 9, 94, 174, 175, 190
compounded .. iii, iv, 6-9, 11-15, 19, 21, 26, 36, 83-85, 89-93, 95-106, 108-111, 115, 123, 125-128, 140, 148, 158
comprehended all at once ... 102
conceiving of the not authentic 105
concept labels 29, 145, 175
conceptual elaborations . 147, 156
conceptual elaborations about emptiness 147
confused mind .. 15, 17, 107, 117
confusion .. 9, 14-17, 22, 25, 93, 96, 106, 107, 113, 114, 117, 119, 132, 138, 175
conquerors .. 3, 5, 37-39, 62, 73, 160, 163
conquerors gone in the three times 3, 62
consciousness .. 8, 12, 13, 16, 18, 32, 35, 90, 91, 93, 100-102, 112, 114, 120, 123, 128, 147, 150, 157, 174-177, 182, 184, 189, 190
consciousness and wisdom .. 18, 91, 120
conventional analysis 28, 35, 144, 157
conventional prajñā 158
correct inference 69
correct logic ... 4, 61, 73, 75, 144
correct reasoning 20, 21, 60, 61, 67, 73-75, 78, 91, 126, 129, 130, 153
cultivating the path . 97, 109, 117
cut exaggerations 4
cutting exaggeration 71
cut-off emptiness ... 74, 141, 145
cut-off empty condition ... iii-5, 26, 140, 145-147
cyclic existence ... 133, 174, 176, 182, 186
declaration of composition ... 56
decrement and increment ... 108
definitive meaning .. vii-xi, 3, 12,

23, 57, 59, 60, 64, 65, 77, 94, 100, 104, 110-112, 116, 117, 132-135, 139, 140, 152-154, 159, 162, 163, 169, 172, 176, 178, 187, 190
definitive meaning essence sutras . . . . vii, 57, 65, 169, 172
degenerate times 39, 163
developed species 91, 92
devotion 34, 37, 38, 161, 162
dharmadhātu . . . 8-10, 12, 21, 24, 28, 30, 39, 49, 51, 75-77, 91-96, 98, 100, 106, 121, 125, 126, 129, 135, 136, 143, 144, 147, 152, 163, 169, 170, 176
dharmakāya . . 6, 9-12, 14-16, 20, 21, 25, 33, 80-82, 84, 95, 97-100, 104, 106, 108-118, 127, 128, 137, 148, 152, 154, 176
Dharmakīrti . . . 67, 112, 113, 169
dharmatā 3, 8, 12-14, 16-22, 24, 28, 31-33, 36, 51, 59, 63, 89, 90, 96, 99, 100, 103-106, 110, 114, 116, 118-121, 125-128, 130, 131, 136, 143, 150-152, 158, 159, 176, 177, 189
dharmatā of superfactual truth 17, 119
dharmatā of the essence's wisdom 116
dharmatā suchness . . 21, 120, 128
dharmin . . . 8, 16, 22, 89-91, 116, 123, 125, 131, 176, 177
dharmin of samsaric mind . . . 116
dhātu . iv, 3, 8-10, 12, 14, 20, 21, 24, 28, 30, 33, 39, 49, 51, 52, 75-77, 91-96, 98, 100, 106, 110, 121, 125, 126, 129, 131, 135, 136, 143, 144, 147, 152, 163, 169, 170, 176-178, 190, 193
diacritical marks . . . . ii, xi
direct perception . 31, 68, 69, 82, 83, 88, 108, 115, 116, 129, 140, 145, 149, 150
direct perception valid cognizer 31, 149
direct sight 60, 177
disconnected result 9, 95
discursive thought 123, 126, 127, 130, 131, 136, 177
dispensing with some mistaken positions . . . . iii, iv
dream . . 18, 28, 32, 114, 120, 150
dreaming 120, 124
dualistic mind . . . viii, 20, 59, 87, 89, 90, 92, 94, 104, 114, 116, 127, 139, 147, 152, 174, 175, 177, 181, 186, 188, 190, 191
Dzogchen . . . viii, xi, xiv, 49, 50, 159, 183
earlier and later . . 14, 17, 21, 24, 32, 136, 151
elaboration 9, 28, 94, 99, 100, 177
electronic editions 195, 196
electronic texts 196
eliminative differentiation . . 23, 134, 178
emancipation . 11, 12, 21, 22, 27, 61, 89, 99, 104, 130, 132, 164, 180, 182
emptiness . . v, vi, viii, ix, 3, 4, 6-9, 11, 16, 17, 23, 24, 26-28, 30, 31, 40, 42, 63-67, 74, 79, 80, 82-84, 86-90, 93, 96, 99, 100, 105, 106, 109, 110, 115, 117-119, 125, 127, 132-135, 139, 141-149, 164, 167, 170, 171, 176-178, 184, 195
emptiness of one and another one

. . . . 27
emptiness of other 142
emptiness of self . . . vi, 117, 142, 171, 195
emptiness of truth 30, 147
empty entity 23, 28, 65, 66, 132, 143
empty of self-entity 27, 142
enlightenment mind 24, 31, 135, 149, 169, 170, 174, 178
entity of sugata essence . 107, 110
Enumerators 112
equal taste . . 12, 19, 20, 33, 101, 123, 125, 127, 151, 152
essence existing within 51
essence of a buddha . . . 5, 25, 51, 54, 56, 77, 78, 128, 137
eternalism and nihilism . . 35, 156
existence and non-existence . 28, 35, 156, 159
extreme of permanence 65
factual sugata essence 91
fictional . . . 13, 93, 94, 103, 107, 108, 116, 118, 123, 129, 131, 179, 180, 191
fictional and superfactual . . . 179
fictional truth . 108, 119, 179, 180
final turning . . . . vi-ix, 23, 48, 57, 59, 60, 65, 77, 86, 88, 111, 117, 132-135, 139-142, 145, 148, 149, 152, 169, 171, 172, 178, 195
final turning of the wheel . . . . vi, viii, 48, 57, 59, 60, 65, 77, 86, 117, 139-141, 152, 169, 171, 172, 195
five paths 33, 82, 152, 180
force of the thing . . . 15, 21, 108, 109, 129, 130, 187
Forder . 11, 27, 99, 138, 141, 180
Forders 26, 31, 39, 138, 140, 141, 149, 180
foremost instruction 181
foremost instructions . 3, 23, 67, 181
formative 22, 79, 131, 181
forward pervasion 97, 98
four reasons 117, 128
fourth aggregate 101
fourth vajra topic 56, 77
freedom from elaboration . . . 99, 100, 177
fully characterized . . 6, 8, 30, 31, 91, 147, 149
full-blown buddhahood 48
garbha . vii, 50, 51, 53, 136, 179, 181
Gelugpa . 82, 85, 86, 92, 140, 193
giving the answer iii-5, 76
good qualities . . v, viii, 3, 6, 9, 11, 14, 15, 17, 20-22, 27-29, 36, 37, 65, 66, 74, 84, 85, 88, 89, 92, 98, 100, 106-108, 110, 111, 113, 116, 117, 127, 130-132, 135, 141, 143, 144, 158, 159, 165, 184
good qualities of a buddha . . . 6, 11, 66, 84, 89, 98, 100, 135
good qualities of buddhahood . . . . viii, 65, 74, 84, 85, 92, 110, 113, 116, 143
gotra . . . . iv, 50, 52, 55, 170, 171, 181, 189
grammar texts 194
grasped-grasping 181
grasping at a self 105
grasping consciousness 114, 147, 157
great actuality of emptiness . . 17, 118

great equality . . 32, 33, 104, 151, 152
great permanence 103
great purity 19, 103, 123
great self 36, 103
great uncompounded . . . 13, 103
Great Vehicle . . ix, 5, 8, 9, 21, 26, 39, 55, 70, 77, 80, 88, 91, 93, 95, 100, 101, 104-106, 117, 119, 120, 124, 130, 138, 163, 166, 169-172, 178, 180, 182, 184, 191, 195
Great Vehicle sutras . . . 8, 9, 77, 91, 93, 95, 100, 104, 106, 117, 119, 120
great wisdom . . 20, 33, 118, 126, 152
ground sugata essence . . 148, 150
guardian 9, 73, 95, 115, 118, 127, 132, 182, 183
hearing and contemplation 4
Heaven of the Thirty-Three 9, 93
highest approach to emptiness 142
Highest Continuum . . . . ix, 5, 6, 9, 14, 15, 24, 25, 37, 55, 56, 77-79, 81, 91, 95, 96, 105, 106, 113, 132, 135-137, 142, 160, 161, 170, 171
honest and correct assessment 74
honest approach to argument . 74
illusion created by a magician 119
impermanent . . . iii, iv, 11-13, 26, 27, 30, 31, 34, 36, 40, 97, 98, 100-102, 105, 112, 140, 147-150, 154, 158, 164
impermanent valid cognizer . 149
impure appearances 122-124
impurity's appearances . . 18, 20, 122, 127
In Praise of Dharmadhātu 9, 10, 24, 75, 77, 95, 98, 135, 170
inconceivable good qualities . . 37
inconceivable qualities 161
individualized beings 71
inference 68, 69, 108, 129
inferential reasoning 69, 108
initial spread of Buddhism . . . 78
innate disposition . . . 10, 15, 32, 33, 96, 151, 152
inner sanctuary 51
inseparability of the two truths 65
inseparable knower and knowable 32, 150
interdependent arisings 103
irreversible from buddhahood 34, 153
Jamgon Kongtrul . 52, 155, 167, 170, 195
Ju Mipham . . . i, iii, v, xiv, 1, 171, 172, 195
Kagyu 79, 85, 86, 109, 111, 183, 193, 194
Kalama Sutra 70, 170
kāya 3, 5, 6, 9-16, 20, 21, 23, 25, 32-34, 42, 56, 66, 77, 78, 80-82, 84, 93-95, 97-101, 104, 106, 108-118, 127, 128, 132, 134, 137, 148, 150, 152, 154, 167, 176, 183, 184
kāyas and wisdoms 3, 23, 132, 134
King Langdarma 78
knower . . . 32, 33, 103, 150, 152, 174, 184, 186, 191
knower and knowables . . 33, 152
knowing awareness 13, 102
knowing awarenesses 102
knowledge, love, and capacity 7, 89
knowledgeability 39, 41, 163, 184
Lesser Vehicle . 70, 80, 159, 180,

182, 184
like the sun and its light rays 106, 110
lion's roar .... i, iii-v, vii-x, 1, 38-40, 42, 45, 57, 60, 87, 117, 142, 162-164, 167, 171, 195
Lion's Roar of Sugata Essence ... 60
Lion's Roar Proclaiming Other Emptiness v, ix, 87, 117, 142, 171
logical proofs 4
Longchen Rabjam .. 23, 134, 169
luminosity . viii, 8, 10, 13-16, 20, 33, 65-67, 74, 90, 96, 102, 105-107, 110, 118, 119, 126, 152, 177, 184
luminosity aspect .. 65, 66, 74, 90
Mahāmati 27, 141, 142
Mahāmudrā .. viii, xi, 49, 63, 183
Mahāti 49, 63
Maitreya ... ix, 23, 48, 55, 64, 73, 77, 78, 80, 91, 95, 115, 118, 127, 132, 170, 171, 183, 187
manifest buddhahood ... 33, 60, 84, 139, 152
manifest wisdom 139
Mañjuśhrī .. 3, 30, 34, 35, 39, 59, 60, 64, 73, 156, 163
meditating on a self 36, 158
meeting and parting .. 10, 23, 96
merit ... 30, 34, 37, 41, 154, 161, 162, 165
merit will arise 34, 154
middle turning .... vii-ix, 23, 64, 86, 94, 132, 134, 135, 141-143, 147, 154
Middle Way 9, 40, 93, 102, 110, 125, 164, 170, 178, 182
migrator 76, 123, 185
mind's purity 14
Mipham .... i, iii, v, viii, x, xiv, 1, 48, 49, 54, 62, 64, 66, 67, 70, 71, 73, 75-79, 81-90, 92, 94-97, 104, 110-113, 116, 119, 120, 126, 127, 131, 132, 136-138, 143, 147-149, 153, 155, 160, 164, 165, 167, 171, 172, 195
Mipham's understanding of "radiate" 109
momentary arising and cessation 33, 151
momentary consciousness .. 8, 91
moments of consciousness .. 102
Nāgārjuna . 9, 24, 73, 75, 77, 95, 104, 111, 135, 146, 169-171, 183
naked ascetics 11, 99
Namgyal .. i, iii, v, xiv, 1, 43, 168
naturally present species ... 8, 9, 15, 91-95, 108
nature of sugata essence 78
Nigrantha Jains 99
nihilistic view 3
nirvana .... xi, 11, 13, 14, 17-19, 24, 27, 28, 32-34, 36, 40, 94, 99, 102, 104, 115, 116, 118-121, 123, 132, 136, 151, 152, 154, 158, 159, 164, 167, 170, 171, 173, 193
no discursive thinking 141
no transformation ... 32, 33, 150
noble ones ... 32, 35, 82, 94, 95, 102, 108, 115, 129, 151, 157
non-affirming negation ... 7, 11, 28, 30, 80, 83-90, 99, 109, 110, 144, 145, 147
non-dual wisdom 13, 101
non-synchronisation ... 22, 113, 115, 117, 132
non-things .. 13, 31, 33, 35, 103, 129, 149, 151, 157
Nyingma ... v, xii, 56, 76, 78, 79,

82, 83, 85, 86, 97, 111, 126, 139, 163, 164, 183, 193, 194
objects of dualistic mind 104
obscurations ... 7, 15, 17-20, 87, 88, 97, 112, 113, 116, 120-123, 126, 187
obscurations to knowledge ... 7, 87, 88
obscured in regard to flesh-eaters 4, 72
one ultimate vehicle 130
ordinary people .. x, 3, 4, 33, 63, 71, 102, 108, 123, 126, 150, 153, 180
ordinary perceptions 101
other emptiness ..... v, vi, ix, 87, 117, 142, 170, 171, 195
Other Emptiness, Entering Wisdom Beyond Emptiness of Self .... vi, 117, 142, 171
output 13, 14, 102, 106, 186
overstatement 66
Padma Karpo Translation Committee . i, ii, v, vi, xii, 169-171, 193, 194
Padmasambhava 78, 188
path of the noble ones ... 35, 157
peaceful nirvana 33, 152, 167
perceived object 16, 19, 123
perceiving subject ... 16, 18, 19, 32, 114, 121, 123, 150
perception of permanence 34, 155
permanence . 3, 5, 13, 31, 34, 36, 65, 66, 101, 103, 141, 148, 154, 155, 158
permanence and nihilism 66
permanent, stable, and eternal 27, 140
personal self-knowing . 9, 32, 94, 151
play of consciousness and wisdom 18
posing the question iii-5, 75
potential to become a buddha 47, 48, 50
practise the path 26, 61, 89, 139, 191
practising the path .. viii, 49, 139, 157
prajñā ... vi, 9, 13, 18, 19, 29, 35, 36, 40, 64, 93-95, 99, 104, 105, 121, 124, 125, 135, 145, 157, 158, 164, 170, 172, 180, 186
Prajñāpāramitā . vi, 9, 18, 29, 64, 93, 94, 99, 105, 121, 135, 145, 170, 172, 180
precursor 54, 55
prefatory matter 56
primordially pure ... 10, 94, 96, 105, 121, 174
pristine state of buddhahood . 49
profound topic of the inconceivable 22, 131
prophesy of irreversibility ... 153
provisional and definitive 4, 134, 187
provisional and definitive meaning 187
provisional meaning ... 23, 110, 178, 190
pure reasoning 5
purity of scripture 4
purity, bliss, permanence, and self 36, 158
rational mind 60, 61, 69, 82, 100, 175, 187
Ratnagotravibhaṅga 55
realization 108, 115, 126, 181, 187
reasoning awareness 102
reasoning of dharmatā ... 17, 20,

119, 126, 127
reasoning of reliance on the result 117, 118
reasoning of superfactual analysis 22, 132
reasoning of the cause doing its work 21, 118, 128
reasoning of the force of the thing 108, 109, 129, 187
reasonings that analyse the ultimate 102
reference and referencing . . . 188
refuge . 12, 34, 100, 154, 155, 160
result existing in the cause . . 112, 115
reverse pervasion 97, 98, 100
roar of a lion 57, 153
same type or same family 52
samsara . . . . xi, 10, 13-15, 17-19, 24, 32, 59, 61, 94, 96, 101, 102, 104, 105, 107, 115, 118-123, 132, 136, 145, 151, 156, 161, 165, 166, 173, 174, 176, 180, 185, 188, 189
samsara and nirvana . . . xi, 13, 17-19, 24, 32, 102, 118-121, 123, 136, 151, 173
satva and sattva 174, 188
scripture . . iv, 4, 8, 11, 28, 48, 62, 68, 70, 77, 78, 90, 91, 98-100, 111, 119, 143, 147
scripture and reasoning . . . . iv, 8, 11, 62, 77, 90, 98, 111
second spread of Buddhism . . . 78
seed of buddhahood . . 48, 50, 84
self of dharmas 107
self of persons 107
self-arising wisdom . . . xi, 12, 15, 33, 36, 50, 100, 107, 152, 158, 189
self-output 13, 14, 102, 106
separated two truths 8, 90
seven kinds of rational mind . . 60
shiftless 37, 161, 189
shrouding 10, 14
single unique sphere . 24, 33, 35, 136, 152, 156
sky flower 28, 144
Songtsen Gampo 78
sophists . 5, 22, 26, 73, 131, 138, 139
species . . 5-11, 15-17, 20, 21, 23, 25, 28, 32, 39, 52, 55, 56, 77, 78, 80-82, 84, 87-95, 97, 98, 108, 110, 117, 119, 120, 125, 127, 128, 137, 144, 151, 163, 189
spontaneously-existing buddha 50
state . . 13, 14, 18-20, 32, 35, 49, 68, 69, 105, 121, 123, 125, 126, 150-152, 156, 166, 174, 175, 178, 182, 189, 190
study and translation of Tibetan texts 196
study program 195
subjective grasping consciousnesses 156
sugata . . iii-v, vii-xi, 1, 3, 5, 7, 10, 13, 14, 17, 18, 21, 23, 26, 28, 30, 35-38, 40, 41, 45, 49, 50, 53-67, 74-79, 81, 83-94, 96-98, 103-105, 107, 109, 110, 113, 115, 117, 120, 121, 124-126, 129-132, 134-148, 150, 151, 153-156, 158-160, 162-165, 167, 171, 176, 177, 195
sugata essence . . iii-v, vii-xi, 1, 3, 5, 7, 10, 13, 14, 17, 18, 23, 26, 28, 30, 36-38, 40, 45, 49, 50, 53-67, 74-79, 81, 83-94, 96-98, 103, 104, 106, 107,

109, 110, 113, 115, 117, 120, 121, 124-126, 129-132, 134-137, 139-148, 150, 151, 153-155, 158-160, 162-164, 167, 171, 176, 177, 195
sugatagarbha vii
superfact .. 9, 14, 17, 21, 22, 24, 35, 116, 130, 131, 156, 157, 172, 180, 189, 191
superfactual .. 17, 18, 22, 24, 28, 86, 93, 94, 102, 104, 107, 108, 119, 120, 129, 131, 132, 135, 143, 144, 179, 189-191
superfactual analysis . 22, 24, 28, 132, 135, 143
superfactual truth ... 17, 28, 86, 93, 102, 104, 107, 108, 119, 131, 144, 189, 190
supreme vehicle .. 21, 38, 39, 41, 42, 130, 162, 163, 167
svabhāvikakāya 9, 93, 94
syllogism 78, 127
synchronisation ... 22, 112, 113, 115, 117, 132
synchronisation and non-synchronisation 113, 115, 117, 132
synchronised .. 16, 19, 113, 114, 116, 122
tathāgata ... iv, vii, 4, 11, 12, 18, 19, 21, 25, 27, 34, 38, 40, 41, 53, 54, 67, 68, 99, 100, 105, 122, 124, 129, 130, 132, 137, 141, 154, 155, 162, 164, 165, 169, 172
tathāgata essence .. iv, vii, 21, 27, 53, 54, 129, 130, 132, 141
tathāgatagarbha vii
tathātā 53, 67, 80
ten bodhisatva levels 123
tenth level .... x, 3, 9, 63, 64, 95
the authentic .. 13, 18-20, 33-36, 103, 121, 124-126, 152, 155-157, 159, 190
the body of the text 56, 62
the element . iii-5, 10, 12, 15, 24-28, 52, 74, 75, 98, 106, 107, 113, 121, 131, 133, 135-137, 139, 140, 144, 190
the expression of worship .. iv, 58
the fact of the authentic . 18, 33, 35, 121, 152, 156
the fictional .. 107, 116, 123, 191
The Five Dharmas of Maitreya 170, 171
the four reasonings 119, 126, 127
the four reliances ... 39, 163, 190
the great permanence 103
the luminosity nature of the empty entity 65
the nine examples 25, 136
the prefatory section 57
the presentations of other traditions .... iii, iv
the prophecy 34, 153
the prostration .... iv, 58
the species is like a seed 6
the story of sugata essence .. 38, 139, 162
the tathāgata as impermanent 34, 154
the three realms are just mind 120
the title ...... iv, 49, 56-58, 171
the vocabulary of buddha nature 50
things and non-things ... 13, 35, 103, 157
things as they are 104, 116, 122, 127
this shore 13, 19, 24, 26, 94,

101, 115, 116, 129, 136, 138, 139
this shore of impurity . . 115, 116
thousand doses . . . . iii-v, viii-x, 1, 45, 57, 58, 171
three analysers 4, 68, 70, 77
three doors of complete emancipation 27
three phases 25, 137
three reasons . 21, 56, 77-79, 81, 96, 97, 109, 117, 127, 136
three reasons and nine examples 56, 77
three-realmed samsara . 24, 107, 132, 136
time and direction . . . 32, 33, 151
total affliction 23, 190
total affliction and complete purification 23, 190
total stupidity 3, 59, 71
transformation . . 31-33, 38, 150-152, 162
true existence . . . 6, 7, 28, 80, 84-87, 89, 90, 109, 143, 147
trust . 3, 4, 20, 26, 34, 55, 65-68, 70, 72, 74, 78, 126, 131, 139, 153
Tsongkhapa . . . vi, 85-87, 91, 93, 94, 110, 140, 144, 169, 195
turnings of the wheel of dharma . . . . vi, 58, 132, 187
twenty-five suchnesses 112
two different meanings of element 52
two interdependent arisings . 103
two obscurations 17, 126
two purities 9, 94, 95
two selves 107
two valid cognizers . 28, 108, 144
Śhākyamuni Buddha 118
Śhantarakṣhita 78
ultimate analysis . 13, 14, 20, 126
ultimate intent . . 33, 56, 152, 153
ultimate kāya 10, 97
ultimate sutra teachings 86
uncompounded . . 6-9, 11, 13-15, 21, 83-85, 89-93, 95, 98, 99, 101, 103, 104, 106, 108-110, 123, 127, 128, 148
uncompounded dharmadhātu 8, 9, 91, 92, 95
underlying actuality 114
undermined 5, 16, 74, 75
understatement 3, 66
unified appearance and emptiness 110
unified appearance-emptiness 23, 28, 42, 134, 144, 167
unity of the two truths 9, 94
universal purity 123, 124
unobscured buddhahood 54
un-assessed emptiness . . 84, 115, 145
un-assessed superfactual truth 93, 102
un-outflowed . . 10, 96, 120, 186, 190
un-outflowed luminosity . . 10, 96
vajra awareness 103
vajra kāya . . . 11, 13, 34, 101, 154
vajra topic 56, 77, 136
Vajra Vehicle 23, 106, 178, 181, 182, 191
valid cognition . 4, 31, 60, 67-70, 72, 112, 115, 129, 148, 149, 169, 191
valid cognizer 28, 31, 35, 67, 115, 124, 143, 144, 148, 149, 157, 191
view of nihilism 66

view of permanence 3, 66
views of Tsongkhapa 85
Warrior Mañjuśhrī 3, 59, 60
way things are and appear . . . 22, 113, 115, 116
webs of elaboration 9, 94
wisdom . . iii, iv, vi, viii, xi, 3, 6-8, 10-16, 18-20, 25, 26, 29-36, 38, 41, 50, 59, 80, 81, 87, 88, 90, 91, 94, 97, 98, 100-104, 107, 108, 112, 116-118, 120, 121, 123-127, 137, 139-145, 147-152, 154, 157-160, 162, 165, 171, 174, 175, 177, 179, 184-186, 188-191, 195
wisdom dharmakāya . . 6, 10, 14, 15, 80, 97, 98, 100, 108, 148, 154
wisdom of noble ones 102
without differentiation . . . 5, 17, 56, 77, 119, 120

Lightning Source UK Ltd.
Milton Keynes UK
UKOW02f1815060515

251018UK00001B/129/P